TESTED
ADVERTISING METHODS

FOURTH EDITION
Revised and Enlarged

John Caples
Vice-President
Batten, Barton, Durstine & Osborn, Inc.

Prentice-Hall, Inc.
Englewood Cliffs, N.J.

Prentice-Hall International, Inc., *London*
Prentice-Hall of Australia, Pty., Ltd., *Sydney*
Prentice-Hall of Canada, Ltd., *Toronto*
Prentice-Hall of India Private Ltd., *New Delhi*
Prentice-Hall of Japan, Inc., *Tokyo*
Prentice-Hall of Southeast Asia, Pte., Ltd., *Singapore*
Whitehall Books, Ltd., *Wellington, New Zealand*

© 1974 by
John Caples

Library of Congress Cataloging in Publication Data

Caples, John.
  Tested advertising methods.

  1. Advertising. I. Title.
HF5823.C18 1974   659.13'2   74-8627

Printed in the United States of America

Foreword

by David Ogilvy
Chairman, Ogilvy & Mather, International

On page 11 of this book John Caples writes, "I have seen one advertisement sell 19 1/2 times as much goods as another." This statement dramatizes the *gigantic* difference between good advertisements and bad ones. You will increase your chances of writing good ones if you read this book, and commit its conclusions to memory.

An earlier edition taught me most of what I know about writing advertisements. For example:

1. The key to success (maximum sales per dollar) lies in perpetual testing of all the variables.
2. What you say is more important than how you say it.
3. The headline is the most important element in most advertisements.
4. The most effective headlines appeal to the reader's self-interest or give news.
5. Long headlines that say something are more effective than short headlines that say nothing.
6. Specifics are more believable than generalities.
7. Long copy sells more than short copy.

These discoveries, and dozens like them, have been made by John Caples in the course of his long and distinguished career as a writer of mail-order advertising. He has been able to measure the results of every advertisement he has ever written.

The average manufacturer, who sells through a complex system of distribution, is unable to do this. He cannot isolate the results of individual advertisements from the other factors in his marketing mix. He is forced to fly blind.

Experience has convinced me that the factors that work in mail-order advertising work equally well in *all* advertising. But the vast majority of people who work in agencies, and almost all their clients, have never heard of these factors. That is why they skid helplessly about on the greasy surface of irrelevant brilliance. They waste millions on bad advertising, when good advertising could be selling 19 1/2 times as much.

John Caples is the only graduate of the Naval Academy at Annapolis I have encountered in the advertising business. Before he became a copywriter, he was an engineer with the New York Telephone Company. These disciplines predisposed him to the analytical methods that have made him such an effective advertising man. He has no theories; only facts.

His methods are empirical and pragmatic. He is also highly *creative*. He has written scores of remarkable advertisements. Every anthology of famous advertisements includes his classic for the U.S. School of Music, with the headline "They Laughed When I Sat Down at the Piano—But When I Started to Play."

In short, John Caples is a very rare bird. He is not only an indomitable analyzer and teacher of advertising, he is also a first-rate copywriter—one of the most effective there has ever been.

Most of the other great copywriters—including Raymond Rubicam, Claude Hopkins, Rosser Reeves, Harry Scherman and Art Kudner—abandoned the hard slog of writing advertisements to become administrators. Not so John Caples. He has stuck to his knitting—*for forty-nine years*. That is how he has been able to accumulate his unique body of knowledge.

This is, without doubt, the most *useful* book about advertising that I have ever read.

How This Book Will Benefit You

The purpose of this book is to tell you how to write advertising that produces immediate sales for your product or service.

In the pages that follow, you will find no rules for writing institutional advertising, slogans, or corporate-image copy, worthy as those forms of promotion may be.

Instead, you will find:

—Twenty-nine ways to get attention.
—How to discover the most effective sales appeal for your product.
—How to write an interest-arousing first paragraph.
—How to create desire.
—How to put enthusiasm into advertising copy.
—Twenty ways to increase selling power.

—How to make small ads pay.

—Thirty-two ways to get inquiries.

—How to get sales that are profitable and plentiful.

The book contains these and many other time-tested methods plus the latest discoveries for getting ACTION.

News, curiosity, and self-interest have always been powerful factors in making good ads. Words such as Announcing, New, Now, Free, Yours, Quick, Easy, Bargain, and Last Chance have never lost their pulling power. People are still interested in health, wealth, popularity, comfort, enjoyment, and security.

At the same time the modern action-getting methods explained in this book have added enormously to the selling power of advertising. For example: business reply mail, telephone response, magazine inserts, newspaper inserts, split-run copy tests, book clubs, record clubs, credit cards, and editorial-style messages, both print and broadcast.

The original edition of the book contained twenty-three pages of illustrations. This new edition contains eighty-two pages of illustrations including:

—An ad that started an industry

—The most quoted ad of all time

—An ad that ran for forty years

—A $15,000 ad that sold $54,000 worth of subscriptions

—An ad that saved a crop

—An ad that became a conversation piece

—Seventeen examples of successful small ads

—Fifteen famous ads that made advertising history

Briefly stated, this book sums up the results of millions of dollars spent in testing the sales effectiveness of hundreds of different kinds of ads, plus the author's forty-nine years of experience in writing and researching advertising for Du Pont, General Electric, U.S. Steel, Lever Brothers, Johnson & Johnson, Rexall, United Fruit, Hormel, Phoenix Mutual Insurance, Liberty Mutual Insurance, Reader's Digest, The Wall Street Journal, Western Airlines, U.S. Navy Recruiting and others.

Thanks are due to my secretary Marie Lauria for her valuable assistance and editorial help in the preparation of the manuscript of the book.

John Caples

Contents

Illustrations

15 Famous Ads

1

The New Advertising Strategy

The most difficult things to discover in the study of advertising are facts. For example:

— What kind of advertising headlines attract the most readers?
— What kind of pictures get the most attention?
— What sales appeals sell the most merchandise?
— What kind of advertising copy is most effective in selling your product or service?

It is easy to get opinions on these questions. It is hard to get facts. The purpose of this book is to answer questions of this kind. And the answers are based on the traceable results from advertising that can be tested and measured.

Advertisers can be divided into two classes:

Class 1: Those who are continually testing their advertisements to find out how much actual business each advertisement brings in, for example, mail order advertisers, classified advertisers, and department stores.

Class 2: The advertisers who, for one reason or another, do little or no testing or measuring of advertising results.

Writes John W. Blake in a booklet entitled, "Blind Advertising Expenditure":

There is just one justification for advertising: Sales! Sales! Sales! Sales that are immediate, sales that are abundant, sales that are profitable. These are the results that mail order houses demand and get from advertising. Why don't you?

In the general publicity field too much copy is judged solely by opinion and appearance. Costly campaigns are launched, and often pay the advertiser well. Yet the advertiser never knows the individual performance of each advertisement. In a campaign of a dozen pieces of copy it is possible for most of the achievement to be accomplished by just one or two advertisements. All the rest could be duds. Not only is this possible, it is very probable. All mail order men who are onto their job know this. Too many literary faddists, and not enough salesmen, write advertising. The general advertiser may question the above statement; yet he knows that in a sales force of a dozen untried men, not all will succeed.

General advertising greatly needs the cold-blooded, analytical, scientific methods of mail order practice.

Perhaps in years to come, more advertisers will use scientific methods. Perhaps more advertisers will run tested copy in tested media. In answer to the question, "What will advertising be like thirty years hence?" a famous advertising man replied, "It will be more exact, more scientific, and therefore more resultful."

There is a trend toward tested advertising. The fact that the nonscientific advertisers have derived benefit from their efforts is a tribute, not to their methods, but to the extraordinary power of advertising.

The first week I worked in advertising, an artist said to me, "Pen and ink drawings are just the thing to illustrate these furniture advertisements. Pen and ink sketches are so modern. They give the product just the style that it needs."

A copywriter said, "We don't use headlines in these perfume advertisements. Headlines would spoil the effect. Besides, headlines are unnecessary for short copy."

I believed these statements. I believed that these men had a real foundation for what they said. I tried to remember the rules they laid down. "Pen and ink drawings are good in furniture advertisements." "Headlines are not needed where short copy is used." Every time I heard an advertising man talk about advertising I listened carefully. I thought I was learning the rules of the business.

Not long after that I began to work on mail order advertising. Each advertisement was tested. Results were tabulated. Each advertisement and each publication had to prove itself in actual sales.

I know now that much of the talk I heard was just talk. Too often the ad men were stating opinions, not facts. And in many cases, the opinions were not even the boiled-down opinions of a large group of people. They were merely personal opinions.

If the real foundation of those opinions could be discovered by psychoanalysis, it would be laughable in many cases. An artist might favor blue backgrounds in advertisements because blue was his mother's favorite color. A copywriter might recommend short copy because his wife once said, "I would never read all that small print, and I don't think anybody else would, either." An advertising manager might put a magazine on the list because he liked its editorials, or because the space salesman was a fine fellow.

In planning an advertising campaign, the first step should be to clear the decks of all opinions, all theories, all conjectures, all prejudices.

The next step should be to find a scientific method of testing the real strength of the different advertisements and the various advertising media, such as publications, broadcasting, direct mail advertising, etc.

This preliminary research takes time. All right. The time is well spent. To get started on the right foot—to find the right appeal and the right place to advertise—is so important that other considerations are insignificant by comparison.

I have seen one mail order advertisement actually sell, not twice as much, not three times as much, but 19 1/2 times as much goods as another. Both advertisements occupied the same space. Both were run in the same publication. Both had photographic illustrations. Both had carefully written copy. The difference was that one used the right appeal and the other used the wrong appeal.

If I were a manufacturer and I hired an advertising agency to do some advertising for me, I would be vitally concerned about getting the right appeal. I would a dozen times rather have a hastily prepared advertisement based on the correct appeal than twenty beautiful pieces of copy with beautiful pictures featuring an ineffective argument.

To discover the correct appeal is often difficult. There may be many wrong appeals and only one right one. If my advertising agent had a year in which to prepare a campaign for my product, I should be perfectly satisfied if he spent eleven months in search of the right appeal, and one month—or one week, for that matter—preparing the actual advertisements.

The question of getting the right appeal is only one of many instances where facts should be searched for and unfounded opinions guarded against. Every logical advertising medium should be tested. Season and location of advertising should be checked. Every single element that is put into an advertisement—headline, subhead, illustration, and copy—should be put there, not because it looks well, not because it sounds well, but because that type of headline or that type of illustration has proved itself to be more successful than any other.

There are some cases where pretesting is difficult. For example, it is difficult to test in advance the long-haul effect of repeating over and over again a certain advertising slogan. However, as matters stand today, many advertisers, large and small, decide by opinion and theory the following major policies:

1. Where to advertise
2. When to advertise
3. What to say in advertisements

Practically everything is based, not on tested methods, but on somebody's opinion. Often this person whose opinion is final is not even an advertising man. He may be a vice president with a flair for writing, or a manufacturer who knows production from A to Z and nothing at all about advertising. What a wasteful, inefficient, stupid, disgraceful state of affairs! Compared with the efficient manufacturing methods of today, many advertising methods are still in the dark ages.

Now let us look at the other side of the picture. There are certain advertisers who waste not a penny on theory, who deal only with facts. These advertisers test every advertisement and every publication on a small scale before they use them on a large scale. Every advertisement and every advertising medium must prove itself by producing inquiries from interested prospects, or leads for salesmen, or mail order sales, or sales in stores. Some of these scientific advertisers spend comparatively small sums in advertising. Yet they have made their products as well known as certain advertisers who spend far more. They make one advertising dollar do the work of several dollars. How do they do this? What is their secret?

The answer is testing, testing, testing. For example, mail order advertisers and department stores watch with eagle eyes the sales that result from every advertisement and every publication. They spend the bulk of their advertising appropriation on tested copy in tested media.

For those who do not know the methods of testing advertising, it might be well to mention that there are a number of methods. For example, when department stores run a newspaper advertisement for a certain article, they can judge the effectiveness of the advertisement by the increase in sales over previous days on that particular article.

Certain national advertisers use test cities. They try out new copy appeals in small city newspapers. The sales in these cities are compared with the sales in nearby cities that are receiving the regular copy. If the new copy causes an increase in sales, it is then used nationally.

Other advertisers use key numbers in the coupons of their advertisements. Notice the coupon in a typical mail order advertisement. Here is how the address in the coupon might read:

Acme Products Co.
200 Park Avenue, Dept. R-1-7
New York, N.Y. 10017

The key number in this advertisement is Dept. R-1-7. The letter R designates the name of the publication in which the advertisement appears. The numeral 1 designates the month of the year, January in this case. The numeral 7 designates the day of the month.

If this manufacturer runs an advertisement in a different publication on the same date, and the designation of the publication is the letter T, the key number in the coupon will be Dept. T-1-7. If this advertiser runs an advertisement in Publication T on a later date, for example, February 10, the key number will be Dept. T-2-10.

In the same manner, every advertisement is given a different key number. The key number is an invention that has done as much for the science of advertising as the X-ray has done for the science of medicine. The value of the key number is that it enables the advertiser to know exactly how many inquiries or how many sales come from each advertisement. The importance of this is far-reaching. It is one of the greatest steps ever made toward taking the guesswork out of advertising.

For example, one of the important things you can learn through the use of key numbers is which advertisements gain the most attention. By running all of your advertisements, each with a different key number, in the same publication, you can discover, by simply counting inquiries or coupon returns, which advertisements attracted the most readers. Then you can discard the nonresultful ads and run only the resultful ads in your entire list of publications. Naturally, in a test of this kind the coupon must not be featured in some advertisements and hidden in others. It must be given the same prominence throughout the test.

"But I don't care about coupon returns!" you exclaim. "What I want is sales." This brings up a fundamental point. It has been proved many times and by many advertisers that in a properly controlled test the advertisements that bring the most inquiries usually bring the most sales.

Advertisers who employ salesmen to follow advertising leads have found this to be true. Daniel Starch, a famous advertising analyst, reached the same conclusion in his analysis of five million inquiries received by 163 firms over a period of twelve years.

There are exceptions, of course. An advertisement with a picture of a free booklet at the top of the page and the headline "Send for This Free Booklet" may bring a large number of low-grade leads. In this case the large number of leads does not indicate the true value of the advertisement.

There is also the professional coupon-clipper to contend with— the man, woman, or child who goes through a magazine and clips some coupons in order to get free samples and free booklets. Fortunately this element is not large, and what there is of it remains fairly constant. Some advertisers eliminate coupon-clippers by omitting the coupon and by using instead a hidden offer buried in the copy. This method will be explained later.

The important thing to remember in testing a series of advertisements is to keep the booklet offer or sample offer subordinated and identical in all advertisements. If this is done, it will be found that in general the advertisements that bring the most inquiries also bring the most sales.

In the following chapters of this book, an effort will be made to do two things:

1. To explain the scientific principles of advertising that have been learned by advertisers who know by actual test what kind of advertisements sell the most goods, what headlines attract the most readers, which publications are best, and what kind of advertising illustrations and layouts are most effective.
2. To explain the methods of testing so that you may determine for yourself just which headlines, appeals, illustrations, copy, and media are best for you.

I read but one newspaper and that more for its advertisements than its news.

Thomas Jefferson

Would you invest $7 to be $1000 richer...without risking a cent?

A Formula for a Successful Ad

Here is a formula: (1) Write an irresistible headline. (2) Back it up with facts in the copy. (3) Make an unbeatable offer in the coupon. This ad did all three, and was extremely successful. Here is the offer in the coupon: "Send me a FREE copy of the 96-page book, '99 New Ideas on Your Money, Job and Living' and enter my subscription to CHANGING TIMES magazine for one year for only $7. Money-Back Guarantee: If not completely satisfied, I won't owe a cent, and may keep the first issue and the free book '99 New Ideas.' "

The years that the locust hath eaten—

A SOLEMN sounding line it is, full of sad significance.

The years when there were no crops, because they were destroyed by the enemies of crops. The years when men worked and made no progress; when the end of the year found them a little poorer than its beginning, because a part of their little span of life was gone and had produced no increase.

In almost every life there are some fruitless years; but the tragedies occur, when year after year, men go along feeding their lives to the locust of indecision, or the locust of laziness, or the locust of too great concentration on a petty task.

In every week of every year the Alexander Hamilton Institute is brought into contact with such tragedies.

"I wish I had acted earlier"

"MY experience with the Alexander Hamilton Institute leaves me only with the regret that I did not make contact with it at an earlier time," says one man.

For that regret there is no healing. The years when one might have acted, and did not; these are the years that the locust hath eaten.

"If I had read your Course before getting mixed up in my mining proposition, it would have kept me out of trouble," another writes.

He might have read it before; the opportunity was offered to him time after time, in advertisements such as this, but he did not act. And Fate exacted payment for those wasted opportunities, the years that the locust hath eaten.

"If I had enrolled with you a year or two ago, I should be better able to han-

IN a very old book named Joel, after the man who wrote it, you will find this line *"The Years that the Locust hath Eaten"*

dle the problems put up to me every day," another says.

He is making progress now, rapid progress. But the progress might just as well have started two years earlier.

The punishment of wasted years

THIS happened just the other day: A man wrote asking that someone call on him who could give him detailed information as to just how the Alexander Hamilton Institute has helped thousands of men to greater success.

The representative found a man past fifty years of age, occupying a modest position in a great corporation. He sat down to explain the Institute's plan and method. And as he talked, naming one and another who now occupy high positions, he looked across at the gray-haired man who was plainly disturbed by emotion

The representative of the Institute turned away his eyes; he knew what that man was thinking. His thoughts were turned back over the fields of wasted opportunity; he was plagued by the thought of the years that the locust hath eaten.

Today you may start forward with thousands of others

THIS can hardly be called an advertisement about the Alexander Hamilton Institute. The facts about its

Modern Business Course and Service have been printed so many times that few men need to have them repeated.

The average man knows that thousands of men, in every state and city of this country are proof of its strength and standing; he knows that business and educational authority of the highest standing is represented in the Advisory Council of the Alexander Hamilton Institute

Advisory Council

THIS Advisory Council consists o. Frank A. Vanderlip, the financier; General Coleman duPont, the well-known business executive; John Hays Hammond, the eminent engineer; Jeremiah W. Jenks, the statistician and economist; and Joseph French Johnson, Dean of the New York University School of Commerce

"Forging Ahead in Business"

TO all men of earnest purpose who seek to avoid these wasted years, the Alexander Hamilton Institute comes now, asking for only one moment of firm decision—one moment in which to take the first step that can begin to turn ordinary years into great years of progress.

A book has been published for you entitled "Forging Ahead in Business."

It is not a book for drifters; but to men who are asking themselves "Where am I going to be ten years from now?" it is offered freely and gladly without the slightest obligation.

Send for your copy today.

Alexander Hamilton Institute

000 Astor Place, New York City
Send me "Forging Ahead in Business" which I may keep without obligation.

Name _____
        Print here
Business
Address _____

_____

Business
Position _____

An Ad That Failed

This ad for a correspondence course in business training was highly praised. The client loved the ad. The salesmen thought it told a great story. The ad was reproduced in advertising textbooks as a classic. Yet it brought few coupons. Why? (1) The headline fails to promise a benefit. (2) The picture of a locust offers no reward. (3) The copy is an essay on human failure—"the punishment of wasted years." For contrast, read the successful Alexander Hamilton ad on page 300. Ads should not be judged on literary value but on sales value.

2

The Most Important Part of an Advertisement

There are eighteen chapters in this book. Four of these chapters, or more than one-fifth of the entire book, deal with headlines of advertisements. But four chapters are not too much space to devote to this vital subject. Headlines are extremely important. They are the telegraphic messages that the advertiser puts into big print for the public to read. The majority of the public reads little else. The success of an entire advertising campaign may stand or fall on what is said in the headlines of the individual advertisments. In an article in a trade magazine, Don Belding wrote:

> Inquiry returns show that the headline is 50 to 75 per cent of the advertisement. So, selling punch in your headline is about the most important thing. It competes with news and articles and other headlines in picking out readers. In fact, your single headline, in the average big-town newspaper, competes with 350 news stories, twenty-one feature articles, and eighty-five advertisements. And it competes in time, because, seen for a second, it is heeded, or passed up, and there is no return by readers. . . .

In discussing the importance of headlines, Bruce Barton told how results were increased by a change of headline on a correspondence school advertisement. Mr. Barton said:

> The old headline was, "John Smith made $25,000 the first year writing motion picture scenarios." The new headline was "John Smith sold his first motion picture scenario for $140, one month after completing this Course." The advertisement with the new headline drew enormously, and the explanation is, of course, easy.

Every reader could imagine himself making $140, but few could imagine themselves making $25,000.

I feel we are in a period when the interesting headline is more indicated than ever before. I believe that everyone who writes a piece of copy ought to put on it the best headline he can and then say to himself, "How can that headline be changed to be more interesting or appeal to more people?"

An Ad That Failed . . . and One That Didn't

Below are two headlines that were tested by a mail order advertiser. One was a success, the other a failure. See if you can guess which is which.

Are you afraid of making mistakes in English?

Do you make these mistakes in English?

The advertisements bearing these headlines were the same in general appearance. And they both had the same copy appeal. The difference in pulling power was due largely to the headline.

Which headline was the successful one? Have you checked one of them mentally? Or do you feel that they are so much alike that it is difficult to choose between them?

As a matter of fact, the second headline is the resultful one. It brought a much larger number of inquiries and sales than the other. Why? What quality does the second headline possess that the first one lacks?

Advertising men have agreed that the use of the word "these" in the second headline is what makes the difference. The headline, "Do you make these mistakes in English?" says in effect to the reader, "There are described below certain blunders in English. Read the copy and see if you make these blunders."

This arouses the reader's curiosity and self-interest. Here is free information. He can read about these mistakes in English and learn to avoid them. He may also find entertainment and self-satisfaction in reading about the blunders of other people and saying to himself, "I would never make such silly mistakes as that."

Now consider the other headline, "Are you afraid of making mistakes in English?" This headline fails to suggest to the reader that there are some interesting blunders described below. It merely suggests that the copy will be a sales talk for a book on English grammar or a course in English. And who wants to read a sales talk?

Few persons, even among some experienced advertising people, realize how much of the effectiveness of an advertisement depends on the headline.

Every copywriter knows what it is to struggle with copy for hours, for days—fixing it, polishing it, rearranging it. We have all been guilty of leaving the headline until the last and then spending half an hour on it—or perhaps only five minutes. I did just that before I had any experience with keyed copy and traceable results. Now, I spend hours on headlines—days if necessary. And when I get a good headline, I know that my task is nearly finished. Writing the copy can usually be done in a short time if necessary. And that advertisement will be a good one—that is, if the headline is really a "stopper."

What good is all the painstaking work on copy if the headline isn't right? If the headline doesn't stop people, the copy might as well be written in Greek.

If the headline of an advertisement is poor, the best copywriter in the world can't write copy that will sell the goods. He hasn't a chance. Because if the headline is poor, the copy will not be read. And copy that is not read does not sell goods. On the other hand, if the headline is a good one, it is a relatively simple matter to write the copy.

What do people see of advertising? Headlines! What do you yourself see of advertising as you glance through a magazine? Headlines! What decides whether or not you stop a moment and look at an advertisement, or even read a little of it? The headline!

Of course, the illustration counts, too. Sometimes a striking picture will make an advertisement good even if the headline is only ordinary. But a good headline can make an advertisement good even if the picture is poor. The combination of a good headline and a good picture is irresistible.

Advertisers who work with keyed copy find that the majority of their most resultful headlines can be divided into three classes:

The best headlines are those that appeal to the reader's self-interest—headlines that offer the reader something he wants. Examples:

Another $50 raise

Retire at 55

The next best headlines are those that give news. Examples:

New features of the Ford truck

Discovered—a new kind of hand cleaner

The third best headlines are those that arouse curiosity. Examples:

Lost: $35,000

Are you playing fair with your wife?

However, the effectiveness of the average curiosity headline is doubtful. For every curiosity headline that succeeds in getting results, a dozen will fail.

Why is it that self-interest headlines are best and the curiosity headlines only third best? You can answer this question for yourself. Suppose you are looking through a newspaper. You see a headline that arouses your curiosity. You will read the copy if you have time. But suppose you see a headline that offers you something you want. You will make time to read the copy.

The headline that makes a definite offer of something people want has a further advantage. It conveys a message to people who read only headlines. And as every advertising man knows, there are scores of people who read only headlines for every person who reads both headlines and copy.

Note this: The following curiosity headline and logotype (company name) convey practically no message to the newspaper glancers who read only the large print:

Here's one question you shouldn't
ask your wife

[Copy and illustration]

ABC Life Insurance Company

Notice the difference in the following self-interest headline and logotype:

You can laugh at money worries
if you follow this simple plan

[Copy and illustration]

ABC Life Insurance Company

By merely reading the headline and logotype of this second advertisement the reader learns that a certain company has a plan that will help him solve his money problems. Actual returns show that this second advertisement brought twice as many coupon inquiries as the first advertisement and twice as many sales.

Occasionally a curiosity headline is produced that does compete successfully with self-interest headlines. For example, an advertisement for a book of etiquette with the headline, "What's wrong in this picture?" was an excellent puller.

Here is an astounding fact. You can look through almost any publication and find headlines that possess not a single one of the necessary qualities such as self-interest or curiosity. Here are some examples of meaningless headlines taken from magazines:

Youth Cries Unto Youth
Blow Hot—Blow Cold
And This Little Girl Went to Market
No Reason Now
Just One Question, Please

Test these headlines yourself. Do they give news? Do they offer you anything you want? Do they arouse your curiosity? No, absolutely no. These headlines would have some value if they mentioned the name of the product advertised. But they don't even do that.

Here are a few more of the same sort of headlines:

Speak Up!
Daylight Saving
A Revelation
Big Business
Oh, Ye Daughters of Eve!

What do these headlines mean? Nothing. What reason do they give you for reading the copy? No reason. What do they offer to the reader? Not a single, solitary thing. Then why are they used? Because somewhere, somehow, some advertiser or advertising agent, through a process of reasoning known only to himself, decided that these were good headlines.

In what way are they good? Usually the purpose of a headline is to get people to read the copy. You can accomplish this either by offering the reader something he wants or by arousing his curiosity.

Quite obviously these headlines do not offer anything. Then they must be intended to arouse curiosity. Do they? Read them over and see for yourself. Does the headline, "Speak Up!" arouse any curiosity? You may reply, "Combined with the illustration, the headline may have meant something." The answer is that this particular advertisement had no illustration. And the illustrations of the other advertisements were of little or no value in making the message clear.

The purpose of these headlines may have been to convey a message to people who read only headlines and not copy. Do the above headlines convey any message? None whatever.

Perhaps the authors of these advertisements would say, "But you should read the entire advertisement. Then you will see how beautifully the headline ties up with the copy." This is laughable. What reader cares how well the headline ties up with copy? Do people read advertisements backwards? No. They read the headline first. And then if they are interested, they read the copy. The business of judging a headline after you read the copy is wrong. It takes for granted that everybody reads the copy.

For example, the headline of the following advertisement taken from *The New York Times* means little or nothing until you read the copy:

It's Sure!
It's Permanent!
It's All Mine!

This is the feeling you get when the monthly Life Income starts under a Retirement Annuity.

The monthly income can begin at any time between 50 and 70. It is a most attractive self-pension plan.

Retirement Annuities are obtainable in $100 investment units. Income is also guaranteed in event of total and permanent disability. A substantial cash return is guaranteed if you do not reach retirement age.

ABC Life Insurance Company

Compare the meaningless headline of the above ad with this homely but effective mail order caption:

Corn Gone In 5 Days or Money Back

There's a headline that says something. There's a headline that stands up on its hind legs and talks to its audience in a language they understand. A picture of a man's foot with a corn plaster helped to make the meaning of the headline absolutely clear.

Analyze that headline. "Corn Gone!" Instantly the man with foot troubles knows he is being spoken to. "In 5 Days!" "Better yet," he says. . . . "Or Money Back." . . . "Sold!" he cries.

The best headlines are the ones that offer something. The headline, "Corn Gone In 5 Days" offers something that certain readers want and want badly.

Another thing: In order to impress your offer on the mind of the reader or listener, it is necessary to put it into brief, simple language. Your prospective customer may be in a hurry. He may be half asleep as he turns the pages or twists the dial of his TV set. His thoughts are a thousand miles from you and your product. No farfetched or obscure statement will stop him. You have got to hit him where he lives—in the heart or in the head. You have got to catch his eye or ear with something simple, something direct, something he wants.

Given a good product, the American advertising industry does an efficient, imaginative and essential job of information and promotion and makes an important contribution.

Dwight D. Eisenhower

HOW I GOT A BETTER JOB

by reading The Wall Street Journal

"What do you think of the news from Washington?" he asked.

I replied by quoting a piece I had read in The Wall Street Journal.

He asked my views on business conditions, on new industries, on new ways of doing business. Several times I was helped by things I had read in The Wall Street Journal.

When the interview was over, he said, "We will let you know!"

A week later, I got a letter. They offered me $15,000 a year.

* * *

A few minutes' daily reading of The Journal has put thousands of men on the road to increased earnings. The Journal helps salaried men making $7,500 to $25,000 a year. It is valuable to small business men. It can be of priceless benefit to ambitious young men who want to win advancement.

The Wall Street Journal is the complete business DAILY. Has largest staff of writers on business and finance. The only business paper served by all three big press associations. It costs $24 a year, but you can get a Trial Subscription for three months for $7. Just tear out this ad and attach check for $7 and mail. Or tell us to bill you. Address: The Wall Street Journal, 44 Broad St., New York 4, N. Y. NYT 9-21

NEXT 90 DAYS CAN CHANGE YOUR LIFE

A Warning from The Wall Street Journal

You are living in a period of rapid changes. The next 90 days will be filled with opportunities and dangers.

Fortune will smile on some men. Disaster will dog the footsteps of others.

Because reports in The Wall Street Journal come to you DAILY, you get fastest possible warning of any new trend affecting your business and personal income. You get facts in time to protect your interests or seize a profit.

If you think The Journal is just for millionaires, you are WRONG! It is a wonderful aid to salaried men making $7,500 to $25,000 a year. It is valuable to owners of small businesses. It can be of priceless benefit to ambitious young men who want to earn more money. Read it for 90 days and see what it can do for YOU.

The Wall Street Journal is the complete business DAILY. Has largest staff of writers on business and finance. The only business paper served by all three big press associations. It costs $24 a year, but you can get a Trial Subscription for three months for $7. Just tear out this ad and attach check for $7 and mail. Or tell us to bill you. Address: The Wall Street Journal, 44 Broad St., New York 4, N. Y. NYT 7-26

Which Ad Made the Most Sales?

These ads were tested by mail order sales. One brought twice as many mail orders as the other. Can you guess the winner? *Answer:* The winner is the ad on the right. Why? It is likely that the ad on the left attracted the wrong audience. The headline sounds like a help-wanted ad.

How to Announce Important News

In order to find the most effective words to announce the publication of the Revised Standard Version of the Bible, several different ads were tested by mail order sales. The above ad was the winner. It was used as an announcement campaign. Notice how the news was made bigger by spreading the headline clear across the page in big type. What happened? A trade ad apologized to booksellers with the headline "The biggest print order in history wasn't big enough."

3

What Kinds of Headlines Attract the Most Readers?

This chapter discusses ten successful headlines and tells what made them successful. Here is headline No. 1.

1. How a fool stunt made me a star salesman

The advertisement bearing this headline sold a large number of correspondence courses in salesmanship. The ad was repeated many times in many publications. Obviously the success of the ad was due largely to its unusual headline. Let us, therefore, examine the headline and see what special qualities it possesses. Perhaps we can inject some of these good qualities into our own future headlines.

This particular headline does two things: (1) It arouses the reader's curiosity by making him want to know what the fool stunt was. And (2) it appeals to his self-interest by offering to tell him how to become a star salesman.

The copywriter could have written the headline this way:

How I did a fool stunt

This is a good curiosity headline and would have attracted a number of readers.

On the other hand, the copywriter could have written the headline this way:

How I became a star salesman

This is a good self-interest headline and would have captured the interest of many prospects.

By combining the two features, curiosity and self-interest, into a single headline—"How a fool stunt made me a star salesman"—the copywriter produced one of the most successful mail order captions of its day.

One other point: In addition to curiosity and self-interest, the headline possesses a third important quality. It suggests that here is a quick and easy way to become a star salesman. If the headline had read, "How two years' training made me a star salesman," it would not have been so attractive.

Let us look at a few other tested, successful headlines and see if we can discover the secret of their success. Take, for example, the headline of one of the best advertisements for a book of etiquette:

2. What's wrong in this picture?

The illustration in the advertisement showed two women walking along the street escorted by a man. The man was shown walking between the two women.

The chief virtue of this headline is its curiosity value. It is a challenge to the reader. The reader suspects that he knows what is wrong in the picture, but he has to read the copy to make sure. Thus the headline accomplishes its main purpose. It gets the reader into the copy.

Another virtue of the headline is its appeal to the self-interest of the reader. The reader takes it for granted that he will find in the text of the advertisement the answer to the question, "What's wrong in this picture?" Thus he will get free information, a free lesson in etiquette.

Here is a successful headline for a course in memory training:

3. How I improved my memory in one evening

This is primarily a self-interest headline. A great many people think they have poor memories. Hence, a method of improving one's memory is bound to be attractive. The headline also suggests that the method is quick and easy, that results may be obtained in a single evening.

Here is a successful headline for a mail order book on the subject of personality development. Although the value of a book of this kind may be questioned by some people, this caption proved to be a powerful one:

4.   Give me 5 days and I'll give you a Magnetic
Personality...Let Me Prove It—FREE

This is a self-interest headline. People want to be liked by other people. They want to be popular with their friends. This advertisement offers to tell the reader how to accomplish this by means of a magnetic personality.

The headline also suggests that here is a quick, easy way to become magnetic. The method is apparently quick because the headline says it takes only five days. The method seems easy, because there is apparently no effort required on the customer's part. The headline does not say, "How you can develop a magnetic personality." It says, "Give me 5 days and I will give you a magnetic personality."

Here is a headline that was used with excellent results to introduce a new business course for executives:

5.   ANNOUNCING
A new Course and Service for men
who want to be independent in the
next five years

This is primarily a news headline. It announces something new. It also strikes a strong self-interest note with the words "for men who want to be independent in the next five years."

Here is the headline for an advertisement selling a device for people who are hard of hearing. This advertisement brought a large number of orders.

6.   The deaf now hear whispers

This is primarily a self-interest headline. It appeals directly to the proper audience and offers them the thing they want; namely, an invention that aids the deaf. There is also curiosity value in this headline. The reader says to himself, "What can this device be that enables formerly deaf people to hear whispers?"

Here is a headline for a mail order course in selling real estate. The advertisement bearing this headline was highly successful and was repeated many times.

7. Wanted—your services as a high paid real-estate specialist

This is purely a self-interest headline. It offers jobs—highly paid jobs. There are plenty of men in this country who are dissatisfied with their work and their pay. It would be difficult for these men to pass this advertisement without reading it.

It should be further noted that the word "wanted" has always been a good attention-getter. The reader instinctively stops to find out what is wanted. He thinks perhaps he can furnish the thing that is wanted, and make a profit for himself.

Here is the headline of an advertisement that brought excellent results:

8. Announcing a New Home Money-Making Plan

This headline is a combination of news and self-interest. The words "announcing" and "new" give the news flavor. The self-interest element is expressed in the words "Home Money-Making Plan."

Here is the headline for an advertisement that was notably successful in selling a set of books containing the World's Greatest Literature:

9. "No time for Yale—took college home," says well-known author

This is primarily a self-interest headline. It is aimed at those who never had a college education and who would welcome an opportunity to continue their studies.

Sometimes a mail order advertisement can be run for years without wearing out. Here is the headline of just such an advertisement. The product being sold is a course in self-improvement.

10. I gambled a postage stamp and won $35,840 in 2 years

Here again is a headline that appeals primarily to the reader's self-interest. Who wouldn't like to gamble a postage stamp and win $35,840?

This headline also contains curiosity appeal. The reader would like to know how on earth it is possible to gamble so little and win so much. Furthermore, the plan seems easy. There is no suggestion in the headline that any effort is required on the part of the reader. All you have to do is to gamble a postage stamp and the same big winnings may be yours.

Advertising men can probably guess the plot of this advertisement. The postage stamp the reader is asked to risk is the stamp necessary to send for the free booklet that tells about the self-improvement course.

What Makes Certain Headlines Successful?

Having discussed ten headlines, all of which were outstandingly successful in their respective fields, let us see what qualities they possess in common. Then, perhaps we can formulate the test of a good headline. Here are the qualities: Two of the headlines were news headlines. Four employed curiosity as a means of getting the reader into the copy. Four suggested that here is a quick and easy way to accomplish certain results. Ten of the headlines—or, in other words, every single headline—offered the reader something he wanted and therefore appealed to his self-interest.

This analysis suggests that there are four important qualities that a good headline may possess. They are:

1. Self-interest
2. News
3. Curiosity
4. Quick, easy way

Self-interest is by far the most important of these headline qualities. News comes next in importance. Department stores and other users of tested copy employ the news angle to a large extent in their newspaper advertising.

Another important point, which has not been mentioned, is believability. In striving to produce an attractive headline, the copywriter should not emphasize the "quick, easy way" to such an extent that the headline becomes unbelievable. One aid to believability is to use specific figures. Note the frequent use of specific figures in the aforementioned successful headlines. For example: "Give me 5 days...," "...in one evening," "...$35,840 in 2 years."

Do Advertising Awards Indicate True Merit?

With these facts in mind, let us consider a headline that won an advertising award. It reads:

> "Kill my cow for an editor? I should say not!"

This is a curiosity headline. Some advertising men hailed it as a masterpiece. Yet not a few intelligent readers were frankly puzzled by it. Said one reader: "What does it mean? The only explanation I can think of is that a newspaper editor has been invited to a farmer's house. The farmer says, 'I refuse to kill my cow to furnish a steak for an editor's dinner.' "

This misinterpretation of the award-winning headline is no reflection on the reader. It is a reflection on the headline. This headline is from a series of public service ads designed to promote medical inspection of cattle. The headline belongs to the class of advertising that causes the sophisticated advertising man to exclaim "Wonderful!" but which is completely over the heads of the greater portion of the reading public.

Now consider a headline that won another advertising award. It reads:

> The call that will wake any mother

This headline quite obviously has no news value, and although it appeals to the maternal interest, it lacks self-interest. It is merely a second-rate curiosity headline.

Four eminent judges selected the 150 "best" advertisements published in a certain year. These advertisements were reproduced in a book called *The Advertising Parade*. The headlines of the three advertisements that received the highest ratings are as follows:

> Fresh and relaxed at the journey's end
> [Blank Motor Company]
>
> Tireless Wings
> [ABC Airline]
>
> An old man and a corporation
> [Transportation Co.]

Not a single one of these headlines has any news value. Not one arouses curiosity. Not one except the first offers the reader anything he wants. The first does contain an appeal to the reader's self-interest. It says in effect, "If you ride in a Blank car, you will be fresh and relaxed at the end of the journey."

Here are the headlines of other advertisements that received high ratings in *The Advertising Parade.* See if you can find self-interest, news, or curiosity in any of them:

In Congress assembled
[Eastern Railroad]

Nuthin' I like!
[Life Insurance Co.]

The male of the species is harder on towels
[Grade A Towels]

Straight and Far
[Meat Packing Company]

If you want a real judgment of the selling power of an advertisement, do not submit it to an advertising jury. There are several good reasons why such a group is apt to select poor headlines:

Reason Number One: Before voting on a headline, the members of the jury read the copy. Thus, the meaning of many an obscure headline is made clear to them.

The reading public uses the reverse method. If the headline is obscure, they do not bother to read the copy.

Reason Number Two: Advertising juries are usually composed of men and women who want to raise the image of the advertising business. This is a praiseworthy undertaking. Nevertheless, every advertising agent must answer this question: Shall I spend my client's money to raise the image of the advertising business? Or shall I spend the money to increase his sales?

Reason Number Three: The following two life insurance headlines were judged by an advertising jury:

What would become of your wife if
something happened to you?

Get rid of money worries for good!

The jury favored the first headline because it seemed to be the more logical for life insurance. Also because it is more altruistic and higher toned. Yet actual sales results showed that the second headline was more effective.

Reason Number Four: Advertising juries give too much weight to fine writing. As a matter of fact, there is little sales value in fine writing. It is what you say that counts, not how you say it. A valid argument presented in blunt language will sway the reader more than a less valid argument beautifully presented.

Reason Number Five: The business of judging advertisements in a conference room creates a false atmosphere. The judges are not buyers. They are advertising critics and as such they cannot always tell which advertisements would sell them.

Reason Number Six: Advertising effectiveness can usually be judged only by sales or by some action that may lead to a sale, such as writing for a booklet or a sample. The real judge of advertising is the woman who says to her grocer, "No, I don't want Blank's Soap. I want that kind I saw advertised in the newspapers last week."

More and more advertising agents and manufacturers are becoming sold on the idea that there should be less guessing and more testing in the advertising business. A well-known advertising agent expressed this view in a trade magazine advertisement. This ad expresses so well the necessity for scientific testing that it is reproduced in part below:

50% OF ALL ADVERTISEMENTS ARE WRONG

A set of mail order ads of known results were submitted to 14 advertising clubs. Each club was requested to present these ads to its members and ask them to pick out the best-selling ads.

About 50 per cent of the judgments of these experienced advertising men in the 14 advertising clubs were wrong when compared with the actual sales results of the ads.

Therefore, it must be reasonable to assume that 50 per cent of all advertisements are wrong and that even expert advertising judgment is unsafe in prejudging the selling power of an ad.

Do not depend on opinions. Use some kind of objective test to determine the relative effectiveness of advertisements.

The spider looks for a merchant who doesn't advertise so he can spin a web across his door and lead a life of undisturbed peace!

Mark Twain

How Split-run Copy Testing Works

Here are two pages from the New York *Daily News* that are identical except for two small ads in the lower right-hand corners of the pages. Each ad appeared in half the press run. Hence the expression, "split-run." The headline of one ad says: "Stop cold misery or your money back." The other says: "Relieve cold suffering at any stage with Rexall Super Anapac." Each ad contains an offer of a free bottle of cold tablets if the reader will mail the ad to Rexall. The purpose of this test was to find out which ad headline

induced the most people to read the copy and send for the product. Since both ads appeared in the same position, on the same page, and on the same day, the only variables in this test are the headlines of the ads. The advertiser can count the number of replies from each ad and get an accurate measure of which headline is more effective. For a detailed explanation of split-run copy testing, see chapter 18.

4

Right and Wrong Methods of Writing Headlines

In the preceding chapter we analyzed ten outstandingly successful headlines and found that self-interest was the principal quality they all had in common.

Below are the headlines of ten advertisements that were outstanding failures. Each of these ten advertisements was tested by running it in a magazine or newspaper in which previous advertisements had been tested. These advertisements brought so few inquiries and so few sales that they were never used again. Let us consider the headlines of these failure advertisements so that we will know what sort of headlines not to write. Here are the headlines:

Ten Headlines That Failed

"No...no...don't call on me!"
[Course in Public Speaking]

The Odds Are 9 to 1 Against You
[Business Training Course]

"I'll never give another party," she sobbed
[Book of Games for Parties]

A Test of How "Well Read" You Are
[Book of Literary Gems]

Is Worry Robbing You of the Good Things of Life?
[Life Insurance]

The Trouble with Many Married Men Is...
[Life Insurance]

Are You Playing Fair with Your Wife?
[Life Insurance]

Are You Living in a Circle?
[Budget Book]

The Years That the Locust Hath Eaten
[Business Training Course]
Letters Wives Don't Write to Their Unsuccessful Husbands
[Business Training Course]

In reading over these unsuccessful headlines, perhaps you decided in your own mind what made them unsuccessful. See if you agree with the following analysis:

1. All ten headlines are primarily curiosity headlines. For example, the headline, "The Trouble with Many Married Men Is..." attempts to get the reader into the copy by making him want to find out what, if anything, is the trouble with many married men.
2. None of the headlines gives news.
3. None of the headlines contains an offer of a benefit that appeals to the reader's self-interest.
4. Seven of the headlines are negative. They paint the dark side of the picture. For example, " 'I'll never give another party,' she sobbed."

Having analyzed ten successful headlines in the previous chapter, we should now be able to set down a few fundamental rules for writing a good headline. Following are the rules.

Five Rules for Writing Headlines

1. First and foremost, try to get self-interest into every headline you write. Make your headline suggest to the reader that here is something he wants. This rule is so fundamental that it would seem obvious. Yet the rule is violated every day by scores of writers.
2. If you have news, such as a new product, or a new use for an old product, be sure to get that news into your headline in a big way.
3. Avoid headlines that merely provoke curiosity. Curiosity combined with news or self-interest is an excellent aid to the pulling power of your headline, but curiosity by itself is seldom enough. This fundamental rule is violated more often than any other. Every issue of every magazine and newspaper contains headlines that attempt to sell the reader through curiosity alone.

4. Avoid, when possible, headlines that paint the gloomy or negative side of the picture. Take the cheerful, positive angle.
5. Try to suggest in your headline that here is a quick and easy way for the reader to get something he wants.

In using this last suggestion—the quick and easy way—be sure, as mentioned previously, to make your headline believable. Here is the headline of an advertisement that was tested by a correspondence school:

To men who want to work less
and earn more

This seems to sum up in a few words what men have wanted ever since the world began. Yet the advertisement did not bring many replies, probably because the headline was unbelievable. It seemed too good to be true.

Additional Aids to Headline Writing

Having set down five fundamental rules for writing a good headline, let us now consider a few other aids to headline writing that have been proved by actual sales tests.

A sensible point of view to take in writing a headline is this: Try to decide what would make you buy the product. Actually try to discover in your own mind what argument would make you, the writer of the headline, part with good money in order to buy the article you are advertising. Then express in a few words this reason for buying. That is your headline.

Do not try to make your headline so short that it fails to express your idea properly. Brevity in headlines may be an excellent quality, but it is not so important that all else should be sacrificed for it. It is more important to say what you want to say—to express your complete thought even if it takes twenty words to do it.

Here is a lengthy but excellent headline for a travel bureau. It tells a complete story:

This Summer the West Is Yours
for as Little as $827 and up...

All-Expense Tours
14 Thrilling Vacations
to Choose from

This headline would have been far less effective if the writer, for the sake of brevity, had merely said:

This Summer the West Is Yours

Here is another lengthy but effective headline. It appeared at the top of an advertisement for the New York Telephone Company:

A 3-hour trip for a $10 order!...
It would have taken 3 minutes by telephone

Avoid the "dead" headline—the type of headline that sounds as if it were written to be carved on a bronze tablet or uttered in solemn conclave by the chairman of the board of directors. Here are examples:

Unusual Times
Unusual Values

The Value in Quality

True Optimism

Avoid the "too smart" headline—the headline that instead of making the reader want to buy your product simply makes him exclaim "How clever!" Examples:

Women! Read this SUMMERY SUMMARY
Banquet Size
Family Wise
Why Not Give Emeralds Away?

Avoid the meaningless headline. Examples:

A Plain Fact for Plain People
When, As and If

One way to persuade people to read an advertisement is to suggest in the headline that the copy contains useful information. Examples:

Advice to Wives Whose Husbands Don't Save Money
Jean Carroll's Page on Hair Beauty
How to Improve Your Handwriting
A Tiny Treatment of Tremendous Importance

It is an old saying that shoemakers' children usually have poor shoes. Below is an example of a modern parallel—a poor advertisement for an advertising man. The advertisement occupied a full page in a trade magazine. The reason it is poor is because the idea that should have been expressed in the headline is not expressed in the headline, but in small print in the last paragraph of the advertisement. Here is the actual advertisement:

ADVERTISER'S NOTE

Mr. A.B. Jones
Director of
X.Y.Z., LTD.
London, England

the well-known and old established international advertising agents, responsible for handling a number of American advertising accounts in various parts of the world, will be in New York from May 12th to 20th. Advertisers and agents wishing to consult him with regard to overseas markets should write to:

Mr. A.B. Jones
c/o Blank Agency, Inc.
Fifth Avenue
New York

The last line of this advertisement contains the words "overseas markets." That is the point of the entire advertisement. It is addressed to advertisers and agents who want data regarding overseas markets. Yet this fact is not mentioned until the end. It should have been mentioned in the headline in order to attract the proper audience. An advertiser who was actually looking for data regarding overseas markets might read the headline of this advertisement and turn the page, not realizing that the copy contained the very data he wanted.

Get the big point of your advertisement into your headline. Use your headline as a hook to reach out and catch the special group of people you are trying to interest.

Although curiosity alone is seldom enough to make a good headline, it is an excellent idea to get curiosity into your self-interest headlines. For example, here are two purely self-interest headlines:

How I saved myself from baldness
Make $60 a day

Notice how these headlines are improved by revising them so

that they arouse curiosity in addition to offering the reader something he wants:

How a strange accident saved me from baldness
Is $60 a day worth a postage stamp?

Advertisements bearing these headlines were used in magazines. The advertisements were extremely successful and were repeated over and over again for years before sales fell off to a point where the cost of the advertising space was greater than the profits from the sales.

Compare the above tested headlines with the following headlines taken from untested advertisements:

Men may not admit it, but...
Children shriek with joy
Look to the Sea!

What hopeless, useless, senseless headlines! They say nothing, mean nothing, sell nothing. Yet scores of advertisers are using headlines that are just as bad. It is unfortunate that these advertisers do not test their copy. Or is it fortunate perhaps? Sometimes ignorance is bliss.

Headlines that are merely a statement of fact are not effective in getting people to read copy. For example:

When dull film covers teeth, smiles lose fascination
[Toothpaste manufacturer]

Nothing rolls like a ball
[Ball bearing manufacturer]

The reason that these headlines are not effective in getting people into the copy is that the reader knows what the copy is going to say without reading it. It is going to say, "Use Brand X Toothpaste"..."Use Brand Y Ball Bearings." However, this type of headline does have the advantage of getting a brief message across to people who read only headlines.

The advertiser's logotype at the bottom of the ad can be considered as part of the headline. After reading the headline, the reader instinctively looks down at the logotype to see what company the message is from. Thus, the headline writer can count on the name of the company to supplement and make clear the meaning of the headline. For example, the four advertisements below all have the same headline, but the headline means something different in each case, owing to the different logotypes.

End Money Worries
[copy and illustration]

The New York Business Training Institute

This advertisement suggests that here is a method of ending money worries either through (1) some system of accounting, or (2) through a course of training that will enable a man to earn more money.

End Money Worries
[copy and illustration]
Life Insurance Company

This advertisement suggests that here is a plan for ending money worries by means of life insurance.

End Money Worries
[copy and illustration]
Macy's Department Store

This advertisement suggests that you may end money worries by means of the money you save through Macy's reduced prices.

End Money Worries
[copy and illustration]
First National Bank

This advertisement obviously is a suggestion to end money worries through some plan for saving money.

The effect of the advertiser's logotype must be considered when writing a headline.

What is true of the logotype is also true of the picture used to illustrate the advertisement. The picture may be used to supplement and help make clear the meaning of the headline. For example, a successful mail order advertisement had the headline, "Fat Men." This headline would not be entirely clear if it weren't for the fact that the illustration showed a fat man being pulled in at the waistline by a reducing belt.

Avoid the "hard-to-grasp" headline—the headline that requires thought and is not clear at first glance. Here are examples:

Dependability—a word that grew out of a fact

Coming and going through New Orleans, the touring thousands pause and refresh themselves

If every wife knew what every widow knows, no husband would be without life insurance

Remember that the reader's attention is yours for only a single, involuntary instant. He will not use up his valuable time trying to figure out what you mean. He will simply turn the page.

Do not run advertisements without headlines. Some advertisers do this in the mistaken notion that it is smart, modern, and sophisticated. Because they do not test their advertising, these advertisers do not realize that about the only person who reads their copy is the proofreader who is paid to read it.

You can't expect people to read your message unless you first give them in the headline a powerful reason for reading it. To run an advertisement without a headline is like opening a store without hanging out a sign to tell people what kind of store it is. A few customers may come into the store, but many prospective customers will be lost.

If there is any exception to this rule, it is where an excellent picture of the product is used. For example, a beautiful, four-color picture of a bowl of delicious peaches with the name Del Monte at the bottom of the page conveys a message without a headline.

Headline Writing Techniques

Write a number of headlines for every advertisement and then select the best one. The man who submits a dozen answers in a prize contest has a better chance of winning than the man who writes only one answer. In the same way, the copywriter who writes a dozen headlines has a better chance of writing a good one than the copywriter who writes only one headline.

If you have time to write as many as twenty-five headlines, you increase still further your chances of writing a good one. Put the headlines away and read them over the next day. Try to take the point of view of the bored customer. Try to decide which headline would be most likely to stop you if you were turning the pages of a magazine or a newspaper and you were not interested in the advertising at all.

Before you make your final decision as to which headline to use, it is a good idea to show your list of possible headlines to someone who has never seen them before. Let some person whose judgment you have found good in the past act as copy chief.

You should not trust your own judgment entirely. You may be prejudiced. You are too close to the headlines you have just written. A headline whose meaning may be perfectly clear to you may be puzzling to someone else.

If you could put your headlines away for a month and then read them, you might be able actually to view them from the customer's angle. But you can't wait a month. Therefore, get the customer's reaction by showing your headlines to someone else.

Often a headline may have two meanings, one of which you do not suspect. For example, a copywriter recently showed me an allegorical piece of copy, the first sentence of which was:

David dropped Goliath

This sentence gave me a mental picture of David holding Goliath up in the air and suddenly dropping him to the ground. That is not the impression the copywriter wanted me to get. He wanted to say that David knocked out Goliath or that David felled Goliath.

How to Handle Long Headlines

As mentioned previously, a long headline that really says something is more effective than a brief heading that says nothing. However, it is important to handle the long headline correctly. Here are two headlines taken from a national magazine showing examples of the wrong way to handle the long headline.

WHY
my second Duplex is the only car
I have ever been able to pay cash for

There's satisfaction in
KNOWING
the appearance of your bathroom
is pleasing to guests

The trouble with the arrangement of these headlines is that the words in large print are words that by themselves mean nothing. If you are going to emphasize certain words in the headline, be sure that they are words that say something.

Here are two headlines taken from a national magazine showing examples of the correct way to handle the long headline. Notice that the emphasized words are words that mean something.

No matter where you live you need ample
WINDSTORM INSURANCE

Brand X's
FINE COFFEE
is served in the home
of each of these surprisingly domestic bachelors

Two ways to handle the long headline are:

1. Print the entire headline in the same size type.
2. Play up one or more important words of the headline in extra-large type.

The trouble with the first method is that a long headline all printed in the same size type gives the effect of a gray tone across the page. It is flat, uninteresting. Nothing sticks out to stop the reader.

The second method is the better. It overcomes this disadvantage. It has three factors in its favor:

1. By their very size, the words printed in the extra large type act as a "stopper."

2. The words in large print, if they are the right words, help to select from the audience the special group who are prospects for your product.

3. These words in large print get a brief message across to these prospects—a message that is almost impossible to miss, no matter how fast the reader turns the page.

Here is another example of the correct application of this

method of handling headlines. Consider the headline below, which sells subscriptions to a weekly book review magazine:

Can you talk about books
with the rest of them?

When this headline was used, it was printed this way:

CAN YOU TALK
ABOUT BOOKS
with the rest of them?

The proper audience was selected and their interest aroused by the message that appeared in extra large type.

Some headlines do not lend themselves to this sort of emphasis. It is impossible to pick out two or three or even five words that tell the story briefly. In cases of this kind there are two things you can do:

1. Recast the headline.
2. Put half the headline in large-size type and subordinate the rest of it.

Here are some more examples of the right and wrong ways to emphasize certain words in headlines:

Wrong	THE SECRET of how to be taller
Right	The Secret of how to BE TALLER
Wrong	THE FINEST QUALITY aluminum railings money can buy
Right	ALUMINUM RAILINGS —the finest quality money can buy
Wrong	NOW IS THE TIME to buy good funriture
Right	GOOD FURNITURE —now is the time to buy it
Wrong	AT LAST a hair spray made for dry hair
Right	At last a hair spray made for DRY HAIR

Wrong   HI-POWER
                automatic electric paint sprayer
Right   Hi-Power automatic electric
                  PAINT SPRAYER

Some of the wrong emphasis that you will find in ad headlines is due to the fact that an ad writer has handed to the artist or layout man a typed piece of copy and left it up to the artist to decide which headline words to emphasize. This is unwise. The writer should sit down with the artist and help him to select meaningful words to put into big print. Artists tend to think in terms of tone values and masses of light and shade. If the balance of a layout is helped by putting the first word or the last word of the headline in large letters, the artist may do it regardless of the meaning or lack of meaning. I once heard the following amusing exchange between a writer and an artist:

"The trouble with artists is that they think ads should be looked at but not read," said the writer.

"The trouble with writers is that they think ads should be read but not looked at," said the artist.

The net of it is that the best ads are produced when writer and artist work together as a team.

Lessons from Current Publications

It is instructive to look through current magazines and newspapers and compare the headlines being used by some of the general advertisers with the headlines being used by the mail order advertisers—the advertisers who can trace the sales results from every ad.

The headlines below are taken from a single copy of a magazine. Notice the vagueness and supposed cleverness of the general headlines (List No. 1) as compared with the simple directness of the mail order headlines (List No. 2).

List No. 1—Headlines used by General Advertisers

Your luncheon on many a summer's day!
What's right with the world when girls just will be boys?
This Nose Belongs to a Thrifty Woman
Blank's Candy—the Fifth that makes the Foursome
Lucky Baby
First you listen! Then just dip in your spoon
It won't go off!

List No. 2—Headlines used by Mail Order Advertisers

Be a Hotel Hostess
Banish Teetering Furniture
Lifetime Floor Coating
Spare-Time Cash
Kill Ant Colonies at Their Source
Spray Your Weeds Away with Weed Out
Maternity Frocks
Learn Dressmaking—Earn Money at Home
Now! Orange Juice for the Whole Family...Quickly!
Easily!
Hollywood's Make-up Secret

Could anything be more simple or more direct than these mail order headlines? They are telegraphic. They get the story to you in a few short words. They are absolutely clear and understandable.

Mail order ads of this kind are repeated again and again. Sometimes they last for years before their effectiveness is worn out.

Advertising nourishes the consuming power of men. It creates wants for a better standard of living. It sets up before a man the goal of a better home, better clothing, better food for himself and his family. It spurs individual exertion and greater production.

Winston Churchill

An Ad That Attracted the Wrong Audience

When Dale Carnegie's famous book about how to win friends was first published, two ads for the book were tested by mail order sales. The headline of one was the title of the book, namely: "How to Win Friends and Influence People." This ad was successful. The headline of the other ad is shown above. This ad failed. Why? Because it attracted people who wanted a book on marriage. When these people read the coupon order form, they discovered that the book was not about marriage but about winning friends. Be sure that the headline of your ad attracts the right audience. *Note:* The successful ad is shown on Page 305.

Which Recruiting Ad Pulled the Most Coupons?

Here are two Navy recruiting ads that offer a free booklet, "Life in the Navy." One ad features the free training appeal. The other features the romantic appeal. Before being published nationally, these ads were given a preliminary test in four states.

In all four states the winning ad was the one with the headline: "Free! Training that is worth $1500." Another winning ad in the campaign had the headline: "Which of These 35 Jobs Do You Want Right Now?" Apparently men who are considering joining the service are practical minded rather than romantic minded.

BUY NO DESK

Until You've Seen the Sensation of The Business Show

Buy no desk until you have seen Skyscraper, the new desk by Shaw-Walker. You'll marvel at the downright cleverness of it. You'll revel in the rich beauty of it. You'll be amazed at the organized features of it. And you'll gladly pay the moderate price asked for it. Your people, too, will thank you for an easier and better day's work.

No wonder the Skyscraper Desk by Shaw-Walker was the sensation at the Business Show.

Every desk-interested person who saw it, whether office worker, executive, official, or professional man, admired the way in which it solves old-time desk problems.

It has a new kind of top—smooth and glove-like. No other desk can have it.

Each drawer is *organized* for the worker's special convenience. One drawer is your "waste basket." Another takes a flat-type interdepartmental telephone. Others hold trays for "In," "Out" and "Pending" mail. Others, special card files, visible indexes, pencils, pads, accessories, etc.

Come see it, or send your man. Or mail the attached coupon for complete information. Shaw-Walker Company, Liggett Building, 42nd and Madison Avenue; Telephone, Murray Hill 5680.

T-4-7

SHAW-WALKER Co.
Liggett Bldg., 42nd St. & Madison Ave.
New York City

Without obligating me in any way, send complete information on the new Skyscraper Desk.

Name_____

Business _____

Address_____

SHAW-WALKER

This Was the First of a Number of "Don't Buy" Ads

When newspaper readers first saw this ad, they gasped with amazement. Never before had they seen an ad that said: "Don't buy." All previous ads had said "Buy...buy...buy." Thus the headline of the ad accomplished its purpose. It stopped people and made them read. The ad was so successful in selling desks that it was used over and over again. In the years that followed, a number of advertisers copied this appeal with headlines such as: "Buy no soap until you have tried this new kind...," "Buy no car insurance until you have compared our prices...," "Buy no Florida land until you read this message."

5

Twenty-nine Formulas for Writing Headlines

Formulas are applied to the writing of stories, plays, and popular songs, and to the creation of dramas that are broadcast daily on television. Can formulas be applied to writing headlines for advertisements?

The answer is yes. Many successful headlines have been written by this method. This chapter presents a checklist of twenty-nine headline formulas that have worked successfully in the past and may be expected to work successfully in the future.

As you review these formulas, with your product in mind, you may find a formula that will give you a good headline you can use. If not, you may be stimulated to invent a new formula. New formulas are being invented all the time. Or you may find that an old formula can be reworked into a new pattern. This list of formulas is not intended to hamper your creative thinking, but to guide your thinking into profitable channels. Use the formulas not as a crutch but as a springboard!

And remember, if you create a good headline, your task is more than half completed. It will be a relatively easy matter to write the copy. On the other hand, if you use a poor headline, it doesn't matter how hard you labor over your copy because your copy will not be read.

The headline formulas listed here can be applied, not only to advertisements in publications, but also to headlines printed on the outer envelopes of direct mail pieces. The same formulas can be used in writing the opening sentences of radio and television commercials.

News Headlines

Let's begin with news headlines. One of the most important functions of advertising is to present new products and to tell about

53

new uses and new improvements of old products. Department stores use news headlines because they bring people into the stores. Mail order advertisers use news headlines whenever possible because they are good pullers. News headlines are effective in getting attention and promoting sales. Therefore, the first seven of these headline formulas are devoted to the presentation of news.

Here is the first formula:

1. Begin your headline with the word "Announcing"

Announcing a great new car
Announcing a new dictionary
Announcing a new selection of Kodak home-movie cameras
Announcing new Firestone tires
Announcing a new help in solving the housewives' problem

The word "Announcing" can take different forms. For example:

Gulf announces a new and different gasoline
An important announcement to homeowners

2. Use words that have an announcement quality

Introducing Salonette Dresses
Presenting new 36" tall ballerina doll
Today's DuPont sponge with mop-up action
Good-bye. . . old-fashioned air conditioners
Just published . . . a new encylcopedia

Whenever a new product or a new improvement of an old product arrives on the market, you should announce that fact. Announce it in a big way! Spread the word "Announcing" clear across the page in large type. People are interested in announcements. They will often read an announcement of a new improvement or a new product regardless of whether or not they have any immediate need for the product.

Announcement copy is not a recent invention. The ancients used it. Many ancient advertisements were announcements in the form of proclamations.

After you have announced your new product or your new improvement, you can continue to retain the news element in later advertisements by using formula number three.

3. Begin your headline with the word "New"

New lemon blossom pie
New! Golf clubs specially sized for youngsters
New idea; Soup-Plate meal
New concept in weight control
New modernized record player
New Black & Decker electric drill
New method of keeping your personal finances

When you have used the word "New" for all it is worth, you can continue to give a news flavor to advertisements by employing formula number four.

4. Begin your headline with the word "Now"

Now sleep under new warmth ... new beauty!
Now you can eat like a king ... in Britain
Now ... a low-calorie Bacardi Daiquiri
Now an opportunity for long-term capital gains

Here is a successful headline which contains both "Now" and "New":

Now comes the new shorthand

5. Begin your headline with the words "At last"

At last! A steam iron with a "Magic Brain"
At last — you can drive all over the U.S. with one
easy-to-follow Map Book
At last — a one-volume world history
At last — a toothbrush guaranteed for 6 months

Using the words "At last" creates the impression that here at last, after long preparation, is a product that many people have been waiting for.

A variation is to put the words "at last" at the end of your headline, like this:

Has a remedy for the common cold
been found at last?

6. Put a date into your headline

Beginning June 1 ... low summer rates at the
Miami Biltmore

July sale of fashion gloves
Monday save 30% to 60% on these books
Why G.E. bulbs give more light this year
A 19— [insert year] warning from
   The Wall Street Journal
Reduce your golf handicap with these new 19 —
   [insert year] golf clubs
How to keep ahead this summer
You can speak French by October 15

7. Write your headline in news style

The wines you loved in Paris are here
Better hearing is suddenly here
The world's first atomic watch
Modern gift from old Mexico
Discovered — amazing way to grow hair

Other words and phrases that give a news flavor are "Just invented," and "Just off the press."

Here is a successful news headline that appeared at the top of an advertisement selling business courses by mail:

Just Published
   a new booklet announcing
   a new series of Business Courses

This headline uses the news formula no less than four times: (1) Just Published, (2) new booklet, (3) announcing, (4) new Business Courses.

Headlines That Deal with Price

Sales tests show that one of the most important factors in any sale is price. Readership surveys show that readers will often skip copy set in big type in order to get to the bottom of an ad and read prices set in small type.

The next three formulas are devoted to price. It is not always practical to mention price in national magazine ads because prices may vary in different areas. However, it is often practical and desirable to mention price in local newspaper ads and in local broadcast ads.

8. Feature the price in your headline

Lightweight G. E. Portable Mixer does all mixing
    jobs...only $17.95
Magnificent all-mahogany dining room...$749
Guaranteed 17-jewel quality watches...$16.95

9. Feature reduced price

This is a formula that is constantly used by retail advertisers, as follows:

Wool twist broadloom usually $12.95 sq. yd.
    ...sale $8.88 sq. yd.
Pigskin executive file case $19.80 (Reg. $35)
Wamsutta supercale sheets...slightly irregular
    ...$3.95 (if perfect $6.95)

National advertisers also use this formula sometimes. For example:

Whale of a coffee sale...25¢ off
Less than half price...stainless steel kitchen sets

10. Feature a special merchandising offer

In this type of headline, you often make an offer that actually causes you to lose money. You do this in order to entice a customer to start using your product. Examples:

Big Perennial offer...10 Delphiniums $1
Special 1/2 price introductory offer...8 months $1
30-day supply of vitamins for 65¢
Any 4 books (value up to $43.95) for only $1

11. Feature an easy payment plan

Sales tests show that the offer to sell merchandise on the installment plan creates many sales that otherwise would be lost. Many ads mention easy payments in the copy. Some very successful ads have featured this appeal in the headline. Examples:

Order now...pay after January 10

Only $2 a week buys this new Cassette Player
No money down ... easy payments when you buy
Cyclone Fence

12. Feature a free offer

A free offer is a device that frequently leads to future sales. The free offer may take several forms as follows: (1) A free trial; (2) A sample of the product or service; (3) A booklet about the product; or (4) A premium that requires the purchase of the product. Examples:

Free 10-day trial of three-record album
Free Plato and Aristotle
Free trial lesson
Free consultation
Free to new members of the Literary Book Club
Free garden catalog
Free map
Free guide book
Free to brides ... $2 to anyone else
Free gift ... Hot Handle Holder attached to every
   can of Johnson's Wax
Free gray hair treatment
Free plans for a clever Valentine's Day party

13. Offer information of value

People buy newspapers and magazines to read articles that give them information. Therefore, it is possible to get high readership by writing your ad in the form of a helpful article. The copy usually consists of three parts, as follows: Part 1: Information without sales talk, Part 2: Information interwoven with sales talk, Part 3: All sales talk. Here are examples of headlines of ads of this kind:

Do you make these mistakes in English?
Straight facts on when to take profits
Two easy tuna "Short pie" dishes with Bisquick
Barron's tell how "soapless soap" is creating new
   markets
Follow this Agrico plan to a greener lawn

14. Tell a story

People buy magazines in order to read stories. Therefore you can get high readership by writing a headline that offers the reader a story. In addition to high readership, this method offers the following advantages: (1) A good story makes your message clear; and (2) A good story makes your message compelling. The effectiveness of stories was illustrated long ago by the parables in the Bible.

Some of the following headlines not only sold merchandise or services, but also became famous.

How I improved my memory in one evening
They laughed when I sat down at the piano
The diary of a lonesome girl
How I became popular overnight
Often a bridesmaid but never a bride

Note: The most successful story headlines (from a sales standpoint) are those that select the right audience. For example, the headline above selling a memory course contains the word "memory" in the headline.

Using Key Words in Headlines

The next eight formulas (15 through 22) deal with key words.

15. Begin your headline with the words "How To"

Certain key words in headlines not only increase readership, but also have a beneficial effect on the copywriter by forcing him to write copy that is in the proper groove. For example, if a headline begins with the words "how to," the copywriter is forced to write copy that tells how to do something, and that is exactly the kind of copy the reader desires.

How to end money worries
How to get a better position
How to be generous to a man at Christmas
How to become an office manager
How to start a backyard garden
How to keep your husband home ... and happy
How to get rid of an inferiority complex

People are interested in learning how to do things. They will eagerly read advertisements that tell them how to do the things they want to do.

The words "How to" have also been found valuable in other forms of writing. One time I said to a magazine editor, "Mail order advertisers discovered long ago that advertisements whose headlines begin with the words 'How to' bring a large number of inquiries."

The editor replied, "We have discovered the same thing in our work. Magazine articles whose titles begin with the words 'How to' are popular with readers. Such articles actually increase circulation."

Closely related to the above headlines are those beginning with the word "How."

16. Begin your headline with the word "How"

How many a down-and-out kitchen has been reformed

How this new invention is revolutionizing concrete construction

How your energy curve responds to the world's quickest hot breakfast

How I earn my living in 4 hours a day

How I started a new life with $7

How Pepperidge Farm Bread helps you keep that radiant look

How can these magnificent Nature Guides be sold for only $1?

17. Begin your headline with the word "Why"

Why these vitamins can make you feel peppier

Why your feet hurt

Why G.E. bulbs give more light this year

Why some people almost always make money in the stock market

18. Begin your headline with the word "Which"

Which is the best battery value for your car?

Which of these five skin troubles would you like to end?

A slightly different handling of this formula is seen in the following:

Do you have these symptoms of nervous exhaustion?

This type of headline has two advantages: (1) It is interesting. It appeals to the reader's keen interest in himself; he likes to find out if his own difficulty is among those mentioned. (2) The mentioning of a number of symptoms enables the copywriter to cover much ground. Almost every reader is likely to have at least one of the symptoms.

19. Begin your headline with the words "Who else"

Who else wants a whiter wash—with no hard work?
Who else wants a kissable complexion within 30 days?
Who else has hair that won't stay combed?

20. Begin your headline with the word "Wanted"

Wanted! Man with car to run store on wheels
Wanted—More bookstores
Wanted—Your services as a high-paid real-estate
    specialist
Wanted—Safe men for dangerous times

The word "Wanted" is a compelling word. It makes the reader curious to know what is wanted. Furthermore, the headline "Wanted — Your services as a high-paid real-estate specialist" suggests a great demand for real-estate specialists. As mentioned previously, this particular headline belonged to a couponed advertisement and appeared again and again in many magazines — proof enough of its effectiveness!

21. Begin your headline with the word "This"

This soothing beauty bath is astonishing to
    fastidious women
This magical lamp automatically lights highway
    turns before you make them
This glistening porcelain washer is distinctly
    up to the minute
This friendly sign . . . everywhere

Beginning a headline with the word "This" has two advantages: (1) It makes the headline specific; (2) It draws attention to the product you are advertising.

A formula that has been proved by advertisers who use keyed copy is to offer advice. This is accomplished by employing formula number twenty-two:

22. Begin your headline with the word "Advice"

Advice to a young man starting out in business
Advice to husbands
Advice to brides

The word "Advice" suggests to the reader that he will discover some useful information if he reads the copy. The headline doesn't ask him to buy anything. It simply offers free advice. Naturally this is an attractive offer. After you have enticed the reader into the copy, you can include sales talk in addition to advice.

The preceding eight formulas employing key words do not exhaust the list of key words you can use. You can find other key words in the headlines you see in daily newspapers and in the titles of books and magazine articles. For example, in the following titles, the key words are printed in italics:

Plain talks with husbands and wives
Common faults in English
Principles of electricity
What every girl should know
Facts you should know about skin care

23. Use a testimonial-style headline

Your headline can be an actual testimonial or it can be a testimonial-style headline. Examples:

Let me tell you how I reduced for keeps
Why I cried after the ceremony
I was going broke — so I started reading
The Wall Street Journal

24. Offer the reader a test

Can your scalp pass the fingernail test?
Can your kitchen pass the guest test?
Can you pass this memory test?
A test of your writing ability

25. Use a one-word headline

Advertisers who run small ads are sometimes able to find a single word that can serve as a headline. This method is successful if the single word is meaningful and selects the right audience. The method has the advantage that the single word can be printed in big type and thus give big display to a small ad. Examples:

Accounting	Law
Aviation	Patents

Diamonds	Nerves
Reduce	Corns
Bashful?	Vitamins

You can take it for granted that these one-word headlines are effective. Otherwise, mail order and patent medicine advertisers would not continue to use them year after year.

26. Use a two-word headline

Sometimes it is impossible to find a single word that will convey a meaningful message about your product or service. In that case you can use a two-word headline. Examples:

Itchy scalp
Diaper rash
Public speaking
Fat women
Head cold

27. Warn the reader to delay buying

Most headlines urge you to buy something. Therefore, a headline advising "Don't buy" is an effective stopper. Examples:

Buy no desk until you have seen the new, all-steel
     executive
Read this before you order your Zoysia grass
Don't buy car insurance until you have read these facts
Buy no more soap until you have tried amazing
     new [name of brand]

28. Let the advertiser speak directly to the reader

Why I offer you this new kind of pipe for 50¢
I'll train you at home for a good job in computer
     programming
I guarantee you results worth $2,000 in one year
They thought I was crazy to ship Live Maine Lobsters
     as far as 1,800 miles from the ocean

29. Address your headline to a specific person or group

To the man who is 35 and dissatisfied
To a $15,000 man who would like to be making $25,000
To car owners who want to cut gasoline bills

To the man who is "making the old car do"
To women whose husbands are wedded to their work
Girls! . . . Want a fast permanent?
Sportsmen! . . . Improve your shooting skill
To young men who want to get ahead
To men who want to retire on a guaranteed income

This type of headline does two important things. First, it selects your logical prospects. Second, it offers the prospect a solution to some problem close to his heart.

Summing Up

Headline formulas are selling ideas that have worked again and again in the past and can be expected to continue to get results in the future. For example, the formula "Begin your headline with the words 'How to' " will probably last as long as advertising exists. Unless human nature changes radically, people will never tire of learning how to do the things they want to do and how to get the things they want to get.

Another form of headline that will probably never wear out is the announcement. As long as human beings inhabit this earth, they will be looking for something new, something different, something better.

Just as the physician uses the same prescription many times with beneficial effect, just as the civil engineer uses the same formulas again and again for building bridges, so can the advertising copywriter use formulas that have worked successfully in the past.

Here is a complete list of the twenty-nine formulas discussed in this chapter. This list can help you in two ways: (1) As a tool to use when you need a headline in a hurry; and (2) As a stimulus to spur your imagination toward the invention of new formulas.

1. Begin your headline with the word "Announcing"
2. Use words that have an announcement quality
3. Begin your headline with the word "New"
4. Begin your headline with the word "Now"
5. Begin your headline with the words "At last"
6. Put a date into your headline
7. Write your headline in news style
8. Feature the price in your headline
9. Feature reduced price
10. Feature a special merchandising offer

11. Feature an easy-payment plan
12. Feature a free offer
13. Offer information of value
14. Tell a story
15. Begin your headline with the words "How To"
16. Begin your headline with the word "How"
17. Begin your headline with the word "Why"
18. Begin your headline with the word "Which"
19. Begin your headline with the words "Who else?"
20. Begin your headline with the word "Wanted"
21. Begin your headline with the word "This"
22. Begin your headline with the word "Advice"
23. Use a testimonial-style headline
24. Offer the reader a test
25. Use a one-word headline
26. Use a two-word headline
27. Warn the reader to delay buying
28. Let the manufacturer speak directly to the reader
29. Address your headline to a specific person or group

*As a profession advertising is young; as a force it is
as old as the world. The first four words uttered,
"Let there be light," constitute its character. All
nature is vibrant with its impulse.*

Bruce Barton

How a Publisher Measured the Effect of a Price Change

Here are two ads offering five children's books at a bargain price, provided the customer agrees to buy a new book each month for four months. The headline of one ad offers five books for $1.69. The headline of the other ad offers five books at a slightly lower price — $1.59. Otherwise the ads are

identical. To measure the effect of this price change, the advertiser split-run tested these two ads in the *National Observer*. This change in price may seem too small to matter. However, when you are selling thousands of books, it is essential to get an accurate measure of the all-important factor of price.

How I Improved My Memory In One Evening

The Amazing Experience of Victor Jones

"*Of course* I place you! Mr. Addison Sims of Seattle.

"If I remember correctly—and I *do* remember correctly—Mr. Burroughs, the lumberman, introduced me to you at the luncheon of the Seattle Rotary Club three years ago in May. This is a pleasure indeed! I haven't laid eyes on you since that day. How is the grain business? How did that merger work out?"

The assurance of this speaker—in the crowded corridor of the Hotel St. Regis—compelled me to look at him, though it is not my habit to "listen in" even in a hotel lobby.

"He is David M. Roth, the most famous memory expert in the United States," said my friend Kennedy, answering my question before I could get it out. "He will show you a lot more wonderful things than that, before the evening is over."

And he did.

As we went into the banquet room the toastmaster was introducing a long line of the guests to Mr. Roth. I got in line and when it came my turn, Mr. Roth asked, "What are your initials, Mr. Jones, and your business connection and telephone number?" Why he asked this, I learned later, when he picked out from the crowd the 60 men he had met two hours before and called each by name without a mistake. What is more, he named each man's business and telephone number.

I won't tell you all the other amazing things this man did except to tell how he called back, without a minute's hesitation, long lists of numbers, bank clearings, prices, parcel post rates and anything else the guests gave him in rapid order.

∗ ∗ ∗

When I met Mr. Roth—which you may be sure I did the first chance I got—he rather bowled me over by saying, in his quiet, modest way:

"There is nothing miraculous about my remembering anything I want to remember, whether it be names, faces, figures, facts, or something I have read.

FREE EXAMINATION COUPON

WALTER J. BLACK, Inc., Dept. 22
2 Park Avenue, New York, N. Y.

Please send me, in a plain container, the Roth Memory Course of seven lessons. I will either remail the course to you within five days after its receipt or send you $3.50 in full payment.

Name ....

Address ....

....

....

"*You can do this as easily as I do.* Anyone with an average mind can learn quickly to do exactly the same things which seem so miraculous when I do them.

"My own memory," continued Mr. Roth, "was originally very faulty. Yes it was—a really *poor* memory. On meeting a man I would lose his name in thirty seconds, while now there are probably 10,000 men and women in the United States, many of whom I have met but once, whose names I can call instantly on meeting them."

"That is all right for you, Mr. Roth," I interrupted, "you have given years to it. But how about me?"

"Mr. Jones," he replied, "I can teach you the secret of a good memory in one evening. This is not a guess, because I have done it with thousands of pupils. In the first of seven simple lessons which I have prepared for home study, I show you the basic principle of my whole system and you will find it—not hard work as you might fear—but just like playing a fascinating game. I will prove it to you."

He didn't have to. His Course did; I got it the next day from his publishers.

When I tackled the first lesson, I suppose I was the most surprised man in forty-eight States to find that I had learned—in about one hour—how to remember a list of one hundred words so that I could call them off forward and back without a single mistake.

That lesson *stuck*. So did the other six.

Read this letter from one of the most famous trial lawyers in New York:

"May I take occasion to state that I regard your service in giving this system to the world as a public benefaction. The wonderful simplicity of the method, and the ease with which its principles may be acquired, especially appeal to me. I may add that I already had occasion to test the effectiveness of the first two lessons in the preparation for trial of an important action in which I am about to engage."

This man didn't put it a bit too strong. The Roth Course is priceless! I can *count* on my memory now. I can call the name of any man I have met before—and I keep getting better. I can remember any figures I wish to remember. Telephone numbers come to mind instantly, once I have filed them by Mr. Roth's easy method.

The old fear of forgetting has vanished. I used to be "scared stiff" on my feet—because I wasn't sure. I couldn't remember what I wanted to say.

Now I am sure of myself, confident, and "easy as an old shoe" when I get on my feet at the club, at a banquet, in a business meeting, or in any social gathering.

The most enjoyable part of it all is that I am now a good conversationalist—and I used to be as silent as a sphinx when I got into a crowd of people who knew things

Now I can call up like a flash of lightning most any fact I want right at the instant I need it most. I used to think a ' air trigger" memory belonged only to the prodigy and genius. Now I see that every one of us has that kind of a memory of he knows how to make it work.

I tell you it is a wonderful thing, after groping around in the dark for many years to be able to switch the big search light on your mind and see instantly everything you want to remember.

This Roth Course will do wonders in your office.

Since we took it up you never hear anyone in our office say "I guess" or "I think it was about so much" or "I forget that right now" or "I can't remember" or "I must look up his name." Now they are right there with the answer—like a shot.

Here is just a bit from a letter of a well-known sales manager up in Montreal:

"Here is the whole thing in a nutshell. Mr. Roth has a most remarkable Memory Course. It is simple, and easy as falling off a log. Anyone—I don't care who he is—can improve his Memory 100% in a week and 1,000% in six months."

My advice to you is don't wait another minute. Send for Mr. Roth's amazing course and see what a wonderful memory you have got. Your dividends in *increased* power will be enormous.

VICTOR JONES.

Send No Money

So confident are the publishers of the Roth Memory Course that you will be amazed to see how easy it is to double, yes, triple your memory power in a few short hours, that they are willing to send the course on free examination.

Don't send any money. Merely mail the coupon and the complete course will be sent, all charges prepaid, at once. If you are not entirely satisfied send it back any time within five days after you receive it; and you will owe nothing.

On the other hand, if you are as pleased as are the thousands of other men and women who have used the course send only $3.50 in full payment. You take no risk and you have everything to gain, so mail the coupon now before this remarkable offer is withdrawn. WALTER J. BLACK, Inc., Dept. 22, 2 Park Ave., New York, N. Y.

One of the Most Quoted Ads of All Time

This ad was written by Wilbur Ruthrauff of the Ruthrauff & Ryan Advertising Agency. It was the most successful of a number of mail order ads for the Roth Memory Course. The ad was published many times over a period of years. The first line of the copy became famous and people often quoted it with a smile. "Of course I place you! Mr. Addison Sims of Seattle."

6

Finding the Right Appeal

Years ago an advertisement like the following brought results:

[Headline] You can make big money easily
[Illustration] Man pointing finger at reader

Today the attitude of the average reader toward such copy is: "I don't believe the scheme would pay me big money. I don't believe the work is easy. It probably consists of selling some trinket to my friends at five times its value."

Like it or not, the public is becoming more sophisticated every year. This does not mean that you can't use an old standby, such as the money appeal. People are as eager as ever to make money, but your advertisements must be believable. An ounce of belief is worth a pound of half-belief.

Here are some believable money headlines:

How a man of 40 can retire in 15 years
[Life Insurance Company]

To men who want to be independent in the next 5 years
[Business School]

A story of spare time and extra cash
[Publishing Company]

There is no element in an advertisement more important than the appeal—the reason you give the reader for buying. If this statement seems to clash with statements previously made about the importance of the headline, remember that the headline and the appeal are usually one and the same. The appeal is usually expressed in the headline:

Effective Appeals

Here are some appeals that have increased sales:

Make more money	End drudgery
Save money	More leisure
Advance in business	Comfort
Prestige	Better health
Enjoyment	Freedom from worry
Reduce fat	Security in old age

Other effective appeals are:

The desire to be popular, to attract people, to have personal charm. This appeal sells a wide variety of products, from lipsticks to books on "How to win friends."

The average person's desire for a bargain is another powerful appeal. Department stores constantly use the bargain appeal.

The desire of one man to outshine his neighbors is an appeal that sells high-priced automobiles, expensive cabin cruisers, luxurious homes, landscape gardening, and fancy swimming pools.

The shame appeal—avoid embarrassment—helps to sell another large group of products: etiquette books, courses in correct English, deodorants, etc.

The money appeal, one of the most effective of all, can be employed in a number of ways. For example, a publisher of business books found that his most effective appeal was "These books will help you make more money." A clothing manufacturer found that of all the appeals he tried the most effective was "Wear these high-grade clothes and you can command a better income." Insurance companies, banks, investment houses, and stock brokers all use the money appeal in one way or another.

Proof of the Importance of the Appeal

The importance of the appeal used in advertising was first brought forcibly to my attention by the following experience. I took all the advertisements I had prepared for a certain client in one year's time and studied the coupon returns from test insertions. Here is the way the coupon returns looked:

Advertisement	Replies
A	218
B	666
C	240
D	191
E	502
F	511
G	263
H	550
I	867
J	194
K	210

I then arranged these advertisements in order of merit, as follows (the poorest advertisement is listed first and the best one last):

Advertisement	Replies
D (poorest)	191
J	194
K	210
A	218
C	240
G	263
E	502
F	511
H	550
B	666
I (best)	867

Notice that the foregoing eleven advertisements fall into two distinct groups:

Group 1.	Group 2.
The following six advertisements brought 263 coupon returns or less:	The following five advertisements brought 502 coupon returns or more:

Advertisement	Replies	Advertisement	Replies
D	191	E	502
J	194	F	511

Advertisement	Replies	Advertisement	Replies
K	210	H	550
A	218	B	666
C	240	I	867
G	263		

Further study revealed this important point: Every advertisement in Group 2—the successful group—had a certain appeal expressed in the headline of the advertisement. No advertisement in Group 1—the unsuccessful group—had this appeal expressed in the headline. In other words, the five successful advertisements, without exception, had a definite quality in common. That quality was a certain appeal around which the headlines were built. The unsuccessful advertisements all lacked this particular headline appeal. The headlines of the unsuccessful advertisements were based on several entirely different appeals.

This analysis pointed to the following logical conclusions:

1. That the appeal around which an advertisement is built is vitally important.
2. That in order to be effective, the successful appeal must be featured in the headline. To get the appeal into the copy is evidently not enough, since some of the unsuccessful advertisements had it in the copy.

One other significant point about this analysis is that Advertisement G, the best of the unsuccessful group, had the result-getting appeal moderately displayed in a subheading.

This method of analyzing a series of advertisements almost always brings out one or more significant points. It is an easy method to follow. Simply take a set of proofs and mark in the corner of each proof the number of replies or the amount of sales brought in by that advertisement. Then lay the proofs in a row in order of merit and study the advertisements to see what quality the most successful advertisements have in common. You will find that the successful advertisements usually possess one or more definite qualities that the unsuccessful ones do not have.

For example, the successful advertisements may all have long copy, whereas the unsuccessful advertisements may have short copy. Or the successful advertisements may all have a certain type of illustration that is lacking in the other advertisements. The important thing is that once you have discovered the result-getting quality, you can enlarge on it and use it to the fullest possible extent in future advertisements.

One way to realize the importance of getting the right appeal is to consider the effect on yourself of two advertisements. For example, suppose the following two advertisements for toothpaste were shown to you:

Ad No. 1: More people buy A's Toothpaste than any other toothpaste in the world

Ad No. 2: B's Toothpaste comes in a specially patented tube, the cap of which is fastened to the tube and cannot be lost

It is obvious that Ad No. 1 contains the stronger appeal. Logic tells you that if more people buy A's Toothpaste than any other in the world, it must be superior. The other advertisement devotes too much emphasis to a minor point.

Now suppose the advertisement that tells you A's Toothpaste is the largest seller is a carelessly prepared advertisement—poor selection of type, no illustration, no use of color, just black and white. Suppose the advertisement telling you about the cap that cannot be lost is a handsome four-color job with an expensive painting for an illustration. Would you alter your decision? Probably not. The basic appeal would sway you more than the manner in which the appeal was presented.

Suppose two advertisements for business schools were presented to you. The first advertisement tells you how this particular business course helps you to make more money. It gives specific examples of men who have made more money by taking the course. It tells what the incomes of these men were before they took the course and what their present incomes are.

The second advertisement speaks in general terms about the value of business training. It fails to give you specific facts and figures and proof of results.

Wouldn't you be much more apt to be swayed by the first advertisement—the advertisement that tells you exactly how much more money was made by the men who took the course? And again, wouldn't the facts the advertisement gave you be more important than the manner in which the facts were presented?

The layout, the illustration, and the style of type wouldn't have nearly as much effect on you as what the advertisement said. The point of all this is that what an advertisement says is more important than how it is said.

Ideas That Sound Good Versus Ideas That Are Good

Another point: Appeals that sound good when an advertising agency man describes them to his client are not always the most effective appeals that can be used. Clever, tricky ideas often sound fine when described in a conference room. But usually some simple, basic, plain-as-the-nose-on-your-face idea will sell more goods.

A nationally advertised business school published an advertisement with this headline:

Letters wives don't write to their
unsuccessful husbands

The advertisement featured the following beautifully written letter:

Dear Fred:

Tomorrow is our eighth wedding anniversary. Haven't the years flown by! How carefree we were, how hopefully we started out just eight years ago! You were going to work so hard and get ahead so fast, remember?

You *have* worked hard. I've seen the tired, worried lines in your face that prove it. And I've worked hard, too, since the children came — worked to make the same old salary enough for the four of us, worked to make one dollar carry the burden of two.

Understand, dear, I'm not complaining. I'm not thinking about *me* — I'm thinking about *you.* Often I've wondered, lying awake at night, why some of the men we know have gone ahead while you haven't — men who haven't any more brains and aren't half as nice as you. Remember that first disappointment when Joe Edwards was made assistant to the president? You wanted that promotion, and you were ahead of Joe. But they told you that he had the all-around training you lacked.

Dearest, it's gone on a long time now. You come home tired at night, and there are bills to pay, and we have a scene, and you say you "simply *must* make more money" — and then you never seem to *do* anything about it. Can't something be done? I want to help you succeed while we are still young. Isn't there a way?

Your loving wife,
Helen

This advertisement brought more praise from advertising men than any business school advertisement in years. Ad men who read it exclaimed, "Wonderful!" Yet the advertisement was an unqualified failure. The coupon returns failed to come in.

Highly-praised advertisements are not always selling advertisements.

Another type of copy that has been found to be ineffective is copy that talks in general terms and fails to get to the point. A few years ago an investment house used advertisements that began like this:

Everyone is entitled to fun in life. Everyone is entitled to the things that make the world worth living in. And yet thousands of people with perfectly normal incomes think of the good things as luxuries they can't afford.

This advertisement rambled on in this strain for several paragraphs. Finally the reader was given a few facts. Today this same advertiser starts his copy off by telling the facts right away. *Result:* Increased inquiries and sales.

Appeals That Create Ill Will

Some appeals not only fail to sell a product; they actually create ill will.

A friend once said, "Do you remember that cigar ad that showed a fat, grinning face? It was a sort of balloon face or moon face, perfectly round, with a silly ogling grin. How I hated that face! It seemed so unnecessarily ugly."

Another man complained about a slogan he didn't understand. He said, "That slogan is meaningless to me. Every time I see that slogan, it annoys me."

Another friend described a display card that bothered him. It was an advertisement for a household insect destroyer showing a picture of a woman smiling and winking one eye. The caption was "I'm wise, are you?" Remarked my friend, "That ad doesn't make any sense to me. What does it mean?"

Experiences of this kind indicate that people actually feel resentment toward advertisements they don't understand. They become positively annoyed at slogans and captions whose meaning is not clear.

The reverse is also true. Advertisements that seem like good advertisements to the reader, and actually do sell him, create a friendly feeling.

It is the same in personal selling. Suppose a salesman tries to sell you a patented necktie presser and fails. You are not anxious to see that salesman again. If you see him on the street, you would just as soon avoid him. On the other hand, you are glad to smile and say hello to a salesman whose product you bought. You have a friendly feeling toward him.

However, a friendly feeling toward an advertising campaign is not always enough to make the customer buy the product. An artist told me how much he admired a certain toothpaste's "Danger Line" campaign—especially an advertisement that showed the old Greek temples on the Acropolis crumbling away. A line was drawn through the base of the temples and nearby appeared the caption "Guard the Danger Line." "What kind of toothpaste do you use?" I asked the artist. With a laugh, he mentioned a different brand!

People often have two judgments of advertising—the conscious and the unconscious. The conscious judgment is their reaction to it from an artistic point of view. The unconscious judgment or real judgment comes to the surface when they go into a store to buy.

In regard to the aforementioned slogan that my friend disliked, it might be argued that the very fact that my friend noticed it, even though unfavorably, was a point in its favor. It might be argued that the slogans he didn't notice and the advertisements he didn't remember, either favorably or unfavorably, were the bad advertisements. A famous copywriter once said, "The greatest crime advertising can commit is to remain unnoticed."

The importance of noticeability is illustrated by a story told by a buyer of women's dresses. The buyer said:

When I am selecting dresses for our store, I find that I can divide all the dresses into three classes. First, those that produce a strong favorable impression on me. Second, those that produce a bad effect on me—that seem actually ugly. Third, those that do not affect me much one way or the other.

I always buy the dresses that have a strong effect on me. I buy the dresses that seem to me either beautiful or just the opposite. I have discovered that not only the beautiful dresses, but also those that seem actually ugly, will always be sure to attract some woman's eye.

The dresses I never buy are the ones that don't affect me one way or the other. I have found that those dresses will not sell.

The Specific Appeal Versus the General Appeal

A dealer in used cars decided to stimulate his business with newspaper advertising. He ran some institutional advertisements with headlines such as:

Better automobile values
Long life at low cost

The advertisements were beautifully laid out, with borders and carefully selected type. But the results were poor. Only a few customers came to the showroom. Said the automobile dealer, "The ads looked like winners, but actually they were flops."

New copy was tried—copy featuring specific car bargains and naming the make, the year, and actual prices. The advertisements were set like the mail order advertisements in the Sears-Roebuck catalogue. Results were surprising. By actual count, three times as many customers answered the ads.

This experience is typical. It is just another indication that fine language and a handsome layout do not in themselves make a good advertisement. What you say is more important than how you say it.

In chapter 18 there are detailed instructions regarding methods for discovering successful appeals. When, after testing, you have found a successful appeal, you can use many variations of it. For example, a financial advertiser tested a number of appeals and found that an advertisement with this headline brought the best results:

Get rid of money worries for good

Similar advertisements were then prepared with headlines that contained variations of the same basic appeal. Here are the headlines:

How to end money worries
This plan has helped thousands of people to end
   money worries
Here's a wonderful way to end money worries
You can laugh at money worries if you follow
this plan

These similar advertisements all brought excellent results.

The technique of finding and using a successful appeal can be summed up in three basic steps as follows:

1. Test a number of different sales appeals.
2. Determine the winning appeal by an analysis of results.
3. Cash in on the winning appeal by featuring it in all your

advertising, whether it be space advertising, broadcast commercials, or direct mail.

This method of finding the best appeal has brought success to some of the world's greatest advertisers. It can do the same for you.

Let your light so shine that men may know your good works.

Bible

DON'T POISON YOUR DOG!

Has it ever occurred to you that in these hot sultry days your dog might be eating foods that poison his system and sap his strength — foods that are truly harmful to his continued good health? We're talking about table and kitchen leavings. Such food was never intended for dogs.

What should you feed your dog? What is a safe summer diet? MILK-BONE is the answer. It's the food specially prepared for dogs. It contains no drugs, no artificial flavoring, no preservatives. Just good clean beef meat, energy-giving cereal, and other valuable food elements.

And it's very economical! Buy a box at your grocer's. Or, send the coupon (or a postcard) for a free gift package. And help keep your dog in sound good health no matter how hot it gets!

COUPON BRINGS FREE GIFT PACKAGE

MILK-BONE
Dog & Puppy Biscuits

Milk-Bone Bakery,
NATIONAL BISCUIT COMPANY
Department 00, 449 West 14th St., New York City
I want my dog to get the right food this summer.
So send that free gift package of MILK-BONE.

Name

Street

City and State

Any veterinarian will tell you that summer is the hardest time of the year for your dog. He'll also tell you that you can keep your dog safe . . . in sound good health . . . if you watch his diet!

Don't feed him table and kitchen leavings these hot days. Such food may poison his system, cause summer complaints, upset stomach, skin trouble. Choose a food that is specially prepared for him . . . MILK-BONE BISCUIT. This famous dog food is helping thousands of dogs fight dangerous summer weather, is saving thousands of owners no end of expense and trouble these hot, sultry days.

You can try it at our expense if you send the coupon below (or a postcard). It brings you a special gift package and a helpful folder on care and feeding. Send now . . . and keep your dog safe this summer!

KEEP YOUR DOG SAFE THIS SUMMER!

MILK-BONE
Dog & Puppy Biscuits

Milk-Bone Bakery,
NATIONAL BISCUIT COMPANY
Department 86, 449 West 14th St., New York City
Certainly I want to keep my dog safe this summer. So please send your special gift package of Milk-Bone to

Name

Street

City and State

Which Dog Food Ad Got the Most Replies?

When two ads are tested to find out which gets the better results, there is a set of facts supporting each ad. The test determines which set of facts is stronger. In this case, the ad "Keep your dog safe this summer" brought 56% more sample requests. This was in spite of the fact that the other ad featured the free offer in a subhead above the coupon.

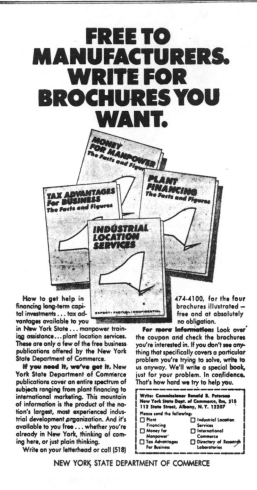

Using Multiple Offers to Increase Response

An ad that offers to send the reader several brochures has several advantages: (1) The reader is given more things to choose from, and is therefore more apt to respond. (2) By counting the number of requests for each brochure, the advertiser can tell which brochures are most popular. The popular brochures can be featured in future ads, and the unpopular ones omitted. (3) If the coupon leads are followed by a salesman, he will know in advance what to talk about. He will talk about the subject discussed in the brochure the prospect sent for.

7

Tested Advertising Versus Untested Advertising

Three groups of people whose job it is to appeal to the public are: (1) professional entertainers, (2) salesmen, (3) advertising writers.

Entertainers have a definite advantage over the advertising writers. Take the case of a nightclub comedian. He tells a joke to the audience. The audience either laughs or remains silent. If the audience laughs, its laughter can be measured. It is either a perfunctory laugh, or a moderate laugh, or a side-splitting laugh. The point is that the comedian knows exactly how well his joke has gone across. If he puts on his act a dozen times a week, he gets a dozen chances every week to test the reaction of the public. He can alter the manner in which he tells his jokes. No matter what he does, he gets an immediate judgment of his efforts direct from the people he is trying to please.

In the case of the salesman the prospect he is trying to sell sits a few feet from him. The salesman can study the prospect's facial expression. He can listen carefully to what the prospect says. He can get a good idea of how well his sales talk is getting across. He can vary the sales talk at any moment in order to suit special conditions. The important thing is that he gets an accurate judgment of his selling effort direct from the person he is trying to sell.

Now consider the case of the advertising writer. He writes what he believes to be an excellent advertisement. It is probably just one of a series. Weeks later, or perhaps months later, the advertisement appears in a publication or in a broadcast commercial. Perhaps a few dealers comment on it. Perhaps a few letters come in from consumers. Is the advertisement a good one or a bad one? Who knows? The product continues to sell, so evidently the advertisement didn't do any actual harm to the business!

Perhaps sales are up. Did the advertisement cause the increase?

Who knows? It is more likely that the entire series of advertisements caused the increase. But who can be sure of even that? Maybe the credit belongs to the sales force. Or maybe it's just a seasonal rise in the business. Or maybe some unknown condition is causing an increased demand. The point is that no matter whether sales are up or sales are down, it is difficult to tell, except in a general way, over a period of years, whether the advertising had much or little effect.

There are many other factors besides the advertising that have a bearing on sales. All we really know definitely is that a number of companies, such as the makers of Wrigley's Gum, Ivory Soap, and Campbell's Soup, who have advertised persistently for years, have built up big businesses.

What has all this to do with the writer of advertising copy? It means that the copywriter's job is different from the jobs of the entertainer and the salesman. The copywriter lacks close and intimate touch with his audience.

This means that the average advertising writer has a difficult job or an easy job, depending on his point of view. If he is a conscientious worker and wants to prepare advertising that will have a definite effect on sales, his job is difficult. He lacks the quick reaction of the customer to guide his efforts into the proper channels.

If, on the other hand, the ad writer is merely interested in preparing some advertising to get an okay from a client, his job may be relatively easy. He can sometimes go on for years writing mediocre copy. The client is never called on by a delegation from the public saying, "We think your ads lack selling power."

There are certain classes of copywriters who are not offered the choice of writing either sales-producing copy or mediocre copy. Among these are the writers of department store advertisements and the writers of mail order advertising. These people must write advertisements that sell, or lose their jobs. The result of this situation is shown by the following bit of conversation that took place between two mail order men:

"I hope we have a rainy Sunday," said the mail order writer to the layout man.

The other laughed. "Why? Do you have an ad running in a Sunday newspaper?"

"Yes," was the reply. "We're starting that new encyclopedia campaign and I want the first ad to bring a lot of orders."

Why do mail order men like rainy Sundays? Because they know by past experience that rain increases coupon returns. When the weather is rainy, people stay at home and read the newspapers.

Naturally they read the advertisements, too. Mail order sales are increased.

Now consider the case of an institutional advertisement on which results are not checked. Does the writer ever say, "I hope it rains on Sunday! I want a lot of people to read my ad." The chances are that no such remark will be made. Yet an institutional advertisement is affected by the weather just as much as a mail order advertisement. A mail order advertisement has to do a complete selling job. And results can be checked. Therefore everybody works hard to make it good. The copywriter works his head off to make the copy pull. The layout man employs every trick he knows to make the advertisement stick out on the page. The account executive has a lot to say about how the advertisement should look and how the copy should read. When the advertisement is finished, the client takes a hand. He criticizes, makes changes, and offers suggestions. He wants to leave no stone unturned in making the advertisement sell. No wonder mail order advertising is efficient. Everybody works so hard to make it good. They even pray for rain!

Consider the attitude of a group of advertising people preparing an institutional campaign. Of course, there is much discussion as to what the advertisements should say and how they will look. But often this discussion is theoretical. It is often based on personal preference rather than on past experience as to what pays and what doesn't pay. The reason is that when advertising results are not tested in some manner, it is difficult to know just what does pay best.

Here is a typical example of how the themes of the more unscientific advertising campaigns are sometimes arrived at. A friend told me that his father was starting a travel bureau in Philadelphia. He wanted to know how best he could advertise so that the people of Philadelphia would learn about his travel bureau and he persuaded to go there to get information on trips abroad.

I made a few suggestions. But I noticed that my friend didn't listen carefully. He was anxious for me to get through talking so that he could tell me his big idea for advertising the travel bureau.

Here's what he said: "Do you remember that Christmas card our class got out during our freshman year at college? It had a beautiful picture of a square-rigged sailing vessel on it. I think we could get up a wonderful advertisement built around an illustration like that. We could make it very artistic, very distinctive. We might be able to work in the initial letters P.T.B. (Philadelphia Travel Bureau) on one of the sails of the ship."

My friend spent a long time describing just how he thought the advertisement should look and how the picture of the sailing ship should be printed in colors on high-grade paper.

I realized that he didn't want my advice at all. All he wanted me to do was to agree with him and say, "Yes, I think that's a wonderful idea."

He said he thought that this sailing vessel picture would look fine in magazines. I told him that if he ran his advertisements in magazines, he would be paying high rates for circulation that went all over the United States and that the only circulation that would do him any good would be the comparatively few copies of the magazines that went into Philadelphia.

This objection seemed to annoy him. All the other objections I made seemed to annoy him. He didn't want objections. He wanted me to get enthusiastic about his big idea.

This is perhaps an extreme case. Yet it contains an example of how clients sometimes force their agencies to prepare poor advertising. The client has a pet idea he insists on using. This idea may be based on something no more substantial than a Christmas card design.

In certain types of advertising you can be as absurd as you want to, and nobody can ever prove that the advertising isn't good. There are no direct returns to indicate the interest or lack of interest on the part of the public.

Now let's look at the mail order situation again. Suppose the client suggests some ineffective advertising stunt. The advertising agency account executive won't hear of it. He uses every possible means to sell his client off the idea. He knows in advance that the advertisements won't pull, and he would rather incur the client's displeasure now than incur it later by running nonpulling advertisements.

In the same way, if either the account executive or the copywriter should suggest an idea that is obviously poor, the client will probably kill it.

This means that every mail order advertisement has to pass the judgment of three severe critics—the copywriter, the account executive, and the client. If an idea is poor, it will be killed by one of these three. No persuasive flow of theories and arguments can sell it.

What is the result of this situation? Open any publication and you can see it. The expensive decorations, the meaningless headlines, the type that is hard to read, the would-be "clever" copy, the big blocks of white space—all these belong to the untested advertisements.

Now look at the mail order advertisements. What do you see? Bold-type headlines that stick out. Text set in type that is easy to read. Copy that is full of effective sales points. And no white space, because mail order advertisers proved many years ago that white space is too often wasted space.

The quotation below, from John W. Blake's booklet "Blind Advertising Expenditure," brings out some important points in regard to tested advertising versus untested advertising:

General advertising (as distinguished from "mail order") is frequently a structure of opinion and unproven theories. A structure without a foundation. These theories are so deeply rooted that they have become gospel. The reasoning that brings about the spending of millions sounds logical enough. The selling propaganda that induces this investment is powerfully persuasive, and let us hasten to say, honestly believed in.

If your advertising is answered by the public, you should test not only the media, but also the individual insertions. Then keep a careful record of results. You will soon be convinced. Simple enough, isn't it? But gravely important to your pocketbook. If you have no way of testing your advertising, if your publicity is designed to send the public to retail stores, you owe it to your money, and to your business, to inject if possible some kind of "reply copy" into your advertising; a "send for circular" appeal. Big money should never be spent on advertising until it has been tested.

Listen to the testimony of another champion of tested advertising:

When an experienced mail order man was called in to help lift the sales curve for a certain soft drink, he announced, after investigation: "The difficulty lies in the fact that the loyal customers are chiefly older people. Old-time products often suffer because friends die. To replace them one must win a new generation of friends. The solution is simple: Sampling . . . New triers . . . New buyers . . . Coupons. Let everything center around coupon costs, and proven ads that pay."

On this basis a complete plan was built and carried out. Coupon costs dropped from $120 each to 65¢, then to 55¢ and later to 24¢. The $120 coupons offered either a full-size bottle of Soft Drink Extracts at 30¢ or a capping outfit at $2.00. The later coupons offered a free sample, sufficient to make 8 bottles of the beverage. The expensive coupons came from full pages in color. The low-cost coupons came largely from quarter-pages. In the year of the expensive coupons the net earnings were $224,854.18. In the year of the 24¢ coupons (three years later) the net earnings were $889,701.60.

All advertisements for this product were tested carefully and then for several seasons subjected to a "breeding" process. Eventually all the high-cost ads were pruned away and good payers were encouraged. Thus the final schedule was built of 15 tested ads.

In a trade magazine, the advertising manager of a large bank described a method of testing bank advertisements. Briefly stated, the method consists of preparing advertisements in poster form and displaying them in bank lobbies and windows. Observers are stationed to keep a record of (1) the number of people who pass the posters; and (2) the number of people who are sufficiently attracted by the posters to stop and read them.

The accuracy of the tests was indicated by the fact that tests of the same groups of advertisements in four different branches of the bank brought almost identical results.

Said this advertising manager in conclusion:

The wide difference in the attention-value of various advertising ideas is often surprising. Of two savings advertisements displayed under similar circumstances, one stopped nine persons out of 1,000 and the other thirty-four. Of two proposed trust advertisements, one stopped six persons and the other sixteen. Some advertisements have stopped one person out of every ten. Some have attracted so small a number as to have practically no value from an advertising standpoint. Others, little different in character, have won large audiences.

One of the lessons we have learned from our display of proposed advertisements is the increased attention-value that a national figure adds to the copy. For a time we tested posters featuring statements of prominent people about thrift and saving. Included in the list were several U.S. presidents and other famous men. All of these attracted attention far above the average. As a test, we removed the name and photograph of one of the famous men from a poster and used only the words he had spoken, not mentioning him as the author. The attention-value dropped 50 per cent.

A question that may be asked regarding our tests is this: Is attention-value the only test of the effectiveness of the advertisement? Of course not. It is, nevertheless, fundamental.

If an advertisement fails to attract attention, there is little else that can be said for it. It may be dignified, beautiful, and filled with sales arguments, but if not read, these good qualities cannot redeem it. The sales appeal of an advertisement, its general effectiveness, timeliness, and matters of that sort are qualities to be discussed after the fact has been established that the advertisement can attract attention. A test of attention-value may show that the advertisement with the best sales copy attracts so few readers as to be almost worthless. Another, almost as strong in sales arguments, reaches many. A third, at the top in the number of readers, is weak in its presentation of a product or service. In making a choice between these advertisements, all of the factors that combine to make a successful advertisement must be considered. Attention-value is one of the most important of these factors.

The lessons of this chapter are twofold:

1. You should find some way to test your advertisements so that you will know for sure which ads are effective and which are not effective. Chapter 18 tells you how to do this.
2. If you are looking for advertising ideas to use in your campaign, don't imitate the fancy art and the fancy language that you will find in the untested ads whose sales results cannot be measured. Instead, you should emulate and borrow from the ads whose sales are measured daily—namely, the mail order ads, the direct response ads, the direct marketing ads, the department store ads. You should give special attention to the tested ads that are repeated again and again. These are the ads that are paying off in sales. These are the ads that contain ideas that will pay off for you.

Advertise, or the chances are that the sheriff will do it for you.

Phineas T. Barnum

How Timely Ads Get Increased Attention

This ad for Betty Crocker frosting mix appeared at the beginning of the school season. The copy says: "Delicious easy-mix homemade fudge is the perfect treat for lunch boxes, after school snacks, or late night studying." Timely ads get increased attention because they tie in with current events, seasons, and holidays such as Valentine's Day, Easter, Mother's Day, Father's Day, Thanksgiving Day, and Christmas. In almost every month of the year you can find a way to make your ads timely.

STEINWAY

The Instrument of the Immortals

There has been but one supreme piano in the history of music. In the days of Liszt and Wagner, of Rubinstein and Berlioz, the pre-eminence of the Steinway was as unquestioned as it is today. It stood then, as it stands now, the chosen instrument of the masters—the inevitable preference wherever great music is understood and esteemed.

STEINWAY & SONS, Steinway Hall, 107-109 E. 14th Street, New York

Subway Express Stations at the Door

Why Institutional Advertising Is Difficult to Measure

This ad is one of a famous series conceived and written by Raymond Rubicam, former president of the Young & Rubicam advertising agency. Advertising of this kind is difficult to measure in terms of sales because the sales results are spread out over a period of years. Said a buyer of a Steinway piano to a salesman: "Ten years ago when I first saw this ad, I made up my mind that some day I would own a Steinway. But it was not until today that I could afford it."

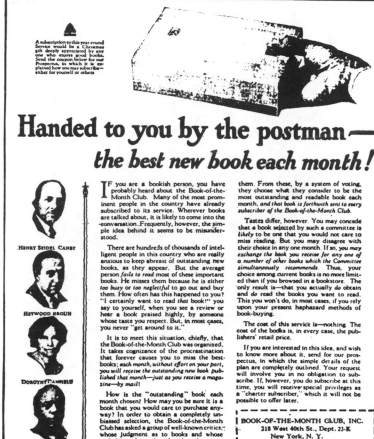

The Evolution of a Famous Series

The old ad on the left is one of the first ever published by the Book-of-the-Month Club. The ad on the right appeared in magazines more than forty-five years later. Note the differences: The old ad shows a mailing carton, and mentions no book titles. The judges who selected the books are pictured. The coupon offers no books. Instead, it offers a "Prospectus outlining the details of the Book-of-the-Month Plan of Reading." The ad on the right is a card

The Book-of-the-Month Club is for people who don't have time for unimportant books

YOU ARE INVITED TO

CHOOSE ANY 4

of the books on these pages

FOR ONLY $1

THE SUGGESTED TRIAL: You simply agree to buy four
Club choices within a year at special members' prices

ONE glance at the Book-of-the-Month
Club's current choices and you'll
see the kind of books that can deepen
your insights, widen your perspectives,
and provide you with solid information
on subjects that interest you. You can
now have any four of these important
new books for only $1, with a trial mem-
bership. And, if you continue after this
trial membership, you will also partici-
pate in our Book-Dividend® Plan, en-
abling you to build a home library you'll
be proud to own while saving as much as
70% over bookstore prices.

47 books to choose from on these 2 pages

FIRST CLASS
PERMIT No. 419
New York, N.Y.

BUSINESS REPLY MAIL
No postage stamp necessary if mailed in the United States

VIA AIR MAIL

POSTAGE WILL BE PAID BY

Book-of-the-Month Club, Inc.

280 Park Avenue

New York, N.Y. 10017

---

insert printed on both sides, and bound into a magazine. Both sides of the
insert contain pictures of books. (Shown here is the front side only.) The offer
is not a prospectus, but "Choose any 4 for only $1." In the lower right corner
is a postcard order form that requires no stamp. These improvements in sales
techniques are the result of years of mail order sales tests.

8

How to Put Enthusiasm into Advertising Copy

One day a young chap came into my office to sell me some stock in a new patent razor company. He was just an ordinary chap—not much personality. And he was not an experienced salesman. Yet he gave me one of the most compelling sales talks I ever heard.

What made him so compelling? His enthusiasm. He believed in that razor stock completely and implicitly. He had bought it himself. He had sold it to his friends. He was absolutely convinced that it would double in value in three months.

Later I found out that the sales manager of the razor company had talked to groups of young salesmen for hours, telling them what wonderful possibilities the new razor had, and how they were doing people a favor by selling them stock in the company. This process of selling the salesmen was kept up until all the salesmen were armed with an enthusiasm more compelling than years of training in the techniques of salesmanship.

Enthusiasm is just as vital in advertising as in selling. Perhaps that is the reason that the toughest part of an advertisement to write is the beginning. It is hard to get started.

An advertising copywriter said, "When I sit down to write an ad, I find myself drawing little designs on the pad. I chew the end of my pencil. I gaze out of the window. I go to the water cooler for a drink of water.

"Finally I write a few lines of copy. Then I stare at the layout for a long time. I wonder if the headline isn't all wrong. I read over the copy I have written. I cross out a word. I rewrite a sentence.

"Later I change it back to the way it was originally. No way I fix it seems right."

Why do so many copy men have difficulty in getting started? There are two reasons:

1. The human brain is like an automobile engine. It works best when it is hot. When you sit down to write an advertisement, your brain is cold.
2. The experienced copywriter knows that the most important part of an advertisement is the beginning. The opening sentences must be good or readers will lose interest.

This means that sitting down and writing a beginning for an advertisement is like trying to drive an automobile up a steep hill with a cold engine.

There are several ways to overcome this difficulty. One method is to say to yourself, "I'm going to write some copy about this product, but I'll probably not use the first few paragraphs that I write. However, I'll start writing anyway and before long I'll write some copy that can be used as a beginning."

Another method is to say to yourself, "I'm not going to start writing this advertisement at the beginning. I'll start in the middle. Then after I have written for an hour, I'll read my copy over and pick out the best paragraph and let that be my opening paragraph."

An experienced copywriter said, "I don't like to write. But I do like to edit copy. Therefore I write fast and get my thoughts down on paper somehow. After that, the job is merely editing."

Do advertising writers ever get "written out"? There is evidence that they do.

One copywriter said to his new assistant, "We need a Christmas ad for the Simplex portable typewriter. I'll be mighty glad to have you help me with it. I've been batting them out for ten years and I'm just about written out.

I've written ads about mother giving a Simplex to her son . . . wife giving one to hubby . . . daughter giving one to dad . . . brother giving one to sister . . . every possible combination. I don't know what else to do."

The problem of what to do when you are "written out" is a difficult one. Some copywriters solve it by changing jobs every couple of years.

A less drastic method of getting your mind out of the rut is to forget Mr. Average Man, that imaginary chap you have been writing to all these years. Write your copy as if you were writing a letter to a friend. Say to yourself, "I've just bought this product and it's good. I think Jim would like to know about it. I'm going to write and tell him about it."

Here is a letter an association president wrote to his friends and to members of the association. Read it and see if you don't feel the quality of enthusiasm in the letter:

Dear Association Member:

You would have been thrilled to have been with me in Montreal on Friday.

Montreal, as you know, is the site of your convention in September. I was there attending a Board of Governors meeting of your Association.

The Queen Elizabeth Hotel, headquarters for the convention, is something to write home about. It was designed specifically to handle conventions—all of the convention facilities (registration, meeting rooms, exhibits, bar, etc.) are on one floor. The hotel is lovely. Beautiful rooms, excellent elevator service, and probably the best hotel food you'll find' anywhere. We had eggs Benedict for the Board breakfast (at 8 a.m.!) and they were something. Rooms are moderately priced. Special telephone service that I haven't seen in the States—special dial numbers for valet, laundry, room service, etc.

This Montreal steering committee has really knocked themselves out. I'm enclosing a copy of their almost-completed program. Real meat in it for both the little guy and the big guy.

Airline arrivals will get their hotel key at the airport (at least those who have the foresight to make their hotel reservations at the Queen Elizabeth early). Both Eastern and Trans-Canada have agreed to "Special Delivery Flights" from all main U.S. entry points. Luggage will receive special Queen Elizabeth stickers and be shipped immediately to the hotel. Identification buttons will be supplied immediately. Rail travelers will arrive directly beneath the hotel—and lucky auto travelers will discover something unique—free parking at the QE. Imagine!

Your wife (and if you don't have one, it would almost be worth it for this trip alone) will get a real treat from the Laurentian Mountain tour including a luncheon and Christian Dior style show. The resort where this activity will take place has a unique feature—a grass roof that is kept "mowed" by two goats. You'd have to see it to believe it. Some of the Board members have actually seen the goats in action!

Chrysler Motors was staging an exhibit the day we were

there and 25,000—count'em—were accommodated in the exhibit area. The beauty of the exhibit area is its accessibility to the meeting rooms, ball room, and registration. It will be the finest deal our convention exhibitors have ever had. We have also appointed a special broker to lessen the problems of shipping exhibit materials through customs.

The program (as you'll see by the attached) is loaded with talent but will leave enough free time to visit some of Montreal's wonderful French restaurants. Incidentally, the program will be printed in both French and English to give it a truly bilingual flavor. Montreal is second only to Paris for French-speaking inhabitants. This alone adds a flavor you just can't afford to miss.

I was so excited after I left Montreal that I thought I'd best tell you about it immediately. If you miss a reservation at the Queen Elizabeth, you're going to miss some of the enjoyment of the convention. Better make that reservation today—I did.

Sincerely,

Bob

The author of this letter wrote it while he was in an enthusiastic frame of mind. He had seen something he was excited about and he wrote about it right away. He didn't give his enthusiasm a chance to cool off. That is one secret of enthusiastic writing. If you are excited about something, you should grab a pencil and get your excitement down on paper immediately.

The same applies in talking. If you have just witnessed an exciting event and you tell somebody about it that same day, your description is much more effective than if you wait a week and tell about it after the details and the excitement have departed from your mind.

Here are some samples of advertising copy that have the quality of enthusiasm:

1. Copy for a Retirement Income Plan

This message is addressed to the man who wants to take things easy some day. It tells how you can provide for yourself in later years a guaranteed income you cannot outlive.

It doesn't matter whether your present income is large

or merely average. If you follow this plan you will someday have an income upon which to retire.

The plan calls for the deposit of only a few dollars each month—the exact amount depending on your age. The minute you make your first deposit, your biggest money worries begin to disappear. Even if you should become totally disabled, you would not need to worry. Your payments would be made by us out of a special fund provided for that purpose.

And not only that. We would mail you a check every month during the entire time of your disability, even if that disability should continue for many, many years—the remainder of your natural life.

2. Copy for a Newspaper Subscription

"A few years ago I was going broke. High prices and taxes were getting me down. I had to have more money or reduce my standard of living.

"So I sent for a Trial Subscription to the *Wall Street Journal.* I heeded its warnings. I cashed in on the ideas it gave me for increasing my income and cutting expenses. I got the money I needed. And then I began to forge ahead. Last year my income was up 40%. Believe me, reading the *Journal* every day is a wonderful get-ahead plan. Now I am really living!"

This experience is typical. The *Journal* is a wonderful aid to salaried men. It is valuable to the owner of a small business. It can be of priceless benefit to young men who want to win advancement.

3. Copy for Boxes of Fruit Sent by Express

Right now as I write this, it is late September, and out here in this beautiful valley our Royal Riviera Pears are hanging like great pendants from those 40-year old trees. We'll have to watch them like new babies from now until picking time—not a leaf must touch them toward the last. Trained men will pick them gently with gloved hands and lay them carefully in padded trays. They'll be individually wrapped in tissue and nestled in cushion packing, and sent in handsome gift boxes lithographed in colors, to reach you—or your friends—firm and beautiful, ready to ripen in your home to their full delicious flavor. I envy you your first taste of Royal Riviera Pears—every spoonful dripping with sweet liquid sunshine.

4. Copy for a Fat-reducing Remedy

In 10 days I'll reduce your weight 5 to 10 pounds. I don't care how stout you are. I don't care how many times you have tried to reduce and failed. My amazing new method will make your excess fat melt away like magic—give you a normal, youthful figure—make you slim, buoyant, energetic, as Nature intended you to be, or the treatment won't cost you a single penny!

No starving—no exercising—no drugs—no external agencies—no mechanical appliances. You just follow my instructions for a few days until your excess pounds disappear, until the scales tell you that you weigh exactly what you should. This method is so simple that anyone can understand how it works. It is so logical, so sensible that the moment you hear about it you will know instinctively that it works.

Send no money. Merely send me your name and address. When the postman brings my complete instructions, "How to Reduce," pay him the special low price of only $4.95 plus a few cents postage. If at the end of ten days you are not completely satisfied—if you do not lose weight rapidly and easily—then simply tell me and your money will be instantly refunded. You risk nothing. WRITE TODAY.

How to Avoid Mental Hazards

One mental hazard that discourages writers is the knowledge that their copy will be judged by the following critics:

The copy chief
The account executive
The advertising manager
The sales manager
The president
And perhaps several other officials

Each critic has his own ideas about copy. Trying to please them all is like trying to drive a croquet ball through half a dozen wickets at one shot. If you want to write enthusiastic copy, you must banish critics from your mind entirely. Ignore them. Forget them. Write the way you want to write.

And write fast. Get steamed up. Make your copy sizzle. Put all the power of a runaway locomotive into it. Later go over it in cold blood and cut out the things your critics will object to. In this way you can produce copy that is both lively and acceptable. If you write with the prejudices and preferences of other people uppermost in your mind, you will produce copy as correct as a school child's essay, but utterly lifeless.

This same plan helps to overcome two other mental hazards:

1. The things you are not allowed to say about the article you are selling.
2. The things you must say as a matter of advertising policy.

Try to put these things completely out of your head. Don't sit down to write copy with a string of "musts" and "can'ts" dangling in your mind.

Use a process of self-hypnotism. Say to yourself that Smith's Pills are the best pills in the world—that no other pills are like them—that they can produce wonderful results in a short time.

Get excited! Get worked up! Tell yourself that you've got the biggest piece of news to tell since man walked on the moon. Remember that enthusiasm is as contagious as measles. It spreads from speaker to listener, from author to reader.

Then start to write. Write fast. Write furiously. Write as if you had to catch a plane. Write as if you had to put all your thoughts on paper in the next five minutes or lose them forever.

Perhaps your first few paragraphs will sound impossible. Never mind. Keep on writing. Somewhere, somehow, you will produce real selling copy. Some of the things you write will work on the emotions of your readers in subtle ways that are perhaps unknown to yourself. Unconsciously you will produce little touches that arouse and stir to action.

Action—that's the vital quality that emotional copy possesses and that "reason why" copy lacks. "Reason why" copy appeals to the reader's intelligence and makes him nod his head in agreement with you. But emotional copy goes deeper. It gets into those lower portions of the brain where love and hate, and fear and desire are.

Both types of copy are important. Skillfully combine the two and you will make the reader get up out of his chair and start for the store.

One more word about enthusiastic copy: Everybody knows that you can tame a wild horse and make the animal useful. But it is impossible to put life into a dead horse. The same is true of advertising copy. An advertisement that has been pounded out in the white heat of enthusiasm can be tamed and made effective. But it is impossible to put life into dead copy.

And remember that the polishing and rewriting you do afterwards are extremely important. Anatole France claimed that he rewrote every paragraph five times. The illustrious Frenchman said, "The first four versions of my writing sound as if anybody had written it. Only after a fifth rewriting does it begin to sound like Anatole France."

Advertising is to business what steam is to machinery—the great propelling power.

Thomas Macauley

Imagine Harry and Me advertising our PEARS in Fortune!

OUT HERE on the ranch we don't pretend to know much about advertising, and maybe we're foolish spending the price of a tractor for this space; but my brother and I got an idea the other night, and we believe you folks who read Fortune are the kind of folks who'd like to know about it. So here's our story:

We have a beautiful orchard out here in the Rogue River Valley in Oregon, where the soil and the rain and the sun grow the finest pears in the world. We grow a good many varieties; but years ago we decided to specialize on Royal Riviera Pears, a rare, delicious variety originally imported from France, and borne commercially only by 20-year-old trees. And do you know where we sold our first crop—and the greater part of every crop since?

In Paris and London, where the finest hotels and restaurants know them to be the choicest delicacy they can serve to discriminating guests. And they serve them at about 75 cents each! Our Royal Riviera Pears went to other distinguished tables too—to the Czar of Russia and to the kings and queens and first families of Europe. We got a great kick out of wrapping big, luscious, blushing Royal Riviera Pears in tissue and knowing they were going to be served on golden plates and eaten with golden spoons.

America's Rarest Fruit— Shall We Ship It Abroad?

But I'm getting away from my story. The idea that kept coming to Harry and me was this: Why must all this fruit go to Europe? Aren't there people right here in America who would appreciate such rare delicacies just as much as royalty? Wouldn't *our* first families like to know about these luscious, golden pears, rare as orchids, bursting with juice, and so big you eat them with a spoon? Wouldn't folks here at home like to give boxes of these rare pears to friends at Thanksgiving and Christmas?

So we made an experiment. We packed a few special boxes of these Royal Riviera Pears and took them down to some business friends in San Francisco. You should have seen their faces when they took their first taste of a Royal Riviera. They didn't know such fruit grew anywhere on earth.

Well, a banker wanted not only a box for home, but 50 boxes to be sent to business friends to arrive just before Christmas. A newspaper publisher wanted 40 for the same purpose, and a manufacturer asked for 25. And that gave us another idea. We sent 11 sample boxes to important executives in New York, and back came orders for 489 Christmas boxes for *their* friends.

A New Christmas Gift Idea

That seemed to indicate there were plenty of men looking for something new as a Christmas remembrance for friends who "have everything." The next year, orders came in for several thousand boxes of these rare pears, and you never read such letters as we got afterward—not only from the men who had *sent* the pears and made such a hit, but from folks who *received* them and wanted to know if they could buy more.

Well, that's how Harry and I got the idea that there must be *enough* discriminating people right here in the U. S. A. who'd like to do the same thing.

So we talked it over the other night and said, "Let's put an ad in Fortune—and see." We got a shock when we found what it would cost us to do it, but here we are—and you are going to be the judge.

Right now as I write this, it is late September, and out here in this beautiful valley our Royal Riviera Pears are hanging like great pendants from those 40-year-old trees. We'll have to watch them like new babies from now until picking time—not a leaf must touch them toward the last—trained men will pick them gently with gloved hands and lay them carefully in padded trays. They'll be individually wrapped in tissue, nestled in cushion packing, and sent in handsome gift boxes lithographed in colors, to reach you—or your friends—firm and beautiful, ready to ripen in your home to their full delicious flavor.

I envy you your first taste of a Royal Riviera—every spoonful dripping with sweet liquid sunshine. And you can just bet that every one who receives a box is going to have the surprise of his life.

We hope that right now you'll make up your list of business and social friends and let us send them each a box with your compliments. We'll put in an attractive gift card with your name written on it, and

we'll deliver anywhere in the United States proper, wherever there is an express office, express prepaid, to arrive on the date you name. And don't forget to include a box for yourself! A "Medium Family" box (10 pounds) is only $1.85. A "Large Family" box (double the quantity) is $2.95. At these low prices these pears cost a mere fraction of what you would pay for them in fine restaurants and hotels. And here's how sure we are you'll be delighted. If, after eating your first Royal Riviera, you and your friends don't say these are the finest pears you ever tasted, just re-

turn the balance at our expense and your money will come back in a hurry. Harry and I have agreed you are to be the final judge—*and we mean it.*

Just one more thing—there are far more folks reading Fortune than there will be boxes of Royal Riviera Pears this year. So, if you want to be sure to get some, we hope you'll send your order right along. We are putting a coupon down below, but a letter is just as good. Only, if you write, please say you saw this in Fortune.

HARRY and DAVID
Bear Creek Orchards, Medford, Oregon.

An Ad that Started an Industry

The secret of the success of this ad is long copy and enthusiasm. Here are typical sentences: "Right now our Royal Riviera Pears are hanging like great pendants from those 40-year-old trees" … "I envy you your first taste of a Royal Riviera—every spoonful dripping with sweet liquid sunshine" … "everyone who receives a box is going to have the surprise of his life." This ad was extremely effective in getting mail orders. It won an advertising award and marked the beginning of a new industry in America: selling fruit by mail.

An Effective Testimonial Ad

One of the best ways to sell merchandise is to quote the experience of satisfied users. You can use testimonials from famous people or from plain people. The testimonials are more effective if signed with actual names. The copy in the above ad ends with this quote: "...why pay more for a sewing machine when you can get one like this Kenmore at Sears?" This statement is stronger, coming from Bonnie Cashin, than it would be coming from the manufacturer.

9

How to Write the First Paragraph

Too many copywriters miss their chance to make a sale by starting an advertisement with a few introductory remarks that lose the reader's interest instead of holding it.

Imagine for a moment that you are interested in buying a TV set. You see a good looking set in a store window. You walk into the store to look at it. Uppermost in your mind are these questions: How much does it cost? Has it good reception? Good volume?

Suppose a clerk should walk up to you and say, "This is an age of beauty . . . charm . . . style." Wouldn't you be flabbergasted? Wouldn't you suspect that there was something wrong with him? Yet those very words, "This is an age of beauty . . . charm . . . style," constituted the opening paragraph of a $16,000 magazine advertisement for a television set. This sort of copy is not exceptional. You have become accustomed to it because you see so much of it.

Millions of pages have been turned and millions of advertisements have been left unread because of first paragraphs like the following:

> The modern woman demands something more than comfort and utility in the appointments of her home. She is a devotee of style and beauty. She knows color and design. Her taste is cultivated and refined. She is informed, detests spuriousness, and expects authentic value for her money.

This bit of philosophy is the first paragraph of a four-color page in a national magazine. Can you guess what product is being advertised? Can you guess what the product will do for you? No. There is no hint, no clue. The copy tells nothing, sells nothing. It is merely a barrier between the reader and what he wants to know.

Often a copy chief can improve the copy of his writers by simply omitting the opening sentences or opening paragraphs that the writer used in his first draft. "Begin here," says the copy chief. And he points to a sentence or paragraph halfway down the page.

Did you ever see a baseball pitcher warming up before he gets into the game? He needs to swing his arms a bit before he is at his best. Some writers are the same way. They need to write a few sentences or a few paragraphs before they really get hot. A copy chief can help a copywriter by pointing out the exact spot in the copy where the writer begins to say something worthwhile.

If you don't have a copy chief to guide your efforts, you can put your copy aside for a day or two and then come back to it with a fresh mind. Perhaps you will find a sentence or a paragraph that will make a more exciting beginning than the one you originally used. Perhaps you will find that you can simply omit your original beginning without losing any of the essential ideas in your ad.

A Lesson from *Reader's Digest*

Not long ago I picked up an issue of *Reader's Digest* and copied down the first sentence of every article in the magazine—35 articles in all. I wanted to find out how the editors of the world's largest circulating publication handle the problem of holding the reader's interest after that interest has been sparked by the title of an article. Many article writers as well as ad writers face this same problem, namely how do you hold them after you've stopped them with your headline or picture?

My experiment with a single issue of *Reader's Digest* was so revealing that I went through a number of issues. I found the same successful formulas repeated again and again. Some of these formulas are just as appropriate for ad writing as they are for article writing. Here they are:

1. Interrupting Ideas

A number of articles begin with a sentence that can be described as an "interrupting idea." What is an interrupting idea? It is a startling statement or a novel twist that breaks through the boredom barrier that often exists in the mind of the reader. For example, an article on deodorizers entitled "It Makes Bad Air Good," began this way:

The hit of the annual Chemical Show held in New York City a few months ago was a pair of skunks housed in a plastic cage.

Here are the opening sentences of four more articles that use the technique of the interrupting idea:

As you sit quietly reading these lines, a whirl of activity is taking place in your body.

While we humans think that penguins look and act like people, there's sobering evidence that they think of us as just big penguins.

Pleasing your tongue has lately become the chief concern of the world's largest industry.

Each day hundreds of thousands of harried young mothers thumb nervously through a dog-eared, oatmeal-splattered volume—one of the most extraordinary ever published.

2. The Shocker

Closely related to the interrupting idea is an opening that is even more striking and can be described as "the shocker." Here are examples:

A Frenchman is rarely seen drunk, but France has the highest rate of alcoholism in the world.

This morning in the United States 8,000 more mouths demanded to be fed than yesterday morning.

I used to think that women who did nothing but have babies were stupid creatures.

There are some crimes a racketeer never commits unless he sees his lawyer first.

3. News

Another type of opening popular with editors is the news opening. Here are five examples:

There is a new committee in Washington.

In the past two years an exciting era of exploration has opened up.

A billion-dollar industrial empire has sprung suddenly into existence along the banks of the Mississippi River.

Two years ago the American people ordered for themselves a new 40-billion-dollar transcontinental highway system.

Something exciting and heartening is happening on the American college campus these days.

4. Preview

Occasionally used as an article opener is a sentence giving you a brief preview of the article. Examples:

Port-au-Prince, capitol of the Republic of Haiti, is the busiest, noisiest, most colorful city in the Caribbean.

Until about 15 years ago Japanese beetles seemed unstoppable.

Intelligently analyzed, our dreams can give us significant insights into our problems and our relationships with others.

5. Quotation

Here is the opening of an article on word power that appeals to everyone who works with words:

Daniel Webster said: "If all my possessions and powers were taken from me with one exception, I would choose to keep the power of words, because by them I would recover the rest."

6. Story

I have not yet told you the most interesting discovery of all. Here it is. Over half of the *Reader's Digest* articles begin with a story. As you know, *Reader's Digest* is not a fiction magazine. It is a nonfiction magazine. Yet over half of the pieces begin with an anecdote or a narrative of some kind. If you will tie this fact up with the fact that many of the most famous ads ever written are in the form of stories, you will have something for ad writers to ponder.

Below are examples of story openings:

One night last autumn a visitor in New York noticed lights burning in a church on lower Fifth Avenue.

The time was one a.m., the place a police station on Chicago's South Side.

On a sunny afternoon in Portland, Ore., I was driving my daughter to her weekly swimming lesson.

From the gallery of the Montreal Neurological Institute's main operating room I recently witnessed a seven-hour brain operation.

At the Eastman Chemical Products laboratories in Kingsport, Tenn., a technician using an eye-dropper placed one drop of a newly developed adhesive on the end of a two-inch steel rod.

Last summer Columbia University student, Alexander H. Ladd, a young man from a well-to-do Boston suburb, spent his vacation working as a grease monkey in a Mobilgas station.

When I dropped my letter into the mailbox, I felt exactly as if I'd tossed a bottled note into the ocean.

As dawn broke over Boston Harbor one day last fall, the tugboat Irene-Mae waddled out into the Atlantic on a strange mission.

On a Saturday not long ago, a physician flying in a sport plane over Springfield, Ill., lifted a pocket radio receiver to his ear, pressed a button and in a moment heard a woman say: "One-five-four, code three, emergency. Location 20."

For 34 tension-drenched minutes on August 8, nine test-crew airmen expected to die at any instant.

Here are some of the things you should notice about the various *Reader's Digest* openings:

1. They are fact-packed.
2. They are telegraphic.
3. They are specific.
4. They have few adjectives.
5. They are curiosity arousing.

The next time you write an opening for an ad, see if you can use an interrupting idea, or a shocker, or a news item, or a story.

Another Formula

If none of the above methods fits the ad you are writing—if you can't find an appropriate story or an interrupting idea—you can fall back on the simplest formula of all, namely: You can write a first paragraph that continues the same thought you expressed in your headline.

For example, if you stopped a reader with a headline about house paint, you can be sure of at least one thing about that reader: He wants more information about house paint. You will not lose him as long as you continue to give him what he wants.

If you want proof of the effectiveness of this method, just glance at the opening paragraphs of a few mail order ads. These ads pay for themselves in actual sales.

Here is the first paragraph of a mail order advertisement selling a remedy for a speech defect. The ad has a one-word headline that selects the proper audience. Notice how the first paragraph continues the thought expressed in the headline:

[Headline]STAMMERING
[1st Paragraph]You can be quickly cured if you stammer. Send 25 cents, coin or stamps, for 288-page cloth bound book on Stammering and Stuttering. It tells how I cured myself after Stammering and Stuttering for 20 years.

A humble subject. A small advertisement. But the first paragraph contains more real selling punch than many a full-page advertisement.

Notice how this piano school gets down to brass tacks in the following first paragraph:

[Headline]LEARN PIANO
[1st Paragraph]Play popular song hits perfectly. Hum the tune, play it by ear. No teacher—self-instruction. No tedious ding-dong daily practice .Just 20 brief, entertaining lessons, easily mastered.

Read the following telegraphic first paragraph taken from an advertisement for a Civil Service school. In addition to continuing the headline theme, this paragraph gets seven sales arguments into three short sentences.

[Headline]GOV'T JOBS
[1st Paragraph] Why worry about strikes, lay-offs, hard times? Get a Government job. Increased salaries, steady work, travel, good pay.

Now, for the sake of contrast, read the following first paragraph:

The ideal toward which great engineers work is not only mechanical perfection, but automatic maintenance of such perfection. Every great mechanical advance in motor-car construction has led us toward a freer enjoyment of motor-car convenience.

This is the sort of copy you would engrave on the cornerstone of the Mammoth Motors Building. Or it might do for an epitaph to be chiseled on the tombstone of a deceased manufacturer. But it is neither of these. It is the first paragraph of a full-page advertisement in a national magazine. The product is an automobile oiling system.

Later in the advertisement these excellent arguments appear:

Each bearing receives only the amount of oil it needs at any given speed.
No alternate periods of dryness or overflow.
No waste.
The System is out of the way, under the dash.
Needs oil only once in every 2,000 miles.

Why couldn't these facts appear earlier? Thousands more people would have seen them.

Here is an example of correct handling. Notice how the first paragraph of this insurance ad continues the headline theme:

[Headline]   How to provide a
                              Retirement Income
                                for yourself
[1st Paragraph]   This new Retirement Income Plan makes it possible for you to retire at any age you wish, 55, 60, or 65. You may provide for yourself a monthly income of $500, $600, or more.

When you catch a reader with a certain idea as expressed in the headline, you may lose him if you introduce a totally different idea in the first paragraph.

Based on mail order experience, here are three simple rules for writing a good first paragraph.

1. Make it short. A long first paragraph discourages the reader before he gets started.
2. Continue the thought expressed in the headline.

3. State in a few words the most important benefit or benefits the reader derives from buying your product. Benefits! Benefits! Benefits! What do I get? What will it do for me? That's what people want to know. That's what makes them read advertisements.

With public sentiment nothing can fail, without it nothing can succeed.

Abraham Lincoln

10

Right and Wrong Methods of Writing Copy

This chapter discusses nineteen different kinds of copy and gives samples of each. Not all of these kinds of copy are recommended. Four are listed as questionable and three are definitely not recommended.

Let us first discuss some types of copy that are recommended.

1. Straightforward Copy

This type of copy presents the advertiser's story in a simple, logical manner. It is devoid of style or rhetoric. It merely states the facts in the most understandable way possible. For example:

PERSONALIZED STATIONERY

100 high-quality, special-size bond note sheets and 100 envelopes are neatly imprinted with any three-line address you designate. Carefully packed and mailed prepaid to your home for two dollars.

2. Story Copy

This copy starts off with a human interest situation. Then comes a story, the moral of which is "Buy the product advertised."

Below is an example. It is taken from an advertisement for a laxative. Note how the short paragraphs and the short sentences make the ad easy to read.

"HE TOLD ME HOW PRETTY I WAS—
AND I THOUGHT HE MEANT IT"

Are all men fickle? He said she was a wonderful girl. She was wild about him. And then—read below the unexpected outcome of this thought-provoking story.

"I met Mr. Haskell at a dance when I was in Florida. He was wonderful—handsome, with a marvelous education, and a good dancer.

"I was crazy about him. And he seemed to like me."

Different at Noon

"But next day—how different!

"We had agreed to go swimming together and take some pictures.

"We chatted for a while on the beach. I saw Mr. Haskell looking at me closely. I couldn't help noticing that he seemed cold and distant.

"It just made me miserable! And I feared I knew the 'something' which was the matter.

"After the swim I asked him to call on me. He just *ignored* the invitation.

" 'Mr. Haskell...' I faltered. 'Why have you changed?'

" 'I guess I'll have to tell you something, little girl,' he said, 'just for your own good.'

Right in the Face

" 'Frankly, I am disappointed in you. Last night I thought you were wonderful. But today when I saw your face in the sunlight I got the shock of my life.... Can't you do *anything* about that complexion?' "

Things like this happen all the time. Girls get careless. They forget that true beauty is impossible without regularity and a smooth-running system. Many girls handicap themselves this way.

3. "You and Me" Copy

In the "You and Me" style of copy the manufacturer speaks directly to the customer, usually in a chatty, friendly way, just as a house-to-house salesman talks to a housewife. Here is an example taken from a direct mail letter selling mackerel fillets by mail order:

FISH HAS BEEN MY SPECIALTY ALL MY LIFE

In my many years as a fisherman, I've seen a lot of fish. Starting with the days when I used to go "mackerelling" in my father's vessel, I've loved the sea and the good things that come out of it.

I remember how father carefully selected the best fish of the catch to take home. I've never forgotten his "fisherman's test" of mackerel and codfish. We'd pick the plump ones with meat so fat and tender they would break apart at the touch of the fork. They always turned out to be so juicy and sweet—tender as chicken.

The letter continues in this vein for several paragraphs and then closes with this appeal:

Let Me Send You These Fillets Now—On Approval
Just check and sign the enclosed card and mail it, and I'll send you a pail containing 10 Fillets of fat, fall-caught mackerel, each sufficient for two or three persons. Freshen one of these Fillets and broil to a delicate brown. If you are not fully satisfied that it is the finest mackerel you ever tasted, send the rest back at my expense and the trial costs you nothing.

4. Imaginative Copy

In this kind of copy the copywriter heightens the reader's interest in the product by describing it in imaginative terms. For example, a successful mail order advertisement written by Bruce Barton for a two-year, home-study course in business described the course as follows:

A WONDERFUL TWO YEARS' TRIP AT FULL PAY—
but only men with imagination can take it
About one man in ten will be appealed to by this page. The other nine will be hard workers, earnest, ambitious in their way, but to them a coupon is a coupon; a book is a book; a Course is a Course. The one man in ten has imagination.
And imagination rules the world.
Let us put it this way. An automobile is at your door; you are invited to pack your bag and step in. You will travel to New York. You will go directly to the office of the president of one of the biggest banks. You will spend hours with him, and with other bank presidents. You will not leave these bankers until you have a thorough understanding of our great banking system.
When you have finished with them the car will be waiting. It will take you to the offices of men who direct great selling organizations. Their time will be at your disposal.

Through other days the heads of accounting departments will guide you. On others, men who have made their mark in office management... [etc.... etc.].
The whole journey will occupy two years. It will cost you nothing in income, for your salary will go right along.

Note: The above is condensed from an ad that brought so many responses that it was repeated again and again for seven years. The complete ad is reproduced on page 300.

5. Factual Copy

A large number of successful retail ads were compared with a number of unsuccessful retail ads. The purpose was to discover what kind of retail copy produces the most sales. Conclusion: The ads that tell the largest number of facts about the product are the ads that make the most sales. Stating it briefly: The more you tell, the more you sell.

Here is an example of successful retail copy. Notice how it sells by piling one fact on top of another.

ENGINEERS' BOOTS
For you outdoor men who demand the best in boots. Ease into these comfortable, weather-resistant Wearmasters. Selected grain leather uppers, oil-tanned to repel water ... stay flexible with repeated exposure to moisture. Leather vamp lining wears longer; gives more comfort across instep. Leather Woodsman's heel, rubber top lift, distributes weight evenly for better balance. Double oak leather soles. Steel shank reinforces leather insole. Outside counter pocket strengthens heel. Top ankle straps adjust. Goodyear welt construction ... retains original boot-shape ... easy to resole.

6. Facts-plus-style Copy

Copy that merely imitates the style of some great master of English prose, and omits the selling arguments, is of little value. On the other hand, copy that has style in addition to selling arguments is acceptable, especially when you are advertising a high-grade product.

Below are paragraphs taken from an advertisement stressing the speed obtainable in a Rolls-Royce automobile. Notice the high speed of the copy. It moves rapidly from sentence to sentence. It has a style all its own, just as a Rolls-Royce has. And every paragraph is packed with facts and selling arguments.

There is not a car made that can measure miles with Rolls-Royce on a cross-country run. And if the run includes every kind of road condition, you only add to Rolls-Royce's advantage. For Rolls-Royce is so vibrationless, so floating-smooth, that it can take rough roads at speeds you would never think of attempting in any other car.

Prove that—at the wheel of a Rolls-Royce! You open the throttle—the scenery takes wings. But where are the rack and rattle that are speed's running mates in most other cars? Absent! You can scarcely hear the motor that is hurrying you on. If you didn't know that the speedometer is as accurate as the finest watch, you wouldn't believe you were going so fast. Rolls-Royce is *so* quiet!

7. Forthright Copy

Sometimes a writer can increase the believability of an ad by admitting that there are some weak points as well as strong points in the proposition he is selling. Here is a classified real-estate ad that uses this method effectively. For this example, the author is indebted to advertising consultant Clyde Bedell.

NEGLECTED
JR. ESTATE
$25,000

Few settings in Los Altos Hills are more beautiful than this full acre. Here you have orchard land and towering shade oaks. The basically charming and comfortable home, however, needs loving attention from a family with the Imagination and Energy to bring it up to modern standards. There are 3 good-sized bedrooms, nice bath, separate dining room, and huge family kitchen—plus breezeway, garage, and rundown solarium with intriguing possibilities. The Guest House sags at the seams, but perhaps You can make it livable. While you're trying, there IS the reward of a relaxing dip in your 16' x 36' Filtered Paddock Swim Pool. Make no mistake—there's much to be done here. But the potential is great, and the price downright tempting, so maybe you should have a look. If you like what you see, we'll help you to own this picturesque property on terms that suit you. Palo Alto school district. Obey that impulse and call now for an appointment.

8. Superlative Copy

In this type of copy you step right out and blow your own horn as loudly as possible. This kind of advertising is effective if you have the facts to back it up. Here are two examples:

Build a library of classics
in replicas of rare bookbindings
decorated in 24 Karat Gold

Choose any 3 of the masterworks on this page for only $1 with trial membership in the International Collectors Library. We make this extraordinary offer to introduce you to one of the greatest ideas in publishing history.

The private libraries of the past have bequeathed to us rare bookbindings of hand-crafted design. Today these originals are found only in museums and in the home libraries of very wealthy collectors. Now the International Collectors Library brings you the great classics of fiction, history, biography, poetry, drama and adventure—in authentic period bindings—replicas of the designs on the priceless originals.

[Etc., etc. . . .]

Yours Free ... Giant New
Spring Garden Catalog

Over one hundred great garden ideas. Your first chance to see the Rose of the Year, plus the new All-America roses and much, much more.

Golden Gate—brilliant intense yellow, outstanding for cutting. THE yellow rose for arrangements.

Brand New Hybrid Teas—White masterpiece, with 6-inch blooms so perfect you'll have to see them to believe them. Here's Heirloom—pure, clear lilac, one of the rarest colors in the garden world; rich with fragrance like ripe raspberries.

[Etc., etc. . . .]

9. Signed Copy

Sometimes the manufacturer himself issues a signed statement regarding the product or service he is selling. This method was used by a famous automobile manufacturer to announce a new car. In another case, a watch manufacturer published an advertisement that was written and signed by a well-known author.

Below are quotes from an advertisement for *World Magazine*. The copy is signed by Norman Cousins, publisher.

An open letter to
the readers of *The New York Times*
Norman Cousins
Two Dag Hammarskjold Plaza New York, New York 10017

My purpose in writing is to tell you that my colleagues and I have decided to launch a new magazine.

Ever since I resigned from the *Saturday Review,* for reasons you may know about, I have been thinking and dreaming about the possibility of starting a magazine that, quite literally, would belong to its readers and editors.

[There followed 16 paragraphs of description of the forthcoming magazine.]

We ask no money now. That can come later. What we need right now is an expression of your interest.

As I said above, in inviting you to join us in what we hope will be an exciting adventure in ideas, we realize we are asking you to take a chance on us. We have high hopes of justifying that confidence. The process begins with the Charter Subscription form below.

Sincerely,

Norman Cousins

Note: The complete Norman Cousins ad is reproduced on page 125.

10. Title Copy

Over a period of years, mail order book advertisers have discovered by trial and error just what titles are most interesting to magazine and newspaper readers. Titles that do not sell are discarded from the advertising. Titles that sell in large quantities are retained. Here are some titles listed in a typical advertisement. Notice what a world of interest is packed into three or four words. And remember that these titles were not selected at the whim of the copywriter. They are the most popular titles—the titles that produced the most sales.

Take your pick of the books
listed on this page

What Every Girl Should Know	How to Write Short Stories
Rhyming Dictionary	A Book of Riddle Rimes
Origin of Human Race	How to Argue Logically

Dictionary of U.S. Slang
Physiology of Sex Life
Common Faults in English
Evolution of Marriage
Manhood Facts of Life
Hypnotism Explained
Self-Contradictions of Bible
How to Love
History of World War II
History of Rome
Principles of Electricity
Queer Facts About Lost
  Civilizations
Story of Plato's Philosophy
Evolution of Sex
A Hindu Book of Love
Book of Synonyms
Puzzle of Personality
Plain Talks With Husbands
  and Wives
Is Death Inevitable?
Best Jokes About Doctors

How to Improve Your Con-
  versation
Psychology of Suicide
Facts You Should Know
  About Music
Art of Being Happy
My 12 Years in a Monastery
Baseball: How to Play
Evolution Made Plain
Develop Sense of Humor
How N.Y. Girls Live
How Not to be a Wall-
  Flower
Novel Discoveries in Science
How to Tie All Kinds of Knots
Short History of Civil War
What Women Beyond 40
  Should Know
Hints on Etiquette
Prostitution in the Ancient
  World
Do We Need Religion?

The next time you write a headline, a subhead, or the title of a free booklet, try to put into it the brevity, the simplicity, and the human interest that are contained in the titles of these books.

11. Teaser Copy

This copy is a challenge to the reader. Instead of trying to sell him, it apparently tries to discourage him. Perhaps the effectiveness of this method is accounted for by its unusualness. For example, here is an extract from a teaser advertisement for a business training school.

MEN WHO "KNOW IT ALL"
ARE NOT INVITED
TO READ THIS PAGE

This page is not for the wise young man who is perfectly satisfied with himself and his business equipment.

This page is a personal message to the man who has responsibilities, who feels secretly that he ought to be earning several thousand dollars more a year, but who simply lacks the confidence necessary to lay hold on one of the bigger places in business.

12. News Page Copy

In this kind of copy, the advertiser buys a full page in a newspaper and devotes a quarter of the page to one of his regular advertisements. The rest of the page is made to look like a typical newspaper page, with news headlines, news items, etc. The only difference is that the news items, instead of being written by a newspaper reporter, are written by an advertising copywriter. Naturally, the product is sold just as hard in the news items as in the regular advertising.

An advertising page like this is useful for an occasional variation in the advertising campaign. If used too often, it would lose its effectiveness.

A maker of automobile accessories who used coupons in his advertising tried a news page of this type and reported that coupon returns were three times as great as the coupon returns he had previously been receiving from his regular advertisements.

Now we come to four kinds of copy that are questionable. These should be used with discretion.

13. Card Copy

Some advertisers use copy so brief that the entire advertisement, although it sometimes occupies full-page space, could easily be printed on a business card. For example, the following full-page magazine advertisement contains only twenty-four words:

BLANK & CO.

Jewelers   Silversmiths   Stationers

Diamond Jewelry
Noted for Quality
From Generation to Generation

Mail Inquiries Receive Prompt Attention

Fifth Avenue
New York

Other frequent users of card advertising are the financial houses, stock brokers, etc., whose advertisements in the financial pages of the daily newspapers consist merely of their name and address and perhaps a slogan, all enclosed in a rectangular box.

This advertising may be heaven for those who work on it. In fact, it should allow its authors practically six months' vacation twice a year. But it goes against the grain of the users of tested advertising who have never been able to get a profitable volume of sales with less than 200 words.

14. Competitive Copy

Here is a table of figures and a paragraph of copy taken from an automobile tire advertisement that speaks right out against its competitors, the mail order houses:

COMPARE
Construction and Quality

	Our Tire	*Special Brand Mail Order Tire
MORE Rubber Volume	172 cu. in.	161 cu. in.
MORE Weight	16.99 pounds	15.73 pounds
MORE Width	4.75 inches	4.74 inches
MORE Thickness	.627 inch	.578 inch
MORE Plies at Tread	6 plies	5 plies
SAME PRICE	(price)	(price)

*A "Special Brand" Tire is made by a manufacturer for distributors such as mail order houses, oil companies, and others under a name that does not identify the tire manufacturer to the public, usually because he builds his "first line" tires under his own name. We put our name on *every* tire we make.

15. Clever Copy

When the copywriter tries to be clever, he is likely to produce one of the following results:

1. He may write an advertisement that is neither clever nor effective. The headline, in its attempt to be smart, may turn out to be obscure and fail to attract readers. The few readers who do read the copy realize that the copywriter has tried to be funny and has failed. Such an advertisement can actually do harm.

2. He may write an advertisement that seems clever to the people who read it from beginning to end. However, in view of the fact that the headline is usually tricky, rather than a selling headline, few people actually do read the entire advertisement.

3. He may write the rare advertisement that contains both cleverness and salesmanship. The following Hart, Schaffner & Marx clothing advertising is an example. The element that kept this advertisement from misfiring is the fact that the headline attracted a large number of readers:

[Headline]	THIS IS PROBABLY THE LOWEST PRICE CLOTHING ADVERTISEMENT EVER PRINTED
[Subhead]	This suit $4.79—and very seasonable, indeed
[Illustration]	[Picture of a man wrapped in a large white cotton sheet]
[Copy]	"THIS SUIT" is really a large white cotton sheet. It covers the body, it launders well—and it costs $4.79.
	Like any other low-priced clothing, it has its disadvantages: it doesn't fit, the style isn't so good, and it wouldn't quite pass at a directors' meeting or at the club—but it will keep you out of jail.
	ON THE OTHER HAND, if you do want to look well-dressed and hold the respect of your business associates, and look like success at a time when success never meant more—pay the price of good clothes.

Copywriters should avoid the so-called "clever" type of copy. It is too often a snare and a delusion. To attempt to write it is playing with fire. The chances are a hundred to one against you when you try to be smart in your advertising. Even the men who are famous for writing clever advertisements turn out a number of duds. Why not be on the safe side and stick to selling copy? The chances are a hundred to one in your favor if you stick to a straightforward and simple presentation of the benefits your product will confer on the buyer.

16. Humorous Copy

Humorous copy, like clever copy, should be avoided by 99 copywriters out of 100. Of the millions of people in the United States, less than half have a sense of humor. And those who do appreciate humor are divided and subdivided into at least a dozen different groups. Each group has a sense of humor of a different kind. What is funny to you is likely to be either idiotic or insulting to the other fellow. This means that when you write humorous copy, you limit your audience to perhaps one-third or sometimes one-tenth of your possible audience.

One of the best-remembered humorous campaigns was published years ago by the makers of Kelly-Springfield Tires. The ads were done in cartoon style with a large picture and a few lines of copy underneath. Example:

[Illustration] [Picture of minister and layman in conversation]
[Copy] "Aren't you sometimes tempted to swear a little when you have tire trouble, Parson?"
"Well, I might be, but you see I avoid temptation by using Kelly-Springfields."

The following types of copy are definitely not recommended.

17. Poetic Copy

There is a type of copy so poetically worded that the chief impression the reader receives is, "The man who wrote that piece is certainly a master word juggler."

The advertisement below is an example. In this ad a copywriter is attempting to sell his own services.

DRILLING

against granite with a point of putty—that's average advertising.

Aiming to pierce, it only bores. It wallows in a welter of sugary stultiloquence. "Thou say'st an undisputed thing in such a solemn way." The formula of average advertising is as unchanging as the jokes in an after-dinner speech. Advertising must shave off its mustache or grow one. It has looked the same too long. Advertising needs a fresh newpoint and a new penpoint or—LeDéluge....Mr. S.Y.Z., declared to be the highest-paid advertising writer, compresses into one luminous sentence what average advertising looks for without seeing. Space is too costly to stop to weigh the fee of supreme ability.

Arrangements for retaining Mr. X.Y.Z. may be initiated through Mr. A.B. C., Director Cliental Relations, 100 Park Avenue, New York.

The above advertisement appeared only once. Perhaps it brought so much business that its author is still busy filling orders. However, the opposite explanation seems more likely—that it brought so little business that it wasn't worth repeating.

Below is an advertisement that was repeated dozens of times in business magazines. It must have pulled or it wouldn't have been repeated so often. It is quoted here not as an example of poor copy, but for the sake of contrast.

SALES PROMOTION

$150 to $50,000 Daily Sales Developed during 28 years for clients by our direct mail campaigns. One product a few years ago was just an idea; this year $100,000 in orders booked. Fifty-year-old concern desired 50 national representatives; we produced 40 in three months. 700 dealers in 10 months at $3 each, for another. Ten years Sales Promotion Manager Larkin Co. Submit Sales problems for free diagnosis. J.C.J., Buffalo.

18. Affected Copy

There is a type of copy that sounds as if it were written by a college sophomore in order to produce an intense effect on the reader. This copy depends on extravagant phrases rather than on real thought or feeling. Here is a sample taken from a jeweler's advertisement for star sapphires.

NOCTURNE

Star Sapphire . . . It is like a cup of night blue, dazed with moonlight and soft shadows, and it bears a promise of the sky. For in its depths stir the six arcs of a veiled silver star . . . eager to fling their beauty to the night.

19. Unbelievable Copy

Copy that strains the credulity of the intelligent reader is not as effective as it was years ago. Most of the advertisers who procured sales through exaggerated and unbelievable claims have been reduced to using 60-line space in a few of the cheaper publications. Or they have gone out of business entirely. Here are the first three paragraphs of a form letter used at one time by a stock promotion advertiser:

Dear Friend:

Thousands of people who have read this letter have

QUICKLY BECOME RICH! My sincere wish is that it will produce the same delightful results for YOU.

I'm going to write to you frankly—just as I would to an old friend—and give you some AMAZING FACTS that you can use to your VERY GREAT ADVANTAGE.

You know and I know that the man who can tell what business conditions are going to be six months, a year, or two years, ahead can make a FORTUNE out of this knowledge. That's exactly what I'm going to tell you.

[Etc. . . . etc.]

Yours for success,

John Doe

The men who prepare advertising have a responsibility to the public. The public places a trust in advertising, and those who betray that trust do harm to their own profession as well as to the business of their clients. Following is a story illustrating this point.

A life insurance salesman tried for ten years to sell a man a policy. One day the prospect walked into the insurance man's office with a printed advertisement for that same policy in his hand and wanted to buy it. The advertisement, by means of printed words, sold the same thing that the salesman had for ten years been trying to sell with spoken words. The prospect felt a confidence in the printed message that he did not feel in the sales talk.

This belief in printed words is trained into a man from childhood. He learns from printed pages that two plus two equal four and that Columbus discovered America in 1492. These things are facts, and during the most impressionable years of a man's life he is trained to believe what he reads.

Advertisers who betray this confidence do harm. For example, let us say that a boy aged twelve sees an advertisement with the headline "Free Roller Skates ... Simply mail coupon." The boy fills in and mails the coupon and immediately begins to think about the fun he is going to have when he gets the roller skates. Then comes the rude awakening. The youngster receives a letter from the advertiser stating that if the boy will sell to his friends thirty sets of beautiful hand-colored photographs at a dollar a set and send in the money, he will receive the roller skates absolutely free.

Thus is created a skeptic, a doubter. Twenty years later, when this individual is in the market for an automobile, the automobile advertiser may find his selling job has been made more difficult by the misleading advertisement that jarred the prospect's confidence years before.

The pre-eminence of America in industry has come largely through mass production. Mass production is only possible where there is demand. Mass demand has been created almost entirely through the development of advertising.

Calvin Coolidge

An open letter to the readers of The New York Times

Norman Cousins
Two Dag Hammarskjold Plaza   New York, New York 10017

My purpose in writing is to tell you that my colleagues and I have decided to launch a new magazine. The magazine will be published every two weeks. It will be called *World Review*.

Ever since I resigned from the Saturday Review, for reasons you may know about, I have been thinking and dreaming about the possibility of starting a magazine that, quite literally, would belong to its readers and editors.

This has never been done before. Usually, new magazines call for a prodigious investment. The reason for this is the traditional way a magazine operates. Magazines and newspapers are the only products sold to the consumer at less than the cost of manufacture. Advertising is expected to make up the difference. What compounds this problem is that the standard way of building a subscription list is through cut-rate introductory offers.

On a new magazine, the subscription list generally consists almost entirely of cut-rate introductory offers. This is why massive outside investment has usually been necessary to see a magazine through to the point where introductory-offer readers can be graduated to full-rate subscribers. Outside investment frequently means outside control—and this is something we want to avoid if we possibly can.

My hope, therefore, is that we can find enough readers willing to take a chance on us by becoming long-term subscribers from the very outset. This would make it unnecessary to seek outside financing. It would also put the reader where he should rightfully be—in a position of ultimate authority.

We decided to put these hopes to the test. I am delighted to say that the first responses to our testing have been favorable beyond even our most extravagant expectations. As a result, we are scheduling our first issue for late in the spring.

What about the magazine itself?

We believe that a magazine is essentially a reading, rather than a viewing, experience. In this sense, we will publish for a readership rather than a flippership.

The new magazine will be concerned with ideas and the arts. Our arena, however, will be the world. We will do more than report on books, plays, movies, music and the arts in just the United States alone. We will attempt to review and report on cultural events on a world scale—cultural being defined in its broadest sense.

We will write about the human condition at a time when the ability of human intelligence to meet its problems is being tested as never before. Our hope is to see the world as the astronauts saw it—a beautiful wet blue ball with millions of factors in the delicate combination that makes life possible. Our dominant editorial concern, then, will be the proper care of the human habitat—whether that means world peace and everything that is required to bring it about, or world environmental deterioration, or overcrowding, or any of the things that indignify and humiliate human beings.

In this connection, I am pleased to announce that U Thant and Buckminster Fuller have joined the Board of Editors.

We will also give major attention to what we believe will be one of the most compelling issues in the years ahead—the waste of human resources, far more costly than the waste of physical resources.

I think I have said enough to indicate that the new magazine will direct its central editorial energies both to the enjoyment of creative living and to the pursuit of vital ideas. But it would be a mistake, I think, to attempt a full description of the magazine. Magazines are not really invented or created. They evolve. They are the product of creative interaction between the special tastes and enthusiasms and concerns of a few editors, and the tastes and concerns of the readers.

In this way, a magazine takes shape issue by issue and year by year. No single issue can really be expected to tell a reader everything he may want to know about the nature of a magazine, its underlying philosophy, or its capacity for growth. Since it might be misleading to try to tell you exactly what our new magazine will be like, what I have tried to do is to tell you something about our approach—and to seek your help in achieving our aims.

Some specifics: The rates will be $12 for one year; $20 for two years.

For pre-publication Charter subscribers we propose a special three-year rate of $25.

The reason we emphasize three-year subscriptions is that this reduces sharply the astoundingly high cost of processing renewals.

Even more important is the fact that long-term subscriptions will free us to do our main job—which is to try to publish a magazine you will read and respect.

We ask no money now. That can come later. What we do need right now is an expression of your interest.

As I said above, in inviting you to join us in what we hope will be an exciting adventure in ideas, we realize we are asking you to take a chance on us. We have high hopes of justifying that confidence. The process begins with the Charter Subscription form below.

Sincerely,

[signature]

Norman Cousins

How $15,711 Spent Sold $54,923 Worth of Subscriptions

This ad ran three times in *The New York Times* and pulled $54,923 worth of subscriptions for *World Review* Magazine at an advertising space cost of $15,571. Here are some of the features that made this ad successful: (1) It looks like editorial material. (2) It is signed by a famous editor, Norman Cousins. (3) It is written in the "you and me" style, like a letter to a friend. (4) The name "The New York Times" in the headline gets attention, especially since the ad appeared in *The Times*.

One of the many magnificent illustrations in the Five - Foot Shelf of Books

This is Marie Antoinette Riding to Her Death—

Do you know her tragic story? Have you ever read what Burke wrote about the French Revolution—one of the great, fascinating books that have made history?

In all the world there are only a few of these books, speeches, letters, poems, essays, biographies that have really *made history*. To read *these* few great works systematically and intelligently is to be really well read.

What are these few great works? The free booklet pictured below answers that question. It tells the fascinating story of how Dr. Eliot of Harvard has picked the few *really worth while* books out of the thousands of useless ones, how he has arranged them as the

Famous Five-Foot Shelf of Books
Now Yours For a Few Cents a Day

One hundred thousand business men are using the pleasant, helpful reading courses which Dr. Eliot has laid out.

They are reading the great histories, seeing the great plays, hearing the great orations, meeting the great men of history with Dr. Eliot.

He says: "I believe the faithful and considerate reading of these books will give any man the essentials of a liberal education, even if he can devote to them only fifteen minutes a day."

This Book Is For You—Free

We want to send you by mail a copy of this fascinating "guide book" to books, *absolutely free*.

It is the most valuable little book of its kind ever written; it shows how to select a library without waste or worry, what books are *worth while*, what are not. It contains Dr. Eliot's best advice to you, on just what and how to read for success.

The book was printed to give away; your copy is wrapped up and ready to mail; no obligation; merely clip this coupon now.

CLIP the Coupon

P. F. COLLIER & SON
416 W. 13th Street
New York

Without any obligation whatever to me please send me a copy of the free "guide book" to books, with Dr. Eliot's story of the Five-Foot Shelf.

P. F. COLLIER & SON, NEW YORK

Putting Drama into Book Advertising

Dr. Eliot, former Harvard president, once remarked that a liberal education could be obtained from a five-foot shelf of books. The Collier Publishing Company asked Dr. Eliot to name the books. He did, and the Harvard Classics was born. The theme of the earliest ads was the joy and satisfaction of owning and reading great books. These ads failed to produce many coupon leads for salesmen. Bruce Barton, then an employee of Colliers, was asked to write some copy. He produced the ad shown above. He said: "Marie pulled eight times as many coupons as any previous ad. She was such a good puller that she continued to run for years."

My friend, Joe Holmes, is now a horse

JOE always said when he died he'd like to become a horse.

One day Joe died.

Early this May I saw a horse that looked like Joe drawing a milk wagon.

I sneaked up to him and whispered, "Is it you, Joe?"

He said, "Yes, and am I happy!" I said, "Why?"

He said, "I am now wearing a comfortable collar for the first time in my life. My shirt collars always used to shrink and murder me. In fact, one choked me to death. That is why I died!"

"Goodness, Joe," I exclaimed, "Why didn't you tell me about your shirts sooner? I would have told you about Arrow shirts. They *never shrink*. Not even the oxfords."

"G'wan," said Joe. "Oxford's the worst shrinker of all!"

"Maybe," I replied, "but not *Gordon*, the Arrow oxford. I know. I'm wearing one. It's Sanforized-shrink-proof. Besides, it's cool. Besides, this creamy shade I chose is the newest shirt color, *bamboo*."

"Swell," said Joe. "My boss needs a shirt like that. I'll tell him about Gordon. Maybe he'll give me an extra quart of oats. And, gosh, do I love oats!"

If it hasn't an Arrow Label it isn't an Arrow Shirt

ARROW SHIRTS

Sanforized Shrunk — a new shirt free if one ever shrinks

Made by CLUETT, PEABODY & CO., INC.

Salesmanship with a Smile

Humor in advertising should be used sparingly. What is funny to one person may seem silly to another. The most powerful mail order ads contain no humor. The most powerful book in the world, the Bible, contains no humor. However, a skillful copywriter can sometimes combine humor and salesmanship effectively. This ad for Arrow Shirts was written by George Gribbin, former president of Young & Rubicam, and a member of the Copywriters Hall of Fame.

A Mail Order Ad That Didn't Pay

Two ads for Sherwin Cody's correspondence course in correct English were tested by mail order response. One had the headline, "Do You Make These Mistakes in English?" It paid extremely well and was repeated for years. The ad is reproduced on page 306. The other ad "The Man Who Simplified English" is shown above. This ad was a failure. It belongs to the type of ads called "manufacturer's copy." These ads talk about the manufacturer, his factory, his salesmen, or about some other feature that has little or no interest to the average person. The most effective ads are those that talk about *you*.

11

Twenty Ways to Increase Selling Power of Copy

This chapter discusses twenty ways to increase the selling power of your advertising. All of these methods have been tested in actual practice and have been found to be effective.

1. Use Present Tense, Second Person

Unless there is a definite reason to the contrary, you should write your copy in the present tense, second person. Don't say, "A man will feel well dressed in a Brooks suit." Say, "*You feel* well dressed in a Brooks suit."

Don't say, "People will enjoy a sense of security when they use Goodyear Tires." Say, "*You enjoy* a sense of security when *you* use Goodyear Tires."

Keep hammering at the reader with—you—you—you.

2. Use Subheads

Practically all mail order advertisers use three or more subheads in every full-page advertisement. Many general advertisers do the same. Subheads accomplish the following results:

1. They tell your story in brief form to glancers who don't have time to read your entire advertisement.
2. They get copy read that might otherwise not be read. For example, a customer might be sufficiently attracted by your headline to read a paragraph or two of your copy, and then turn the page. But at that moment an interesting subhead catches his eye and he reads further.

Here are the headline and subheads of a beauty product advertisement. Notice how the subheads tell a brief story as well as arouse interest.

Headline: What Is the Critical Age of a Woman's
                 Skin?
Subhead No. 1:   New York doctor shows how to correct
                 the 4 defects that age your skin.
Subhead No. 2:   Why old-style treatments fail.
Subhead No. 3:   How pore-deep method acts.
Subhead No. 4:   Send 25¢ for book, "New Faces for Old."

3. Put Captions Under Illustrations

In newspaper articles, you will always find captions printed under the illustrations. These captions get high readership because they add to the interest of the illustrations and help to explain their meaning. In magazines such as *Time* and *Playboy*, you will also find scores of illustrations with captions under them. These captions attract readers.

The point is that people are in the habit of reading the brief messages that are printed under pictures. This habit dates back to the reading of school textbooks, which have always had captions under the illustrations. The advertiser should take advantage of this habit. Don't run pictures without putting captions under them. Put a brief selling message or a human interest message under every illustration you use. (See Schweppes ad at end of this chapter.)

4. Use a Simple Style of Writing

In his *Philosophy of Style*, Herbert Spencer gives advice to writers that every advertising writer should take to heart. A copywriter could do himself a favor by typing the following passage on a sheet of paper and keeping it handy so he can reread it from time to time until the message becomes part of his own mental makeup.

Regarding language as an apparatus of symbols for the conveyance of thought, we may say that, as in a mechanical apparatus, the more simple and the better arranged its parts, the greater will be the effect produced.

In either case, whatever force is absorbed by the machine is deducted from the result. A reader or listener has at each moment but a limited amount of mental power available. To recognize and interpret the symbols presented to him requires part of this power; to arrange and combine the images suggested requires a further part; and only that part that remains can be used for realizing the thought conveyed.

Hence, the more time and attention it takes to receive and understand each sentence, the less time and attention can be given to the contained idea; and the less vividly will that idea be conceived.

This quotation from Spencer is not the simplest piece of writing in the world. Nevertheless, the idea that you should reduce to a minimum the amount of time the reader must devote to figuring out what you are trying to say is absolutely sound.

Roy Durstine in his book, *This Advertising Business*, expressed the same idea, perhaps more potently than Spencer expressed it:

The most important job of an advertisement is to center all the attention on the merchandise and none on the technique of presenting it.

5. Choose Simple Words

Use short simple words to express your meaning. Educated readers understand short words just as well as long words, and the masses understand short words much better. Even where it is necessary to substitute three or four short words for one long word, it is usually wise to do so.

POMPOUS WORDS

For some years, folks have been finding in the attics of old houses bits of furniture that are priceless. Abandoned farm houses, gaunt and bald, have revealed, with a bit of coaxing, a purity of line and form and a generous sturdiness of build, which are almost lost arts.

When restored, one of these fine old houses stands out from its modern neighbors of Spanish, French, Italian, Tudor, and Mission design, with the calm dignity of a patrician in a rabble.

Since the days of Chaucer and Shakespeare, we have had stored away in the attic a simple, crude language that was made to order for advertising. It consists mostly of one- and two-syllable words—odd, native, little words that barbarians used to express their uncouth thoughts.

About the time this jargon was in flower, a gang from the Mediterranean muscled in and, with sword and monk, laid the groundwork for modern civilization in England.

Then they began to put together that collection of mongrel words known as the English language. The rude, vulgar, native words had to answer for the masses and so stayed in use, but people with any pretense to culture gradually fixed up a lot of words with fancy Latin fronts, Greek centers and a dash of Turkish in the rear.

For the last thousand years, education in England has consisted chiefly of learning Greek and Latin. We have been about as bad in this country. The result is curiously shown in our writings. Young men who join us each year from big universities for a while find it hard to express themselves in writing with anything less than five-syllable words.

Yet, strange to say, when people are just talking back and forth they still use the old Anglo-Saxon almost entirely.

You see, these built-up words don't, as a rule, mean anything in particular. Take that last word, "particular." That's one of them. It is an adjective or noun and can be made into a verb or adverb. The dictionary gives it something like fifty different meanings. So it really doesn't mean a thing. It is little more than a sound. It started two or three thousand years ago in some wild Latin tribe as "par." The Roman intelligentsia dressed it up into "particula." Then the French made it "particulier." The word has been rolling round for so long that it's all moss and no stone.

Of course, Latin is a beautiful language and has given us a lot of nice little words that are almost Anglo-Saxon in simplicity and clarity. But they are not pompous words.

The reason we use short words to talk with is that they mean exactly the same thing to talker and hearer. When we drag in a lot of jointed words, we forget before the sentence is finished just what it was we were trying to say; and the other fellow never does find out. For the same reason, we use short words to think with.

Now, in advertising, it is vital that the reader shall grasp, in a split second, whatever it is that you want him to know. You can't afford to waste a single syllable just to impress him with your intellectual culture. Broadcasting offers a good example of what we mean. Someone got gorgeous and produced "superheterodyne." One Latin word and two Greek ones. Isn't that a nice word to work into a snappy selling talk? A manufacturer, who likes to have the public know what he is talking about, built his appeal on "Golden Voice."

Short words are easy and pleasant to read. The eye picks up their meaning without conscious effort. But the average reader stumbles over pompous words and loses his mental balance. They annoy and bore him. After about two staggers, his interest wanders and he turns to the next page. A short word takes up about one third as much room as a pompous word. When you are paying forty dollars a line, that is quite an item. (From an ad by BBDO, Inc.)

6. Give Free Information

One way to arouse interest is to give free information as well as sales talk in your copy. In doing this, your advertisement should be arranged so that the free information comes first and the sales talk second. If the sales talk is placed first, the reader may never reach the free information section.

Here are the headline and opening paragraphs of a business school advertisement. Notice that the copy starts off, not with a sales talk, but in an editorial style. It might be the beginning of a magazine article:

A WARNING to men
who would like to be independent
in the next five years

You can tell a $100-a-week man how to make $150 a week.

You can tell a $150-a-week man how to make $200 a week.

But you can't tell a $15,000 man how to make $25,000. He's got to know.

Between $15,000 and $25,000 a year is where most men of talent stop.

Health, youth, good appearance, and brains will carry a man far in business.

But you cannot draw forever on that bank account unless you put something else in. Somewhere between $15,000 and $25,000 a year you will stop dead.

Business today is new and complex. The old rules will no longer work. A whole new set of problems is presented by production. Foreign markets have become a vital issue. An entirely new conception of selling is replacing the old hit-or-miss way.

7. Selling Copy versus Style Copy

Two types of copy in use today are:

1. style copy
2. selling copy

Style copy is based on the assumption that customers are swayed by flowery language and elaborate adjectives. Here is an example of style copy taken from a soap advertisement:

> Try this soap for a week. Revel in its sculptured smoothness, its deep-piled fragrant lather. How exquisitely soft your skin is after its use—how fresh and clear! Doesn't your mirror show you, a little more clearly each day, the natural charm men love to dream about?

Now read a piece of selling copy taken from another soap advertisement:

> This soap is made of olive and palm oils—no other fats whatever. No artificial coloring. No heavy fragrance to mask other odors. It is a pure soap—as pure and wholesome as the complexions it fosters. So pure, in fact, that more than 20,000 beauty experts the world over have united to recommend it.

Notice how style copy consists mainly of unsupported claims, whereas selling copy supports its claims with proof. The first example of soap copy says, "Revel in its sculptured smoothness." The other says, "Made of olive and palm oils—no other fats whatever."

If there is any doubt in your mind as to whether to use style copy or selling copy, remember that advertisers who can trace the sales results from their ads use selling copy.

8. Arouse Curiosity

Curiosity is a powerful selling tool when properly used by the copywriter. On the other hand, the copywriter who satisfies the reader's curiosity, instead of arousing it, is apt to lose customers.

Not long ago I read a review of a new novel . This review aroused my curiosity about the novel and I considered buying it. A few days later I saw an advertisement for the same novel. The advertisement contained several long quotations from the book itself. I read these quotations. They revealed so much of the plot of the story that my curiosity was satisfied and I decided not to buy the book. A book review had practically persuaded me to buy the book. An advertisement lost the sale by satisfying my curiosity.

Here are examples of the proper use of the curiosity appeal. These are taken from ads for adventure books. Notice how these sentences tell enough of a situation to arouse your curiosity; but they refrain from satisfying your curiosity by telling you the outcome of the situation.

> This book tells what happened when an exiled white man and a beautiful native girl met, far from civilization.

> Read the story of how a millionaire's yacht was stranded helpless on a cannibal island.

Here are some curiosity-arousing paragraphs from a successful advertisement for a book on how to develop a magnetic personality:

> This singular book wields a strange power over its readers by showing them how to develop a magnetic personality almost instantly.

> A strange book! A book that seems to cast a spell over every person who turns its pages!

> A copy of this book was left lying on a hotel table for a few weeks. Nearly 400 people saw the book—read a few pages—and then sent for a copy!

> In another case a physician placed a copy on the table in his waiting room. More than 200 of his patients saw the book—read part of it—and then ordered copies for themselves!

> Why are men and women so profoundly affected by this book—so anxious to get a copy? The answer is simple. The book reveals to them for the first time how any man or woman—old or young—can develop a magnetic personality. It explains how to gain the personal charm that attracts friends—the self-confidence that insures success.

In the above paragraphs, notice that the method by which the reader is given a magnetic personality is not explained. You have to buy the book in order to discover that.

The curiosity appeal can be used with free booklets, too, booklets that you want people to send for. Here is an example:

GET THIS FREE BOOK

A 24-page free book tells how you can become financially

independent—how you can provide an income to retire
on—how you can end money worries—how you can do
these things and many other things, no matter whether
your present income is large or small.

This plan ... is explained in the free book. There's no
obligation. Send for your copy now.

Notice that the financial plan is not explained. The reader is
merely told that there is such a plan and that it is explained in the free
book. If the advertisement told what the plan was, the reader might
say, "Oh, is that all it is! I've known about that all my life." An advertisement that gives away its secret in advance is like a magician
who shows the audience the secret of his tricks before he performs
them.

9. Make Your Copy Specific

Anybody who works on tested advertising will tell you how
important it is to be specific in your copy. For example, the statement
that "97,482 people have bought one of these appliances" is stronger
than the statement "Nearly 100,000 of these appliances have been
sold." The first statement sounds like a fact. It tells the reader that a
strict and accurate count has been made of the actual number of
customers. The second statement—100,000 have been sold—sounds
like a copywriter's claim—and possibly an exaggerated claim.

The reason there are so many general claims used in advertising
copy is that it requires time and trouble to collect specific data.

In a trade magazine article, Mr. Marsh K. Powers listed some
good examples of specific copy. Here they are:

Montreal rivals New Orleans in observing the pause
that refreshes. In one year the number of bottles of Coca-
Cola served in each was: Montreal, 66 million; New
Orleans, 69 million.

158 victories in 165 public taste-tests of the four
leading brands. [Popular brand of cigarettes]

It costs only 3/4 of a cent per building dollar more than
the cheapest rustable pipe—for example, about $75 more
for a $10,000 house. [Brass pipe]

The only truck ever sold at less than ten dollars per
horsepower. [Truck]

This car has been in the constant service of the former
Governor and his family for 14 years. [Automobile]

A recent count on the highway between Chicago and Milwaukee showed 587 gasoline pumps, of which 119, or one-fifth, were our brand.

It will take you 3 days. It will cost you 25 cents.

The Spoon is the Enemy of the Highball. Ask Billy Baxter about his self-stirring Club Soda and Ginger Ale. His booklet tells all.

Comments Mr. Powers: "The single word 'self-stirring' gives the message a specific interest that no amount of 'deliciouses,' 'refreshings,' 'piquants' or less usual synonyms laboriously culled from a thesaurus could possibly have achieved."

Here is a story taken from an advertisement for a New York advertising agency. It indicates the cash value of specific statements:

This is the report of a local campaign so powerful that the industry's association requested that the copy, though true, be toned down.

A national producer of a building material had opened a new mill and appropriated $15,000 for introductory local advertising in this market.

Study of the process of manufacture showed that the product averaged 52.7% higher than the U.S. Government standard of quality, a simple fact that might carry conviction. It was decided to feature this fact and let the reader draw his own conclusions. For every customer who would accept an advertiser's claims in praise for his own product, there would be ten who would act on their own inferences based on a tangible fact.

The 52.7% point was visualized by a simple and easily remembered graphic chart.

Newspaper space in selected cities and towns around the mill was scheduled for a two months' campaign.

Meanwhile the strategy of the plan was developed:
1. Each county was analyzed and assigned a "value" showing annual total consumption of all brands.
2. An unselfish feature was incorporated in each advertisement: space to list in display type five or six other fast-selling items.
3. Salesmen were instructed to release the newspaper schedule in local papers over the names of local dealers who placed carload orders.

The salesmen took hold of the plan enthusiastically and

within a few weeks booked 150 carload orders, largely from new accounts...Soon the newspaper advertisements appeared...dealers became actively interested...buyers noted the facts presented...contractors, engineers, architects and public officials began to talk...sales to consumers followed...reorders multiplied. Results far exceeded expectations—at a cost of less than half of the budgeted appropriation.

Then a curious situation arose. The head of the National Association insisted that the copy, though true, be modified. It was feared that new rulings, raising the government standard to an unreasonable level, might result; there were rumors that local mill owners, aroused by the competitive force of the 52.7% copy, might start a vicious price-cutting campaign.

The advertising staff was instructed to "soften" the appeal, remove its sharp selling force. So the figure "52.7%" was changed to "over 50%." Immediately the "kick" was taken out of the advertising. Demand fell off to a fraction of its former strength. Word-of-mouth comment died out. Local competitors and association officials were satisfied.

Note how "52.7%" was accepted as definite proof of quality and value, while "over 50%" was discounted as a mere claim in praise of a product.

10. Use Long Copy

Whether to use short copy or long copy is a question that is difficult to answer with definite rules. So much depends on your special situation and on what you are trying to accomplish with your advertising. However, in general, you can observe the following situation in the advertising in most magazines and newspapers:

1. The short-copy ads, set in poster style, and containing only a few words of copy or a slogan, are usually used by advertisers who are unable to trace the direct sales results from their advertisements.

2. Advertisers who can trace the direct sales results from their ads use long copy because it pulls better than short copy. For example, the book club advertisers, the record clubs, the correspondence school advertisers, and the makers of various items sold by mail use ads containing 500 to 1500 words of copy. Also, you will find that real-estate advertisers, patent-

medicine advertisers, and classified advertisers put as much selling copy into their ads as the space will allow. These people cannot afford to run so-called "reminder copy." They have to get immediate sales from every ad. (See long copy ad at end of this chapter.)

Advertisers who sell their goods and services by means of direct mail letters also have found it profitable to use long copy in their advertising. For example, Frank E. Davis, who made a fortune in selling seafood by mail, started his business with brief letters. Later on he gradually shifted to longer letters because he found that long letters brought in more orders from customers. (See one of his successful letters on pp. 111-112.)

Here is the brief sales letter which Mr. Davis used in the beginning:

Dear Sir:

I wish to call your attention to the "Davis Star Brand" of choice selected Fat Mackerel.

I should be pleased to deliver a package to your address (expressage prepaid by me).

All are of the same quality, differing only in size; are prepared for cooking, and are delivered.

You will find a 20-lb. pail of either Number 1 or Number 1 Extra a desirable size.

Hoping to receive your order, I remain

Yours respectfully,

Frank E. Davis

That is the 75-word letter Mr. Davis sent out in his own handwriting when he first started in business. After years of sales testing, Mr. Davis found that he could get more and more sales by adding more and more copy. Eventually Mr. Davis sent to prospective customers an envelope containing the following:

1. A 750-word letter
2. An order form
3. A four-page folder

The four-page folder contained fourteen pictures, four main headlines, twelve subheads, eight testimonial letters, and approximately sixteen-hundred words of selling copy. In his years of experience in selling by mail, Mr. Davis found that long copy pays better than short copy.

This does not mean that long copy should be used merely for the sake of filling space. Long copy should be used in order to crowd in as many sales arguments as possible.

Here are some additional points in regard to length of copy:

1. Advocates of short copy say, "I don't think anybody will read all that small print. Let's cut the copy down to a couple of paragraphs and set it in 18-point type."

   What the advocates of short copy should say, if they want to be accurate, is this: "I don't think everybody will read all that small print." This is perfectly true. Everybody will not read it. But the fact is that the very people you are most interested in will read your ad. These are the prospects who will buy your product or service if you tell them sufficient reasons for doing so.

2. It is entirely unnecessary to set copy in 18-point type. People buy magazines and newspapers to read the stories and articles contained therein. These stories and articles are set in 6-point and 8-point type.

3. The question arises: Why wouldn't it pay the short-copy users to make their advertising do the utmost selling job by including more sales talk? *Answer*: The chances are that it would pay them.

Here is a solution to the problem of long copy versus short copy that should satisfy the champions of both sides of the question. Put a brief selling message into your headline and subheadings. Put your detailed message into small print. In this way you accomplish two things: (1) You get a brief message across to glancers with your headline and subheads. (2) You give a complete message in small print to the person who is sufficiently interested in your product to read about it.

11. Write More Copy Than Is Necessary to Fill the Space

Said the copy chief of a large advertising agency specializing in testing advertising:

We find that copy improves in quality when we cut it. That doesn't mean that we favor short copy. It means that the copywriter should write more copy than is necessary to fill a given space and then boil it down.

For example, we run our new advertisements in full-page size first. If the advertisement is successful, we repeat it as many times as it will pay. When sales fall off to such an extent that it doesn't pay to repeat the advertisement in full-page size, we cut it to half-page size. Usually it can be made to pay for a couple more insertions in this reduced space.

When the advertisement is no longer effective in half-page size, we sometimes reduce it to 60 lines and squeeze out a few more sales.

I have noticed again and again that the quality of the copy improves when we cut it. In the full-page size there are a number of unessential words and phrases. Sometimes there are whole paragraphs that are not essential to the sales story.

When the copy is cut to half-page size, these unessential elements are omitted. This strengthens the copy—gives it greater sales punch.

When the copy is cut to 60 lines, we have to omit everything but the bare essentials. The copy becomes telegraphic. Every paragraph is packed with selling arguments. The 60-line version contains the best copy of all.

As an illustration of this story, here are the headline and opening paragraphs of a couponed advertisement as it was first tested in large space.

RETIRE ON AN INCOME

You don't have to be wealthy to retire on an income. You don't even have to be wealthy to be financially independent and free from money worries for the rest of your life.

This company has perfected a new Retirement Income Plan that enables any man of moderate means to provide for himself a guaranteed income for life.

The income begins at any age you say—55, 60, or 65. It can be any amount you wish—$400 a month, $500, $600, or more.

This copy brought good results. However, it can be cut. In a reduced-size advertisement, the three paragraphs were cut to two paragraphs as follows:

RETIRE ON AN INCOME

This new Retirement Income Plan enables you to provide for yourself a guaranteed income for life.

The income begins at any age you say—55, 60 or 65. It can be any amount you wish—$400 a month, $500, $600, or more.

Later this copy was put into small space and the message was reduced to a single sentence, as follows:

RETIRE ON AN INCOME

This new Retirement Income Plan enables you to retire at 55, 60 or 65 with a monthly income of $400, $500, $600 or more, guaranteed for life.

This discussion on cutting copy is not to be considered an argument in favor of short copy. If you have space for long copy, it is advisable to use long copy. The point of this discussion is that copy usually improves when you cut it. Therefore, if you have space for 500 words of copy, don't just write 500 words. Write 1,000 words and boil it down to 500 words. If you have space for only 50 words, write 200 words and boil it down. A piece of copy is like a pot of broth. The more you boil it down, the stronger the flavor gets.

12. Avoid Helping Your Competitors

An advertisement for a TV set that describes in general terms the enjoyment of television helps to sell not only your own TV sets, but your competitor's sets as well.

Suppose you sell a man the idea of buying a TV set and he goes to a store where TV sets are displayed. He may buy the type of set you are advertising. But the chances are equally good that he will buy a competitive make. Your advertising will help your sales more if you sell your particular TV set, its tone, its picture quality, its power, or some other special feature.

The same is true in other lines. An automobile advertisement that sells your particular car is better than an advertisement selling the idea of owning an automobile. An advertisement that sells your own special brand of cigarettes has more effect on your sales than an advertisement describing the pleasures of smoking. This seems like an elementary rule. Nevertheless it is often violated.

13. Use Mail Order Methods in Direct Mail Advertising

The problems of direct mail advertising are almost identical with the problems of mail order advertising. In each case you are trying to get attention, arouse interest, and induce action. The vehicle carrying your message is the only thing that varies. In direct mail advertising your message comes to the prospect in an envelope addressed to him. In mail order advertising your message comes to the prospect by means of a page in a magazine or newspaper or via broadcasting.

This means that the rules of mail order advertising apply with equal force to direct mail. Rules for headlines, first paragraphs, use of subheads, length of copy, type of copy, etc., all may be applied to direct mail. In a direct mail letter, however, the first sentence is your headline. Just as the headline of a mail order advertisement decided whether or not the prospect will read the copy, so the first sentence of a direct mail letter usually decides whether or not the prospect will read the letter.

Here are some letter beginnings that were used by successful direct mail advertisers:

Dear Sir:

Do you know what "The Lost Books of the Bible" are? How they came to be? Why they are attracting such widespread interest?

Dear Reader:

I met a man the other day who, through sheer skill and hard work, has amassed a considerable fortune and has risen far beyond his original associations.

Dear Friend:

Here is a letter with a selfish motive. Selfish on my part for I shall gain—and, oddly enough, gain through actually saving money for you.

Dear Friend:

Somehow we failed you.
A few weeks ago, dissatisfied with your personal progress, or ambitious for quicker progress, you wrote us asking whether we could help you.

Dear Friend:

Enclosed find check for $200.
We all like to get letters that begin that way, don't we?

One advantage you have in direct mail advertising is that you can enclose a number of different pieces of advertising material in the same envelope.

For example, the envelope may contain the following:

1. A letter printed on white stock
2. A four-page folder printed on cream-colored stock
3. A leaflet of testimonials printed on green stock
4. A page of newspaper clippings reproduced on newspaper stock
5. An order form, printed on yellow stock
6. A business reply envelope printed on red stock

You may ask, "Why use six separate and distinct mailing pieces printed on different kinds of stock? Why not incorporate the entire message, testimonials, news clippings, order form, and everything in a 16-page booklet?"

The answer is that all large users of direct mail such as correspondence schools, record clubs, and book publishers have found the other method more effective. The reason is this: Much direct mail advertising goes directly to the wastebasket. However, a prospect will rarely throw all of your mailing pieces into the wastebasket without at least glancing at them. If your entire advertising message is contained in a single circular or a single booklet, the prospect will devote a few seconds to it and if it doesn't arouse his interest, he will throw it away. On the other hand, if your envelope is stuffed with half a dozen different mailing pieces, the prospect will probably glance at each piece before throwing it away. People hate to throw things away without at least glancing at them. They want to avoid disposing of anything valuable. Therefore, your six different inserts give you six opportunities to catch the interest of the prospect instead of only one opportunity.

14. Overstatement Copy Versus Understatement

Advertising copy today is showing a trend toward understatement, and in some cases understatement copy has shown greater pulling power than the other kind. Here is an example of the old-style "overstatement" copy taken from an advertisement for an electrical school:

I WILL TRAIN YOU AT HOME
TO FILL A BIG-PAY JOB!

Be an Electrical Expert. Learn to earn a big salary. Get in line for a top job by enrolling now for my easily learned, quickly grasped, right-up-to-the-minute, Spare-Time, Home-Study Course in Practical Electricity. You don't have to be a College Man; you don't have to be a High School Graduate. As Chief Engineer of the Chicago Engineering Works, I know exactly the kind of training you need, and I will give you that training. My Course in Electricity is simple, thorough, and complete and offers every man, regardless of age, education or previous experience, the chance to become, in a very short time, an "Electrical Expert," able to make big money.

Compare the above copy with these conservatively worded and convincing paragraphs taken from a business school advertisement.

TO THE MAN WHO IS 35
AND DISSATISFIED

From thirty-five to forty is the age of crisis. In these years a man either marks out the course that leads to definite advancement or settles into permanent unhappiness. There are thousands who see the years passing with a feeling close to desperation.

They say, "I must make more money," but they have no plan for making more.

They say, "There is no future for me here," but they see no other opening.

"I am managing to scrape along now," they say, "but how in the world will I ever educate my children?"

To men whose minds are constantly—and often almost hopelessly—at work on such thoughts, this page is addressed. It is devoid of rhetoric. It is plain, blunt common sense.

Let us get one thing straight at the very start—
We do not want you unless
you want us

There is the dissatisfied man who will do something and the one who won't. We feel sorry for the latter, but we cannot afford to enroll him. We have a reputation for training men who—as a result of our training—earn large salaries and hold responsible positions. That reputation must be maintained. We can do much, but we cannot make a man succeed who will not help himself. So rest assured you will not be unduly urged into anything.

In most advertisements that offer a free booklet, there is a paragraph at the end that urges the reader to send for the booklet. Here is such a paragraph taken from an advertisement. It is a good example of overstatement copy.

REMARKABLE BOOK, "PRACTICAL SELLING" SENT FREE

With my compliments I want to send you a most remarkable book, "Practical Selling." It will show you how you can easily become a Master Salesman—a big money-maker—how our system of Salesmanship Training will give you years of selling experience in a few weeks; how our FREE Employment Service will help you select and secure a good selling position when you are qualified and ready. And it will give you success stories of former routine workers who are now earning amazing salaries as salesmen. Mail the coupon today. It may be the turning point in your life.

Now read a very different kind of paragraph, also offering a free booklet:

A booklet has been prepared that tells about this new Course and Service. Its title is "What an Executive Should Know." It should be read by every man who faces the responsibility of shaping his own future. It is free. We will send you this booklet if you will simply give us your name and address on the coupon below. But we do not urge you to send for it. If you are the type of man for whom the new Course and Service has been constructed, if you are determined to take advantage of the rich opportunities of the next five years, you will send for it without urging.

Even in the selection of testimonials, the copywriter must make up his mind whether overstatement or understatement will be most effective in convincing his particular type of prospect. Here is a typical overstatement testimonial:

PLANT ENGINEER— PAY RAISED 150%

"I was a dumbbell in electricity until I got in touch with

you, but now I have charge of a big plant including 600 motors and I direct a force of 34 men—electricians, helpers, etc. My salary has gone up more than 150%."

Here is the other type of testimonial, the conservative type. Notice how the copywriter has injected comments that help to sell in parentheses:

We wish you could read the letters that come to us in every mail. Here is one, for example, from Victor F. Stine, of Hagerstown, Md.: "I was floundering around without a definite goal," he says, "and was seriously considering a Civil Service appointment." (You can tell from that how hopeless he was.)

"The study of your Course and Service was not a hardship," he continues, "rather it was a real pleasure, because it is so practical and inspiring throughout." (The method of the Institute makes it practical and inspiring.) "Added self-confidence and increased vision gained from the Institute's work," says Mr. Stine, "enabled me to accept and discharge added responsibilities successfully."

He is Secretary now of the organization in which he was once a dissatisfied "cog."

If it is important to avoid overstatement in copy, it is also important to avoid the appearance of overstatement. When a manufacturer brings out a new product, the best advertisement for it is often a simple news write-up in which the headline clearly states the most important feature, the subhead the next most important feature, and the copy the other features.

Do not try to gild the lily. Do not weaken your entire advertisement by giving the impression that you are trying to make your proposition sound better than it really is.

Below is a news item about a new kind of alarm clock taken from the shoppers' column of a daily newspaper. Notice that the reporter who wrote the news item has also written an excellent advertisement.

NEW CLOCK
WAKES YOU
WITH MUSIC
Tuneful notes replace strident
clangor, with loud alarm
in reverse

No longer is it necessary to have one's morning ripped open with imperious jangling that is little short of cruelty to the sleep-softened nerves. A new Westclox product approaches the subject of awakening, tunefully and softly at first.

The sleeper thus amiably roused, shuts off the alarm and faces the day in a pleasant mood. Should this musical awakening go unheeded, the clock waits a few moments and rings again, this time right stridently.

15. Avoid Trick Slogans

Avoid slogans and catchlines that are obviously untrue. For example, a manufacturer of mint candies used the slogan "On every tongue." This is obviously untrue. Everyone knows that these candies are not on every tongue. It is merely a trick phrase. Some less clever but true selling argument, such as "The flavor lasts," would be more effective.

16. Get Help from Others

It is helpful to take an advertisement or a headline you have just written and show it to someone else and get his opinion. But be sure to get his true opinion. Most people don't want to hurt your feelings by telling you that your idea is terrible and should be thrown into the wastebasket. They will be most likely to nod their heads and say, "That's a fine idea." Sometimes you can find a person who will give you his frank, unvarnished opinion. He is a rare bird, and useful.

The trouble with most critics is that they are too optimistic. One way to overcome this difficulty is to never show a critic just one piece of copy or one headline. Show him two pieces of copy, or two headlines and ask him which one he likes better. Then he will praise one and criticize the other. In this way you can get his true opinion.

It is also helpful for the copywriter to work with his client in preparing copy, instead of sending a salesman to sell it to the client.

17. Do Not Say That Salesman Will Call

Some advertisers offer a free booklet in their advertising in order to get the names and addresses of people interested in the product. After the free booklet has been mailed, a salesman calls on the prospect. If this is your plan of action, do not mention in the advertising that a salesman will call. To do so will cut down your coupon returns at least 75 per cent.

18. Study the Selling Copy in Mail Order Catalogues

The large mail order houses, such as Sears Roebuck and Montgomery Ward, Inc., are masters of the art of selling goods by means of printed words and pictures. The next time you are puzzled as to how to sell some product, study a mail order catalogue and see how the mail order people approach the subject. In the large mail order catalogues you will find excellent sales talks for almost every product you can think of.

19. Make Every Advertisement a Complete Sales Talk

It is an old rule but a good rule to write every advertisement as if it were the first and the last word to be said on the subject. Do not depend on the reader having read any previous advertisements for the product you are selling. Do not assume that the reader will learn from future advertisements the selling arguments that you fail to include in today's advertisement. Make every advertisement a complete sales talk. Bring in every important sales argument.

Suppose a financial house is selling an investment plan that enables a man to do any or all of the following:

1. Provide an income for his wife in case of his death.
2. Provide money to send his son to college.
3. Provide money to leave his home clear of debt.

Suppose a salesman for this financial house has three prospects to call on. He has never seen these prospects before. He knows nothing about them. Suppose the salesman should plan his calls as follows:

"I will talk to Prospect A about leaving an income for his wife" (regardless of whether Prospect A is married or not).

"I will talk to Prospect B about sending his son to college" (regardless of whether he has a son or not).

"I will talk to Prospect C about leaving his home clear of debt" (regardless of whether or not he lives in a rented apartment).

No salesman would work under such a disadvantage. Yet every advertisement is a salesman. Every advertisement is sent out to call on a prospect. Why handicap the advertisement by deciding in advance that it will discuss only a single sales argument? Put every important selling point into every advertisement.

20. Urge the Reader to Act

Every mail order advertisement ends with a strong urge to "Act Now." Unless there is a definite reason to the contrary, the general advertisement should end with a similar urge. You have caught the reader with your headline. You have interested him with your copy. Do not leave him hanging in midair. Tell him what to do. If you can give him a definite reason for immediate action, such as "Price is going up" or "Supply will soon be exhausted," so much the better.

Advertising has induced progress in the use by manufacturers of new materials, new tools, and new processes of manufacture by calling their attention to economies which could be achieved and to the new uses to which they could be put. Without such advertising, information of this kind would take years to reach all of those who might benefit by it and progress would be delayed.

Harry S. Truman

Copy Under Pictures Gets High Reading

This ad for Schweppes Quinine Water, written by David Ogilvy, got very high reading. The ad is a skillful combination of a good headline, exciting pictures, and informative picture captions. Readership studies show that people will often skip the big print in an ad and read the small print under a picture. This habit is formed in childhood. The child's attention is caught by pictures in storybooks. His interest in the pictures causes him to read the picture captions. Never fail to put captions under your illustrations.

LESS THAN **34¢**

Reader's Digest

ARTICLES OF LASTING INTEREST

Enjoy the next 12 issues of Reader's Digest for less than 34¢ a copy.

PLEASE RETURN BEFORE MAR. 31

Detach and mail this card today . . . to get Reader's Digest for the next 12 months at only $3.97—less than 34¢ a copy. Send no money . . . your subscription will start with the next issue and we'll mail you a bill later. Simply print your name and address below and mail this card today.

Mr.
Mrs.
NAME Miss _____
                              (print plainly)
ADDRESS _____
CITY _____ STATE _____ ZIP _____

71548

How to Get Quick Response

This *Reader's Digest* ad got quick response by setting a time limit: "Please return before Mar. 31." Here are other ways to get people to act. (1) If the price is going up, say so. (2) If the supply is limited, say so. (3) Use action words such as: Act at once ... Don't put it off ... Delay may be serious ... Order today. (4) Offer a reward for promptness. For example, a book club ad offered a free bonus book "to new members who enroll at this time."

Attracting Readers with Free Information

This ad for Hellmann's Mayonnaise attracts readers by picturing good things to eat, and by including five recipes in the copy. Naturally, all the recipes call for Hellmann's. Other advertisers can use the same technique. A gasoline ad told how to save gas. A furniture ad gave home-decorating hints. An ad for a correspondence course in correct English included a free lesson. A supermarket ad listed eight ways to get more for your money at any supermarket. People are always looking for helpful hints. If you help them, they will be more apt to help you by buying your product.

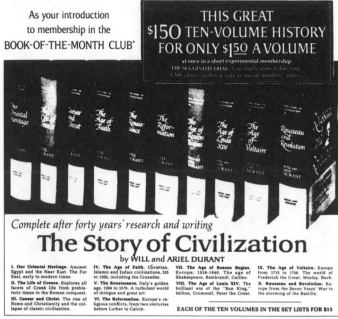

As your introduction
to membership in the
BOOK-OF-THE-MONTH CLUB*

THIS GREAT
$150 TEN-VOLUME HISTORY
FOR ONLY $1.50 A VOLUME
at once in a short experimental membership
THE SUGGESTED TRIAL: You simply agree to buy four
Club choices within a year at special members' prices

Complete after forty years' research and writing

The Story of Civilization
by WILL and ARIEL DURANT

I. Our Oriental Heritage. Ancient Egypt and the Near East. The Far East, early to modern times.
II. The Life of Greece. Explores all facets of Greek life from prehistoric times to the Roman conquest.
III. Caesar and Christ. The rise of Rome and Christianity and the collapse of classic civilization.

IV. The Age of Faith. Christian, Islamic and Judaic civilizations, 325 to 1300, including the Crusades.
V. The Renaissance. Italy's golden age, 1304 to 1576. A turbulent world of intrigue and great art.
VI. The Reformation. Europe's religious conflicts, from two centuries before Luther to Calvin.

VII. The Age of Reason Begins. Europe, 1558-1648. The age of Shakespeare, Rembrandt, Galileo.
VIII. The Age of Louis XIV. The brilliant era of the "Sun King," Milton, Cromwell, Peter the Great.

IX. The Age of Voltaire. Europe from 1715 to 1756. The world of Frederick the Great, Wesley, Bach.
X. Rousseau and Revolution. Europe from the Seven Years' War to the storming of the Bastille.

EACH OF THE TEN VOLUMES IN THE SET LISTS FOR $15

THE EXPERIMENTAL MEMBERSHIP suggested here will prove, *by your own actual experience*, how effectually membership in the Book-of-the-Month Club can **keep you from missing,** through oversight, books you fully intend to read.

As long as you remain a member, you will receive the Book-of-the-Month Club *News,* a literary magazine published by the Club every three to four weeks. The *News* announces the coming Selection and describes scores of other important books, most of which are available at substantial discounts – up to **40%** on more expensive volumes. All of these books **are identical to the publishers' editions in format, size and quality.** If you wish to purchase the Selection, do nothing and it will be shipped to you automatically. However, there is no obligation to purchase any particular volume. If you do not wish the Selection (or any other book) – or if you want one of the Alternates offered in the *News* – simply indicate your decision on the convenient form provided and mail it so the Club

receives it by the date specified on the form. The *News* announcing each Selection is mailed in time to allow members at least 10 days to return the form if they do not want the Selection. If you, because of late delivery of the *News,* should ever receive a Selection without having had the 10-day consideration period, that Selection may be returned at Club expense.

BOOK-DIVIDENDS: A library-building plan every reading family should know about. If you continue after this experimental membership, you will earn, *for every Club Selection or Alternate you buy,* a Book-Dividend Credit. Each Credit, upon payment of a nominal sum, often only **$1.00 or $1.50** – somewhat more for unusually expensive volumes or sets – will entitle you to a Book-Dividend® which you may choose from over a hundred fine library volumes available over the year. This unique library-building system enables members to save **70% or more** of what they would otherwise have to pay.

INCLUDED WITHOUT CHARGE

A brilliant summary of all the Durants learned during their forty-year study of world history... and an invaluable supplement to *The Story of Civilization.* A copy will be included, free, with each set sent to new members who enroll at this time. **Pub price $5**

How to Get Immediate Action

An effective action-getting device is printed just above the coupon in this ad. The copy says—"INCLUDED WITHOUT CHARGE—A brilliant summary of all the Durants learned during their forty-year study of world history...and an invaluable supplement to The Story of Civilization. A copy will be included free, with each set sent to new members who enroll at this time. Pub price $5...." A picture of the free book is shown. It is entitled: "The Lessons of History." An offer of this kind, which prompts the reader to act at once, can often make the difference between a sale and no sale.

Don't Be Afraid to Use Long Copy

This ad is typical of hundreds of long-copy insurance ads that started a revolution in the insurance business. Formerly, insurance ads of medium length were used to get coupon leads for salesmen. The salesmen called on the prospects and closed the sales. The above ad contains a complete sales talk and eliminates the salesmen. The coupon is not merely a device for offering free literature. It is an order form that requires the customer to answer a questionnaire and mail a down payment. This ad contains more than 3,000 words of copy.

12

How to Solve Special Problems in Copywriting

Dramatizing Dull Products

Often the copywriter is handed a tough assignment in the shape of an uninteresting product that must somehow be dramatized in the advertising. There are described below a number of instances of how such dull products as cough drops, disinfectants, statistics, sewing machines, and even grave vaults have been made exciting.

Advertising a Statistical Service

Suppose you were asked to prepare an advertising campaign for a statistics company, a company whose business is to furnish statistics to investment houses and other business concerns. Wouldn't you consider it a difficult job? Statistics are so dull—no human interest, no drama.

The Standard Statistics Company published a series of advertisements as dramatic as a motion picture thriller. The series was called, "Famous Wrong Guesses in History."

Here is a sample:

When Millions of Dollars Were
Thrown into the Gutter

Forty-five hundred miles of canals costing over $200,000,000. And barely one in ten actually paid. Small wonder men called them "The most expensive gutters in the world"!

The copy tells how the canals of 1830 were doomed by the steam locomotive—how "sure things" fail today just as in 1830—how in the long run, facts and facts alone make for lasting success.

Advertising a Disinfectant

A class of products dull in themselves, but sometimes dramatically advertised, are the disinfectants, for example, the halitosis campaign for Listerine. Another disinfectant campaign consisted of a series of "horror" advertisements for Lysol. Here is one:

A CROSS ON THE DOOR SEALED THE DOOM OF ANOTHER HOUSEHOLD

London was a nightmare of horror that summer. The Black Death raged through the city. Victims died so fast that condemned prisoners collected the bodies by the cartload.

In a subsequent paragraph, the product being advertised was introduced:

200 years later the medical world discovered that disease is caused by germs. Today, science wages war upon germs, and one of its weapons is "Lysol" Disinfectant.

A Lesson from Shakespeare

In some of his plays, Shakespeare permits the audience to learn, not only what a certain character is saying, but also what he is thinking. This is done by letting the actor make a remark directly to the audience. The remark is labeled an "aside." Eugene O'Neill also used this method in some of his plays.

This same trick has enabled copywriters to inject drama into dull products in the form of "hidden thoughts" copy.

For example, a cough drop is not an exciting article, yet cough drops were dramatically brought to the reader's attention in a Luden's series called, "If he said what he thought."

A typical advertisement pictured a salesman coughing across the desk of a purchasing agent. The purchasing agent flies into a rage and orders the salesman out. Underneath the picture is this headline:

If he said what he thought:
"Get out ... I'm tired of you salesmen giving me colds!"

Advertising Paper Towels

Paper towels are another product that, at first glance, seems to lack dramatic possibilities. What can you say about them? Softness? Smoothness? Absorbency? These are the things everybody expects you to say, and are consequently commonplace.

Here is how a paper towel manufacturer put human interest into his copy:

HE NEVER KNEW UNTIL HE
OVERHEARD THEM

[Illustration: Office Manager overhearing talk in employees' washroom.]

"Plenty of hot water, good soap—but these things they give us for towels—."

"Second the motion—we ought to be paid to use 'em."

A Hand Lotion Campaign

The makers of a hand lotion decided to tell the world that their product was good for chapped hands. But a dozen manufacturers of skin lotions have claimed the same thing. This advertiser wanted to be different. A dramatic "Shame on You" campaign did the trick. Typical headlines:

She hid her hands in her lap ... shocked at their
rough, chapped redness against the snowy cloth.
She sat out every dance ... ashamed of her chapped
hands.

Advertising Cellophane

Another product that seems to offer little drama is cellophane, the transparent film used to wrap candy, cake, and cigars. What can you say about cellophane? That it keeps products clean and safe from handling? Or that the customer can see what he buys when it is wrapped in cellophane? This is good copy material, but not dramatic.

The makers of cellophane boldly compared their man-made wrappers with the protective wrappers produced by nature—and to nature's disadvantage! For example:

Corn hides behind its husk ... but nothing is hidden
when wrapped in transparent Cellophane.

The Cocoanut's Package calls for X-ray eyes ... but anyone can see what's wrapped in Cellophane. Nature shows her onions ... She gives them a protecttive, transparent skin almost as good as Du Pont Cellophane itself!

Grave Vault Copy

Perhaps the most difficult product in the world to dramatize is a grave vault. Try to think of some dramatic treatment yourself. Then read how the Clark Grave Vault Company handled the problem.

THE TREMENDOUS POWER OF STEAM ... BUT METAL CONTROLS IT!

[Illustration: Locomotive rushing head-on toward reader]
Rails sing as the railroad train hurls its thousand-ton weight across the continent. Steam rages to be free from the monster's belly, but steel confines it.

Wherever there must be imperviousness to water in any form—metal never fails. Naturally the Clark Grave Vault is made of metal—12-gauge copper steel.

Beverage Copy

At one time the makers of a chocolate beverage powder used four-color pages to tell people that their product was nourishing— that it contained Vitamin D—that children loved it. Sales were falling off. Then the makers of this product started using dramatic situations to bring their chocolate milk drink to the attention of the public. Sales increased. Here is a typical advertisement:

HELEN DISLIKED THE VERY SIGHT OF MILK.... NOW I GIVE IT TO HER A NEW WAY AND SHE LOVES IT

[Illustration: Angry mother exclaiming to child, "Drink that milk or go straight to bed!"]
"My little girl was underweight. My husband's sister suggested this milk and chocolate beverage. How glad I am! Helen loves it ... put eight pounds on her already ..."

Sewing Machines

Sewing machines were used by our grandmothers. One would think that all the possibilities of advertising them dramatically would be exhausted by now. Not so. There is drama that will appeal to any woman in the "Dress Attractively" series published by the Singer Sewing Machine Company. For example:

"YOU WERE WONDERFUL TONIGHT"

It was like old times to hear him say it. Not in months had Bob said one word about her clothes...
Are you, too, dreaming of the clothes you want, but can't afford?...The modern Singer Electric has made sewing a joyous adventure....

Course in English

How can an advertising man put drama into a correspondence course in English grammar—a subject often considered dull?
A dramatic campaign for a correspondence course in English showed the way. The headline of a typical advertisement said, "What are your mistakes in English?" The illustration showed a young lady talking to her male escort. Ugly mistakes in English were popping out of her mouth: "I ain't ... He don't ... It's me ... You was ... Can't hardly."
Proof of the effectiveness of this advertising was found in the fact that although comparatively little money was spent for space in magazines, many people became familiar with the campaign. Each advertisement got as much attention as three or four ordinary advertisements.

Office Stationery

The C. H. Dexter Company, makers of writing paper, sell a lightweight paper for office use. *Questions:* How do you dramatize it? How do you impress executives with the fact that this paper enables you to send multipage letters at low cost? The following headline accomplishes this purpose:

NOW YOU CAN SEND A 12-PAGE LETTER FOR A SINGLE AIR-MAIL STAMP

The copy makes this offer: "Just by way of proof—ask your secretary to write for a sample and we shall send 12 letterhead sheets by air mail."

Sea Cruise

For years the steamship companies—sellers of travel—have been singing the same song with headlines like these:

An ideal winter cruise
Follow the sun to South America
Come with us to Mexico
Live where winter's smile is sunniest

One steamship line added a dramatic touch to its advertising by using copy like this:

WATCH YOUR HUSBAND ...
IS HE A DRAWING-ROOM SPHINX?
Conversation is a lost art with many a successful businessman, unless the talk turns to business.
The unfailing remedy is a winter cruise. Sea travel takes a man's mind completely off his business concerns ...

The copy sold sea voyages to entirely new prospects. It caught the attention of people who never before had considered an ocean trip.

Summing Up the Value of Drama

What can drama do for advertising? By its attention value it can make a small advertising appropriation do the work of a large appropriation. It can attract new customers—people who would not normally be customers. It can give emphasis to some particular feature of your product or service. It can put new life into a worn-out theme.

One of the most popular of the dramatic methods seems to be the "domestic drama"—little dramas involving husbands and wives. The "hidden thought" type of copy and the "Shame on You" theme are also popular.

The next time you write an advertisement for a dull product, try to dramatize it. And remember, many products are dull until some advertising man puts life into them.

Problems with Headlines

How can a life insurance company explain in a few words the fact that a small down payment on a life insurance policy can immediately increase the size of a man's estate? Here is a headline that does this:

Today...add $10,000 to your estate—
for the price of a new hat

How can an automobile brake relining service emphasize the high value and the relatively low cost of its service in terms of accidents avoided and lives saved? The following headline puts the story into a few words:

Is the life of a child worth $1 to you?

A correspondence school selling a mail order course in business training had this problem:

1. Experience showed that the ads that pulled best were those that featured salary increases as a result of taking the course.
2. It was not possible to make a specific promise in the ads such as "You can add $5,000 to your income" because some of the students who took the course did not receive salary increases.

The advertising manager said: "Our problem is—how can we talk about salary increases in the headlines of our ads without making a specific promise?" The following headline was devised to accomplish the desired purpose:

To a ten-thousand-dollar man
who would like to be making $25,000

Notice that the headline skillfully implies the possibility of a raise in pay without making a definite promise.

Here is another successful device:

[Illustration: Photograph of an executive in a handsome office.]
[Headline]: This private office with salary to match may be waiting for you.

The suggestion of a benefit without actually making a specific promise can also be accomplished by putting your headline into the form of a question.

For example, a beauty product manufacturer was so excited about a new product that he wanted to claim that he had discovered the fountain of youth. But a specific claim to this effect would have been censored by publications and disbelieved by readers. However, a successful ad was prepared with a headline in the form of a question, as follows:

Has the secret of eternal youth been discovered at last?

A medical advertiser wanted to tell people how he could cure nervous disorders. However, the promise of definite cures is not permitted. So this advertiser prepared a successful ad with a headline in the form of a question:

Do you have these symptoms of nervous exhaustion?

The advertiser of a stock market guide wanted to say "How you can make money in the stock market." However a toned-down headline was used that was more believable and therefore more effective?

Why some people almost always make money
in the stock market

You can prepare a qualified but effective ad by writing testimonial style headlines as follows:

How a new kind of clay improved my complexion
in 30 minutes
How I improved my memory in one evening

These headlines cause the reader to say to himself: "Maybe I can get the same results." However, the headlines do not specifically promise that everybody will get these results.

Another way to qualify a promise is to include a money-back guarantee in your headline as follows:

Get rid of dandruff in 10 days or no cost
Hands that look lovelier in 24 hours or your money back

Using Coupon Offers to Attract Store Customers

From time to time, retail stores advertise special offers to induce customers, old and new, to come to the store.

For example, in one city, a W.T. Grant store ran a small newspaper ad offering a ten-speed bicycle at a reduced price. The ad contained a coupon that the reader was instructed to bring to the store. Printed in the coupon was a picture of the bicycle, and the following copy:

$48.88—Reg. $69.95.
Coupon good Washington's Birthday only.
Limit 1 per customer.

All the bicycles on hand were sold out the first afternoon. Over 200 coupons were redeemed, with total sales in excess of $10,000. Yet the ad cost only $140.

A number of merchants have successfully used the same device, namely, a small newspaper ad containing a coupon to be clipped out and brought to the store. An attractive offer is printed in the coupon. Here are some typical offers, together with the sales results obtained:

Sambo's Restaurant: 2 chicken dinners for the price of one. Over 750 returns. Sales: approximately $1,300.

Checker Auto Parts: Oil filter 99¢. Over 1,000 returns. Sales: over $1,000.

Kennedy's Firestone: Service offer: (1) Complete lubrication. (2) Oil change. (3) New oil filter. (4) Rotate tires. (5) Adjust brakes. (6) Repack outer front wheel bearings. (7) Check wheel alignment. (8) Complete safety inspection ... All for $5.88. Six stores booked solid. Sales: over $1000.

Robo Car Wash: One free car wash. Over 2,000 returns. Sales: approximately $4,500.

Antoine's Sheik Restaurant: $2 off on each $6.95 combination dinner. Over 150 returns. Sales over $800.

Vaughn's Clothing Store: 10% off on all suits, coats, slacks, shirts, sweaters, pants, etc. Sales: over $1,600.

A.N.A. Photo and Appliance Center: FM/AM Radio $16.95, reg. $37.95 ... Minolta Camera $169. Reg. $265. Over 70 returns. Sales: approximately $1,500.

Worth's Clothing Store: Wet-Look Coats $13. Reg. $30. Over 100 returns. Sales: over $1,300.

Pizza Palace: $1 off any large pizza. Over 1,200 returns. Sales: over $3,600.

Fish Monger—Food to go. 1¢ Special. Buy one at reg. price

and pay 1¢ for the 2nd order (Fish & chips 1.35; Sword-
fish steak 2.75; Halibut steak 2.45). Over 1,100 returns.
Sales: over $2,200.

How to Make Store Coupons Effective

Here are some points to notice regarding coupon promotions:
Many advertisers set time limits. Examples: "Coupon good thru
[date].." "Offer expires [date].." "Coupon good 1-day only [date]."
Some stores set restrictions. Examples: "Limit 2 items per
coupon" ... "Limit 1 per customer" ... "Not valid for take-out or-
ders."
Some stores specify that the customer must bring the coupon.
Examples: "$5.88 with this coupon" ... "This coupon entitles, [etc.]"
... "Come clip us—with coupon."
Some stores include items like these: "Please phone for ap-
pointment" ... "Supply limited" ... "First come! First served" ...
"Free Charlie horse pony ride for the kids."
A big advantage of a coupon is that it becomes a *reminder* to the
customer after he has torn it out and put it into his pocket or purse.
He can't forget it because it is right there staring at him.
Another advantage is that the customer needs to do little or no
talking when he approaches the dealer. The customer merely hands
the coupon to the clerk or storekeeper. Many people are not ar-
ticulate. They don't like to walk up to a proprietor and say: "I understand that you are offering a complete lubrication, oil change, new
oil filter, brake adjustment, wheel alignment, etc. all for $5.88." The
coupon does the customer's talking for him. He doesn't have to say a
word if he doesn't want to.
Question: Briefly stated, how can you use special coupon offers
to induce customers to take the first important step, namely, to step
into the store? *Answer:* Make an irresistible offer. Print the offer on a
coupon. Put the coupon into the hands of as many prospects as
possible, and at the lowest possible cost.

*American advertising has learned to tell the truth
attractively about American products. When the
product is good, and the truth is told, we have the
appealing combination that secures sales and
keeps the wheels of industry turning.*

Norman Vincent Peale

THE AMBULANCE ARRIVED ONE BREATH TOO LATE...

If a heart attack were to strike in your home or office, five minutes without oxygen and there would be no hope.

The LIFE PROTECTOR is a new portable oxygen kit that provides more than thirty minutes of oxygen, enough to last until medical aid arrives. It represents needed security when emergency strikes, particularly for those who suffer from cardiac, asthma, emphysema and other respiratory ailments.

Easy to operate, it weighs just 9 lbs. in its polyethylene carrying case. No special training is necessary to administer the LIFE PROTECTOR. Simply place the form-fitting mask over nose and mouth, turn the handle, and oxygen flows at a medically-prescribed rate.

The LIFE PROTECTOR is refillable at registered oxygen supply stations or through SEI. As such, it is ideal for offices and homes where mobile medical aid may not be immediately available after an accident or cardiac attack.

You are invited to examine the LIFE PROTECTOR in your own home for 10 days by completing and mailing this order form. Or call (212) 593-2275 collect.

Dramatizing the Product

An oxygen kit is not an exciting item in itself, but when dramatized by a skillful copywriter, it can become exciting. Note the 10 days free examination offer in the coupon; also the credit card method of payment. More and more mail order marketers are selling high-priced items by the use of credit cards.

How to Sell Books by Mail Order

It is difficult these days to produce a mail order ad that will sell just one book at a profit. The space cost of the ad is usually too great for the profit margin on the book. The way to sell books profitably is: (1) Start a book club, (2) Run ads that offer a lot of books, and (3) Make an attractive offer such as the above, namely: "any 6 of 99 best sellers for only 99¢ with a short 6-month trial membership."

How to Get Expert Copywriting Help

Suppose you have to write an ad for a product you know little or nothing about. For example: camping equipment, dishwashers, fishing tackle, lawn mowers, movie cameras, sewing machines, or tape recorders. Look up these items in mail order catalogues. There you will find words, sentences, and copy writing ideas that have been tested and proved successful by mail order sales.

13

Thirty-two Ways to Get More Inquiries
from Your Advertising

Sometimes in advertising it becomes advisable to secure as many inquiries as possible. For the sake of ready reference and at the risk of repetition, thirty-two effective methods for increasing ad replies are listed below.

These methods may be divided into two general classes:

1. The methods that increase inquiries by increasing the total effectiveness of your advertising. For example, the use of long copy plus an interesting headline increases the total effectiveness of an advertisement, and the increase in replies is merely a by-product of a better advertisement.
2. The methods that increase ad replies but do not increase the total effectiveness of your advertising. For example, a picture of a free booklet with the sub-caption "Get This Free Book" will get more inquiries, but it does not make your advertisement any better.

The methods are explained in detail on the following pages and summarized at the end of this chapter.

1. Mention the offer in the headline

Suppose your headline is "How to retire on an income." You can increase response by changing it to read "Free booklet tells how to retire on an income."

Suppose your headline is "Stout Women." You can increase response by changing it to read "Free to Stout Women."

Here are other examples:

Yours for only 1¢—this lovely box of greeting cards
Free sales kit—Make up to $50 a day
Given to you—The Oxford Dictionary
Free Ski Guide
Home repair book—read it 7 days free

2. Emphasize the word "Free"

You can increase replies by putting the word "Free" in big print or in capital letters. In broadcast advertising and in printed advertising, you can repeat the word "free" several times. Or you can frequently repeat phrases that mean essentially the same thing, such as "Send no money," "Don't pay a penny," or "Yours without cost." However, the FTC requires that "the terms or conditions imposed are conspicuously disclosed in immediate conjunction with the offer."

3. Mention the offer in a subhead

The subhead may follow immediately after the main headline like this:

[Main headline]   New electronic calculator
[Subhead]   Free 10 day trial

Or the subhead may be placed in the middle of the ad or near the end. Here are typical subheads:

Send for liberal supply
The facts are free
Write for booklet
Special $1 offer
Free talent test

4. Show a picture of the booklet or sample

If you have lots of room, you can show the booklet or sample package in large size. Your layout can include eye-catching devices such as an arrow or a hand pointing at the booklet.

The speed with which an offer registers on the eye of the reader is important. Therefore, one of the best inquiry-getting layouts is a picture of the booklet with the word "Free" printed alongside of it or under it.

In small ads you can save space by reducing the picture of the booklet down to the size of a postage stamp. You can even cut it in half and show only the top half of the booklet. If your booklet title is hard to read in reduced size, you can reset the title on the ad artwork in readable type before you make your reduced size cut.

In TV commercials you can have the announcer hold up the booklet or gift and show it to the audience. Or else you can have him hold up the gift all wrapped and ready to mail. He can point to the address label and say "Send me your name and address so I can put it right here and mail this free gift to you."

Incidentally, the phrase "free gift" is especially good in both printed and broadcast advertising because this phrase says free twice in just two short words.

5. Mention the offer in the first paragraph

Most copywriters remember to include a description of the free booklet at the end of the ad. But many forget to include a brief mention of the booklet at the beginning of the ad. Some of the best-pulling ads mention the free booklet twice: (1) A brief mention early in the ad; and (2) A complete description at the end of the ad.

In broadcast advertising, the announcer can use this technique by saying at the beginning of the program: "Get pencil and paper ready. In a few minutes I am going to offer you a free gift."

6. Use an attractive booklet title

Just as ad headlines are often the deciding factor in getting people to read ads, so are booklet titles often the deciding factor in getting people to send for booklets. Here are some attractive booklet titles:

Accountancy—the profession that pays
New beauty for you
How to protect your invention
Your future in Computer Programming
How to get a government job
New York vacation guide
How to care for your dog

7. Include an attractive description of the offer

In writing a description of a booklet, you should sit down with the booklet in front of you and turn the pages and write down every good thing you can say about it. Then take your list of items and condense it into a paragraph. For example:

Booklet contains 32 pages, 14 illustrations (5 in color), 9 sketches, 4 diagrams, 7 case histories, 2 maps, a list of do's and don'ts, 5 chapters (including complete instructions), a chart for predicting results and an appendix containing scores of useful items.

The "table of contents" technique is also effective. You can include a panel of copy like this:

Auto Mechanic's Book Tells

How to fit pistons	Page 3
How to locate engine knocks	Page 7
How to service main bearings	Page 12
How to recondition valves	Page 14
How to adjust fan belts	Page 20
How to rebuild a clutch	Page 22
How to service brakes	Page 25
How to adjust steering gear	Page 27
How to time ignition	Page 29
How to tune up an engine	Page 31

In broadcast advertising you can use the "table of contents" technique by having the announcer hold the booklet and turn the pages and say "On Page 3 you will find instructions on how to fit pistons. On Page 7 you will find out how to locate engine knocks. On Page 12, how to service main bearings," etc.

Hint: Some booklets are difficult to describe attractively because they contain only sales talk. In these cases, it may be worthwhile to revise your booklet and include some information of a helpful nature. A garden seed advertiser made his seed catalogue ads pull better by putting in a chapter of gardening advice.

8. Include a booklet foreword by a famous person

A booklet on hearing aids was made more attractive by including an introduction by a popular author who used a hearing aid himself. A music school booklet contained a foreword by a well-known conductor. A booklet on beauty care had a chapter written by a movie star. A recipe booklet featured favorite recipes of famous chefs.

9. Include testimonials

An ad for an income tax-guide included testimonials from a homeowner, a salesman, a professional man, a housewife, etc. For example:

Salesman: "I use my car for selling and do a lot of entertaining. I thought I had deducted everything until your Income Tax Guide showed me 18 deductions I never thought were allowable."

Housewife: "Saving on my husband's salary isn't easy. I thought tax returns were a man's job until your Income Tax Guide showed me how many of our expenses are deductible—like the clothes I donate to the Salvation Army."

10. Sweeten your offer

The ad for the income tax guide mentioned above contained this paragraph:

Special Free Bonus: Filled-in Tax Forms ... To give you every possible tax saving—and to save you time and trouble you will also receive a 16-page booklet of sample tax forms, completely filled in for your guidance. This is yours to keep, even if you return the Income Tax Guide for refund.

A series of ads for G.E. light bulbs offered "a booklet about light and seeing." It was desired to increase replies and so a free gift was offered in addition to the free booklet.

An airline wanted to increase replies from ads about flights to Bermuda so that sales literature could be mailed to as many prospects as possible. A free booklet offer did not pull sufficient replies, and so the following offer was used and brought excellent results.

Absolutely free—a Bermuda Vacation Kit. The kit contains detailed map of Bermuda and photographs and descriptions of the big, new luxury Air Liners. Included in the free Kit are a pair of Bermuda sunglasses.

If you have been charging 25¢ for your booklet, you can, of course, increase replies by reducing the price to 10¢. If you want to get 10¢ for your booklet and at the same time feature the word "free," you can use the following wording: "Free booklet. Enclose 10¢ to help cover cost of handling and mailing."

11. Include a coupon

A coupon printed in an ad helps increase returns in several ways. It draws attention to the offer. It makes the offer clear and simple. It indicates to the reader that you really want him to write and that he is fully entitled to receive your booklet or sample. It gives the reader a convenient form in which to write his name and address. When torn out of the ad, the coupon serves as a continuing reminder until it is mailed.

In a small ad, where space is limited, you can gain some of the advantages of a coupon without using one. You can say, "Tear out this ad and write your name and address in the margin."

Caution: If your coupon leads are followed by salesmen, you should be careful not to put too much emphasis on getting a large number of coupon returns. Do not build your entire advertisement around your coupon. If you do, you may find that the quality of your coupon leads will suffer. You may find that your salesmen are wasting valuable time following up prospects who are primarily interested in getting a booklet or a sample rather than in buying your product.

On the other hand, if you are actually selling your goods by mail, and if the customer has to send money with the coupon or agree to pay money, you can put as much emphasis on the coupon as you wish.

12. Print the value on the coupon

Some advertisers print "Value 10¢" or "Worth 50¢" or some other value on the coupons in their ads. An ad published by a greeting card manufacturer had this headline: "This giant $2.75 greeting card assortment yours to keep for 25¢." Printed across the top of the coupon was the line, "This coupon worth $2.50."

13. Include some selling copy in the coupon

Examples:

Book League of America

Please send me—FREE—the brand-new giant Webster's New World Dictionary of the American Language, over 2,000 pages, weighing 10 lbs., containing over 140,000 definitions, 1,400 illustrations, maps, etc., and enroll me as a member.

American Technical Society (Publishers since 1898)

Please rush me the following books I'm checking below to examine at home. If I'm not convinced these books will help me save thousands of dollars by doing my own building and planning, I may return the books and owe nothing.

14. Print your address twice in each ad

Did you ever pick up a magazine in a dentist's waiting room and find a coupon missing from one of the ads? Suppose you wanted to answer that ad? You wouldn't know where to address your reply if the only address in the ad was contained in the missing coupon. To guard against loss of replies, some advertisers include their address twice— once in the coupon and once elsewhere in the ad. For example, in a full-page ad for the Coyne School, the address and key number appeared in a coupon in the lower right-hand corner of the ad as follows:

Coyne School, 500 S. Paulina St.
Dept. 62-73H, Chicago, Illinois 60612

In the lower left-hand corner of the ad, the address and key number were repeated in the form of a logotype as follows:

Coyne School
500 S. Paulina St. Dept. 62-73H
Chicago, Illinois 60612

15. Include a telephone number

Some people like to act fast and they like to make inquiries by telephone. If you are advertising in newspapers or using local broadcasting, you can include a local telephone number in your ad. A school advertiser found that putting a telephone number in his ads not only increased inquiries but also improved the quality of the inquiries. He found he could sell only one out of five people who wrote for a school catalogue, but he could sell one out of two people who telephoned. By asking discreet questions, he could find out the special problems of people who telephoned and offer to solve their problems. He could say, "We have many students who have the same problems that you have. We are starting a new class next Tuesday night at 8 p.m. You are invited to sit in and listen. If you will tell me where you are located, I will tell you the easiest way to reach the school."

If you are using national advertising in magazines or via broadcasting, you can say, "See the Yellow Pages in your telephone book." Or you can use a toll-free "800" number. For example, an Air Force recruiting ad said: "Send in the postcard or call toll free 800-447-4700."

16. Emphasize "No obligation"

Here are sample phrases you can use in copy or in coupons:

No obligation
Send me without obligation
I understand that this does not obligate me
I am under no obligation, now or ever
I understand this book is mine to keep and sending
    for it does not obligate me in any way
No salesman will call

17. Offer certain information in a plain envelope

Here are examples of the type of information people prefer to receive in an envelope that does not identify the product:

1. Hearing aid booklet
2. Data on personal loans
3. Personal hygiene booklet
4. Maternity booklet

18. Urge immediate action

Some advertisers increase inquiries by offering a reward for immediate action. For example:

> Fill in the coupon below and mail it for your free copy of 32-page Information Booklet. If you act at once, we will include Success Booklet and Chart, which supply additional information you should have. All will be sent postage paid.

Other action-promoting devices are sentences such as "Supply is limited," or "For a short time only." Or you can use simple urges to action such as the following:

Mail coupon today
Act now—offer expires April 30th
Rush your name for free outfit
Get free book by sending coupon NOW

19. Include a Business Reply Postcard

A number of advertisers include in their ads a business reply postcard that requires no postage stamp. Examples of these may be found in *Reader's Digest, TV Guide*, and other publications. Often the reply card is printed on a separate insert that is bound into the publication and is adjacent to the ad.

20. Include a fold-over coupon

A less expensive way to get some of the effectiveness of a business reply postcard without paying the premium rate for it is to include a pre-addressed business reply coupon that is double the size of the normal coupon. The prospect simply tears out this double coupon, folds it over, seals it, and mails it with no postage stamp. In effect, this is a do-it-yourself business reply card.

21. Include a Business Reply Envelope

Some publications permit a business reply envelope to be placed adjacent to an ad. This increases response from customers who are asked to send money.

22. Use a free-standing insert

What is it that catches your eye and falls into your hands when you open your Sunday newspaper? A free-standing insert. This device is made to order for a mail order advertiser. If you have an extra-long message, your free-standing insert can be a multi-page booklet or even a complete mail order catalogue. If your message is not so long, you can use a single-sheet insert of stiff paper and print your message on two sides, front and back. The insert can contain a business reply postcard or order form. Free-standing inserts cost more than ordinary ads, but they bring more response. They combine important elements such as attention value, long copy, and an easy-to-mail order form that requires no postage stamp.

23. Test several different offers

One way to step up returns is to test the pulling power of two or more different offers in one publication and then run the best-pulling offer in your entire list of publications. To get the most accurate test you should use the facilities of some publication offering split-run copy testing whereby one offer appears in half the circulation and the other offer appears in the other half of the circulation on the same day and in the same position. More than 1,600 newspapers offer split-run copy testing; so do certain magazines.

As a rule you will find that offers of food samples and soap samples pull well, whereas offers of drug samples, such as cold remedies and headache remedies, pull poorly.

Another way to test offers is to make two or more different offers in your coupon and say, for example:

Check with pencil the offer you want
_____Sample can of floor wax
_____Sample polishing cloth

If you are selling insurance, for example, you can test offers by listing several different pamphlets in your coupon, as follows:

Check with pencil the pamphlet you want
_____How to provide money to send a child to college
_____How to provide money to pay off a mortgage
_____How to provide an income in case of disability

After you have found out which offer pulls best, you can feature that offer alone in future advertising.

24. Test several different ads

After you have discovered the best-pulling offer, you can test several different ads containing the offer. In a series of ads containing the same offer, you will often find one ad that, due to better headline or better picture, will pull twice as many inquiries as the other ads.

You can test your advertisements in inexpensive space before you run them in expensive space. For example, you can get a quick, low-cost test in a daily newspaper. After you have found your best-pulling ad, you can run it in your entire list of newspapers and magazines and adapt it for use in radio and TV commercials.

25. Use the most effective media

In some cases, publication ads will bring inquiries at lower cost than broadcast commercials. In other cases, broadcasting will do better than publications. Your judgment and experience will often enable you to select the best medium. However, sometimes you will have to run actual tests of media.

After you have found out whether broadcast advertising or publication advertising is best for your proposition, you can further refine your testing and find out which broadcasting stations or which publications are most efficient.

26. Skim the cream from various markets

After a few ads have run in a certain publication or on a certain broadcasting station, you may find that your cost per inquiry is rising because you have skimmed the cream off of that particular market. If you are using broadcast commercials, you can try shifting to a different time of day in order to reach a different group of listeners. Or you can try different stations. If you are using publication advertising, you can try different publications.

Mail order advertisers find that readers of certain magazines are so responsive that it is profitable to run an ad every month. On the other hand, certain magazines can be used only once or twice a year if inquiry costs are to be kept down. This system of shifting media is something like fishing. The experienced fisherman shifts from one location to another in order to catch more fish.

27. Use the most effective space size

Certain propositions, such as book clubs, get the most sales per dollar of space cost by using full-page ads, whereas other propositions, such as vacation guide books, do best with ads measuring one-half column or smaller. Apparently it takes long copy to sell the idea of a book club, whereas a small ad is sufficient to induce people to send for a free vacation guide booklet. What size space is most efficient for your proposition? You can determine this by testing ads in several different sizes.

28. Use long copy

After you have found your most efficient size ad, you should jam your space full of copy, no matter whether it is a one inch ad or a full page ad.

Brief, reminder-style copy consisting of a few words or a slogan does not pull inquiries as well as long copy packed with facts about your product or service.

If you want to see efficient use of space, you should look at a mail order catalog or at the mail order ads in magazines or in your Sunday newspaper. Some of the strongest pulling mail order ads have contained as many as 1,200 words of copy set in small print. Don't be afraid to use long copy or small print. Just be sure that your copy is interesting. Remember the saying, "The more you tell, the more you sell."

29. Use the best season

During certain seasons, people read publications and listen to broadcasting more often than during other seasons. Good months for high mail order returns are January, February, and March. The summer months are not as good. One test of couponed ads where the same ad appeared in January and August showed that January pulled twice as many replies as August.

The day of the week makes a difference in newspaper advertising. One test showed that Sunday newspaper ads pulled 40 per cent more replies than daily newspaper ads.

30. Use the best-pulling positions in publications

In checking ad returns, you will find that there is a logical relationship between position and pulling power. The financial page in newspapers pulls best for financial and business items. The women's page is usually best for household items. Position alongside food articles is good for food ads. Pages 1 and 2 and the back page are good in newspapers. The top of the page is better than the bottom of the page. The magazine sections of Sunday newspapers usually have good pulling power. In national magazines, pages 1, 3, and 5 are usually excellent.

31. Study the offerings of your competitors

If you are just starting out and have no experience in a particular line, it is important to study the keyed ads of other advertisers—especially mail order advertisers. No mail order secret can long be kept secret from the eyes of an observant student of advertising. The reason is because the survival of a mail order business depends on repeating the best-pulling ads over and over in the best-pulling media. Therefore, if you want to know which is the most resultful ad of a certain mail order advertiser, all you have to do is to look in the back files of publications and see which ad he has run most often. If you want to know which publications are best, for him, just make a note of the publications in which he spends the most money. Information of this sort gives you a head start in placing inquiry-getting ads for your own proposition.

32. Keep records of your results

Of course, you should key all of your ads and keep careful records of results. You can key your ads by saying in the address

"Write to Dept. 1" or "Write to Dept. 2," etc. Or you can print in the coupon a tiny key number such as RD-5, which would mean *Reader's Digest*, May issue. It is good to use a card file system of small filing cards. Make out a separate card for each ad. Include the essential facts about each ad, namely, headline, size of ad, cost of ad, publication, date, position, and number of inquiries. Divide the cost of the ad by the number of inquiries and enter the cost per inquiry at the top of each card. File the cards according to cost per inquiry, beginning with the lowest cost. Then review your card file at regular intervals and determine which ads and which media are doing best for your proposition. In this way you will be able to plan your future efforts to avoid failures and repeat your successes.

Summary of 32 Ways to Get More Inquiries from Your Advertising

For your convenience, the 32 ways to increase ad inquiries are summarized below.

1. Mention the offer in the headline
2. Emphasize the word "Free"
3. Mention the offer in a subhead
4. Show a picture of the booklet or sample
5. Mention the offer in the first paragraph
6. Use an attractive booklet title
7. Include an attractive description of the offer
8. Include a booklet foreword by a famous person
9. Include testimonials
10. Sweeten your offer
11. Include a coupon
12. Print the value on the coupon
13. Include some selling copy in the coupon
14. Print your address twice in each ad
15. Include a telephone number
16. Emphasize "No obligation"
17. Offer certain information in a plain envelope
18. Urge immediate action
19. Include a business reply postcard
20. Include a fold-over coupon
21. Include a business reply envelope
22. Use a free-standing insert
23. Test several different offers
24. Test several different ads

25. Use the most effective media
26. Skim the cream from various markets
27. Use the most effective space size
28. Use long copy
29. Use the best season
30. Use the best-pulling positions in publications
31. Study the offerings of your competitors
32. Keep records of your results

The advertising profession is an integral part of the life of a free nation. It has helped create markets where markets did not previously exist. It has not merely sold products which the public wanted, it has sold products which the public did not know it wanted. More important still, it has made possible the only free method for the large scale manufacture of goods on a mass basis.

Thomas E. Dewey

A Four-page Center Spread in TV Guide

If you want successful selling ideas, study the ads that mail order advertisers repeat again and again. This ad has been repeated a number of times in *TV Guide*. It is a four-page insert, printed on heavy paper. Inserts of this kind, in the full circulation of more than 18 million, cost upwards of $150,000 each. At that price, you may be sure that the advertiser is not merely testing copy. He is cashing in on an ad that has been tested and proved successful. The two top panels are pages 1 and 4. The two bottom panels are the center spread of the insert.

A Free-standing Insert

Shown here is the front cover of a four-page circular that was inserted in every copy of a Sunday edition of *The New York Times*. This circular, or free-standing insert, is an ad for *Cue* magazine, the New York entertainment guide. Attached to it is a business reply postcard offering 40 issues of *Cue* for $3.98. "Subscription sales were 60% greater than projected," said the Ad Manager. Hundreds of millions of inserts of this kind have been distributed throughout the U.S. The inserts range in size from a single sheet to 16 pages or more. They are not part of the regular newspaper, but are dropped into the paper by an inserting machine. Inserts are one of the most effective advertising devices ever discovered. They have great attention value. They give the advertiser an opportunity to use long copy, lots of pictures, and an easy-to-mail order form that requires no stamp.

14

How to Appeal to the Masses

One of my earliest advertising assignments was to prepare an advertisement for Mr. Blank's Hair Growing Treatment. In attacking this problem, I reasoned thus: If everyone realized that this treatment actually grows hair, we would make thousands of sales. Therefore, our problem is to prove that the treatment works. Why not let the public know that if the treatment does not grow hair, Mr. Blank, the manufacturer, would be criminally liable for fraudulent advertising?

With this idea in mind I produced this headline:

I would be in jail if my treatment didn't grow hair

To add a dramatic touch, I illustrated the advertisement with a picture of Mr. Blank actually behind prison bars.

The advertisement produced loud laughs from a fellow copywriter. "So that's the way you spend your time!" he exclaimed, "making fun of our clients!"

I concluded that if my advertisement was misunderstood by one of our own copywriters, it would certainly be misunderstood by the public.

The average reader makes a snap judgment in interpreting an advertisement. Therefore, for the sake of clarity, the headline and the illustration of an advertisement should tell the same story.

In this case the headline said, "I would be in jail," but the picture said, "I am in jail." My copywriter friend reacted to the picture before he read the headline. Pictures convey their message faster than print.

Here is an example of a mail order book ad where the headline and the picture do tell the same story:

[Headline]: This is Marie Antoinette riding to her
death.
[Illustration: Picture of Marie Antoinette riding to
her death].

This ad dramatized a scene described in The Harvard Classics. The ad drew eight times as many coupon replies as any previous ad for this set of books.

Three Aids to Pulling Power

Three well-known and often neglected aids to pulling power are:

1. Short paragraphs
2. Short sentences
3. Short words

There is nothing more discouraging to the eye than a block of solid type. Break your long paragraphs up into short ones. Short paragraphs invite the eye. A long sentence forces the reader to do tiresome mental gymnastics. It forces him to keep your opening thought in mind while he absorbs half a dozen other thoughts.

As for short words, the following story illustrates their value. A publisher of children's books wanted to know the secret of the popularity among children of a certain history book. Children preferred this particular history book to any other. Some even read it in their spare time when lessons did not require it.

The publisher questioned the author of the book. The author replied, "When the manuscript was finished, I gave it to a ten-year-old child and asked him to cross out all the words he didn't understand. I then substituted simpler words."

Other Ways to Make Copy Easy to Read

Do not clutter up your copy with too many contractions such as "We're" instead of "We are," "We'll" instead of "We will," "He'll" instead of "He will."

Contractions tire the eye. They force the eye to take the tiny apostrophes into consideration. To the careless reader, "We're" looks like "Were." "We'll" looks like "Well." "He'll" looks like "Hell."

Other contractions such as "Shan't," "He's," "It's," "You'll," "They'll," etc., may not look like other words, but they tire the eye just the same. In the following columns, you will notice that it is just a bit easier to read the words in the right-hand column:

Shan't	Shall not
He's	He is
It's	It is
You'll	You will
They'll	They will

Do not use too many exclamation marks. An exclamation mark looks like the letter "l." Consider this headline for a popular beverage:

Here's how!

The word "how" with the exclamation mark coming immediately after it looks like the word "howl."

Consider this headline:

How to get your name on Uncle Sam's payroll!

To the careless eye, the word "payroll" looks as if it were spelled with three "l's." Result: slight confusion.

A Plan for Avoiding Difficult Sentences

When you have finished writing a piece of copy, give it to someone to read aloud. An agency executive received a written solicitation from a magazine. Here is the opening paragraph:

The purpose of this letter is to demonstrate the market an analysis of *Blank Monthly* readers presents to advertisers.

The chances are that you stumbled just a little in reading that paragraph. If the writer of the letter had given it to someone to read aloud, that person would have stumbled, too. The paragraph could then have been changed to read like this:

The purpose of this letter is to show you the type of readers you can reach by advertising in *Blank Monthly*.

A piece of advertising writing should not only be grammatically correct and properly punctuated, but it must read smoothly—swiftly. There must be no need to go back and read certain portions over again. The reader should not be forced to keep an eagle eye out for commas and apostrophes. Avoid sentences that require complicated punctuation.

Small irregularities in your copy may confuse the reader for only a second. But a second's confusion multiplied by a million readers is a lot of confusion.

Style-conscious Copy

Read this paragraph taken from an advertisement:

> You haven't tried Blank's Biscuits? ... Try them, like them—and thereafter you'll find them always the same, all around the world, unchanging and good.

This is a mild example of style copy—the kind of copy that pays more attention to how a thing is said than to what is said. Consider the first sentence. You do not know it is a question until you come to the question mark. Up to that time you have been reading the sentence as a simple statement. Result: slight confusion.

The last sentence of the copy says: "You'll find them always the same, all around the world, unchanging and good." Does this mean that you can buy Blank's Biscuits anywhere in the world? Or does it mean that if you take a package of Blank's Biscuits around the world with you they will not spoil in any climate?

There is much of this style copy being written. It gives the reader the impression that something brilliant has been said, but just exactly what has been said the reader cannot remember.

The weakness of style-conscious copy can be seen in the following headlines. Each headline expresses the same thought. But the thought comes out strongest in the third headline, which contains no style, just plain English.

1. To a $15,000 man with $25,000 potentialities.
2. When you reach it, $15,000 is just another milestone.
3. To a $15,000 man who would like to be making $25,000.

Here is a sentence that conveys an idea in a rather complicated style: "It is unlawful to appropriate, for your personal use, any property that rightfully belongs to other individuals."

Here is how the same idea is expressed in simple language: "Thou shalt not steal."

The simplicity of the latter wording is not offensive to the sophisticated reader, no matter how many college degrees he has. And the simple wording is clear to readers who have little schooling.

In order to increase the pulling power of your advertising, your copy should be simple, not subtle. You will not offend educated readers by making your advertisements understandable to all readers.

Words That Need Explaining

The manager of a department store prepared an advertisement for some household articles. Before publishing the ad, he handed it to an advertising agency man for suggestions.

At the beginning of the copy, this sentence occurred:

Most of these articles are exclusive with this store.

The advertising man added four words to the sentence, making it read:

Most of these articles are exclusive with this store— cannot be obtained elsewhere.

Further on in the copy, this sentence occurred:

Every one of these articles is guaranteed.

The ad man expressed the sentence in fuller detail as follows:

Every one of these articles is guaranteed. If any trouble develops within a year, we will replace the article with a new one. Or, if you prefer, your money will be cheerfully refunded.

The ad man said: "Words like 'exclusive' and 'guaranteed' have appeared in advertisements so often that they have lost their original force. Furthermore, there are plenty of people who never did know the real meaning of the words. Therefore, it is wise to explain them."

Presenting Thoughts Simply

Here is a plan that can be used effectively in writing advertising copy. Read the following paragraph:

> This chapter tells some methods for making advertisements simple. The average reader understands only simple advertisements.

Now read a slight rearrangement of the same paragraph:

> This chapter tells some methods for making advertisements simple. Simple advertisements are the only kind that the average reader understands.

The difference between the two arrangements is this: In the first arrangement the second sentence begins with the words, "The average reader." In the second arrangement the second sentence begins with the words, "Simple advertisements."

Arrangement number two is slightly easier to understand. Here is why: The first sentence ends by leaving the thought "simple advertisements" in the reader's mind. The second sentence begins with the same thought.

Proof That Simplicity Is Vital

The necessity for simplicity in appealing to the masses is proved by the experience of other businesses besides the advertising business.

Consider the motion picture business. It is well known that the sophisticated motion pictures are, more often than not, box-office failures.

Compare the circulations of the great national magazines. Those that reach large audiences are not the sophisticated magazines. For example, the circulation of the *Atlantic Monthly* is only a fraction of the circulation of *Family Circle*.

Take the case of the tabloid newspapers. These journals have gone the limit in simplicity by telling the news primarily in pictures instead of words. What has been the result? The New York *Daily News,* a picture newspaper, has the largest circulation in America.

Broadcasting is another example. The Federal Bureau of Education, after making a study of the average listening audience, issued to broadcasting stations an instruction sheet that said: "Do not overrate the intelligence of your listeners."

More Proof

There are a number of people in the advertising business who are not sold on the value of simplicity. These people continue to write *New Yorker Magazine* copy for *Reader's Digest*.

There are other writers who admit that simplicity is valuable. Yet they continue to write difficult copy because it is easier to write. They are like the man who at the end of a long-winded letter added this P.S.: "Please pardon this long letter. I didn't have time to write a short one."

During wartime, millions of men have been given intelligence tests. What was the result? It was found that the average man has a lower intelligence than was generally supposed.

In spite of this fact, scores of advertisers continue to print advertisements that are over the heads of readers. Here are some ad headlines that were published in magazines:

For a Discriminating Clientele
The Giant and the Pygmy
Give your toothpaste Proxy to her

Does the average citizen know the meaning of clientele, pygmy, or proxy?

Modern advertising copy is full of words like these: fastidious, distinctive, exhilaration, virtual, veritable, heritage. It is full of phrases such as: Sophisticated cuisine...Beautifully appointed interiors...Craftsmanship in volume production. Is this the language of the masses?

What advertising man has not read (or perhaps himself written) a paragraph like the following, which appeared in an ad:

In the big centers where a multiplicity of power broadcasting stations embarrasses less selective receivers, the full range selectivity of the Excelsior Receiver simplifies reception by banishing overlapping.

The next time you write a paragraph like the above, or the next time you write a clever advertisement, give it to someone of average education and see what he gets out of it. His reaction will tell you more clearly than words why it is not clever to write clever advertisements.

When a young writer first enters the advertising business he often rebels at the advice: "Write simply. Use short words and short sentences." There is a temptation to write clever advertising that brings praise from fellow copywriters, from account executives, and from clients. In fact, some writers never recover from this temptation.

I once made a marketing investigation in several small cities in Ohio. The job consisted of going from house to house and asking housewives if they used a washing machine, and if not, why not.

One night while at a hotel in the city of Ashtabula I received this telegram from the advertising agency that employed me: "Ask one hundred women if they know what a Pianola is." I smiled to myself. What a silly question! Of course, the women would know. Everybody knows that a Pianola is an old-style mechanical piano. I recalled a popular song—vintage of high school days:

> And we'll tickle a tune
> upon the Pianola

The next morning when I had finished asking the first housewife her opinion of washing machines, I grinned a bit sheepishly and said, "Do you know what a Pianola is?" She looked at me blankly—as if I had asked her to explain Einstein's Theory of Relativity. I looked back at her blankly. I could scarcely believe that she did not know. Finally I managed to smile and say, "I guess you never heard of it. They are not very well known. Thank you. Good day."

The second housewife I spoke to also looked blank and could give no answer. The third asked if a Pianola was a new kind of washing machine. The final tally showed that only one woman out of ten knew the meaning of Pianola.

In writing advertising copy, use words you would expect to find in a fifth-grade reader.

A Misunderstood Advertisement

A manufacturer of radio receiving sets prepared a billboard poster featuring the fact that his particular radio set had power. The poster consisted of the following elements:

1. The name of the radio. Let us call it the Acme Radio.
2. A picture of a powerful speed boat traveling at such high speed that the bow of the boat was lifted out of the water.
3. The single word "Power."

This diagram shows how the poster looked.

```
┌─────────────────────────────┐
│         ACME RADIO          │
│   [picture of motorboat]    │
│           POWER             │
└─────────────────────────────┘
```

The poster caused advertising men, including myself, to say "Wonderful."

One day while riding in a bus I passed one of these posters. I heard this conversation behind me:

"What kind of motorboat is that Acme Motorboat?"

"I don't know. She sure cuts through the water."

What can you do with people like that? There are millions of them—lazy readers, careless thinkers. To them a picture of a motorboat is an advertisement for a motorboat. And nothing on earth—not even the word "Radio" in huge letters—can make it an advertisement for a radio.

When you are advertising motorboats, show pictures of motorboats. But when you are advertising radios, show pictures of radios.

Here is another incident. One evening while riding in a bus along Riverside Drive, New York City, I heard a woman behind me read an advertisement aloud to her companion. The advertisement consisted of three sentences flashed from a Mazola Oil electric sign facing the drive. One of the sentences was, "You will like its smooth, bland flavor." Here is how the woman read it: "You will like its smooth, bl — — flavor." She started to pronounce the word "bland," hesitated and gave it up. What a pity it is that we copywriters are not more frequently brought into contact with the mental limitations of our readers.

What a News Commentator Found Out

A writer of news commentary discovered the need for simplicity in appealing to the masses. When he first started in the business of news writing, he tried to inject humor, such as describing a notorious gangster as a "One-man crime wave." He found to his disappointment that many of his humorous comments did not bring a laugh. The only remarks that caused merriment were those based on the oldest and simplest jokes, such as jokes about the mother-in-law or jokes about the thriftiness of Scotsmen.

A Lawyer's Secret

A successful lawyer discovered by experience the value of simplicity in winning lawsuits. He said, "Half the cases that go to court today are not presented to a jury. Instead, each lawyer presents his side of the case directly to the judge in the form of a written brief. I am always glad to work on this type of case because I have learned how to write a more effective brief than many of my opponents.

"The way I accomplish this is to make my brief very simple. I omit all legal language such as 'the party of the first part' and 'the party of the second part' etc. I write my brief as if I were writing a letter to a friend who did not understand legal terms. I have considerably increased my percentage of successes in this manner."

A Misunderstood Headline

I once wrote an advertisement for a book called *Courage*. The book told how to banish fear and develop self-confidence. In searching for a striking headline I reasoned thus: One of the best known examples of courage is the bulldog. And one of the most striking words for expressing the idea of courage is the word "grit." I put these two ideas together and produced this headline:

I will give you Bulldog Grit

In preparing the layout, a picture of the author of the book was placed above the headline like this:

[Picture of Author]
I will give you
Bulldog Grit
[copy]

This arrangement gave the impression, so desirable in mail order advertisements, that the author of the book was speaking directly to the reader.

I showed the advertisement to a friend. "How does this ad appeal to you?" I asked.

My friend nodded approvingly. "It sure would stop me if I owned a bulldog."

I stared at him. "What has owning a bulldog got to do with it?"

"Well, isn't that Bulldog Grit a brand of dog food?"

I went back to my desk and changed the headline to "I will give you Bulldog Courage."

How to Make a Good Headline Better

On page 230 are two ads for a gasoline additive. The ad at the top "Save one gallon of gas in every ten" pulled a large number of requests for a sample of the product.

It was then decided to try a more selective approach. The two words "Car owners" were inserted at the beginning of the headline as follows:

"Car owners! Save one gallon of gas in every ten"

There was no other change. The copy in both ads remained the same.

The two versions of the ad were split-run tested in a daily newspaper. The second version, beginning with the words "Car owners" pulled 20% more sample requests than the first version.

This test is just one of many experiments that have been tried over the years involving changes in headlines. In a number of cases, these headline changes have resulted in appreciable improvements in results. The following are examples of these successful changes.

Headline: "Hay Fever"

A maker of a hay fever remedy got good response from a sample offer contained in a small ad headlined "Hay Fever." This advertiser then tested other ads containing the same copy, but with different headlines. One of the new headlines was "Dry Up Hay Fever."

Here are the results of a newspaper split-run test: The ad with the headline "Hay Fever" pulled 297 sample requests. The ad with the headline "Dry Up Hay Fever" pulled 380 sample requests. This is a 27% increase obtained by merely adding two words. These two words "Dry Up" added a promise of a benefit to the purely selective headline "Hay Fever."

Headline: "Retire In 15 Years"

A retirement income advertiser seeking leads for salesmen got good response from an ad headline "Retire in 15 Years." This ad ran successfully for several years. Then the advertiser changed the headline to "How a Man of 40 Can Retire in 15 Years." The response was increased. And equally important, the quality of the leads was improved. The replies came from men ages 35 to 45—just the age group that insurance salesmen like to call on. Many men in this age bracket have both the desire to start saving for retirement and the means to do it.

Headline: "How to Have a Cool, Quiet Bedroom"

A manufacturer of portable air conditioners ran ads with the headline "How to Have a Cool, Quiet Bedroom." The ads contained a telephone number and offered further information. The telephone replies were switched to salesmen who invited prospects to come to the manufacturer's showroom. Later on four words were added to the headline of the ad as follows: "How to Have a Cool, Quiet Bedroom— Even on Hot Nights." This change made the headline more dramatic and strengthened the promise of a benefit. Replies and sales increased.

Headline: "How to Repair Cars—Quickly, easily, right"

At an advertising conference, a mail order copywriter told this case history. An ad with the headline "How to Repair Cars—quickly, easily, right" was successful in getting orders. Then the word "Repair" was changed to "Fix." The new headline was "How to Fix Cars— quickly, easily, right." Orders increased 20%. Apparently the word "Repair" sounded like hard work, whereas the word "Fix" sounded quick and easy.

Headline: "Five Acres and Independence"

A book publisher planned to bring out a book on country home ownership entitled *Five Acres.* The publisher tested two titles as follows:

1. *Five Acres*
2. *Five Acres and Independence*

The latter title *Five Acres and Independence* was the winner by a wide margin. The book was published and it sold well.

Headline: "How I Raised Myself from Failure to Success in Selling"

Here are two more book titles that were tested:

1. *How I Raised Myself to Success in Selling*
2. *How I Raised Myself from Failure to Success in Selling*

The latter title containing the words *from Failure* was the winner. This book became a best seller.

A Lesson from Magazine Publishers

The next time you buy a magazine that has a paper sticker attached to the front cover, read the article titles printed on the sticker and then open the magazine and read the actual article titles. Sometimes the wording is different. For example:

"How to Beat Insomnia Without Sleeping Pills," was the title of a magazine article. "How to Sleep Without Pills" was the shorter and simpler title printed on the front cover sticker.

It is the job of the circulation department of a magazine to sell as many copies as possible, and so they sometimes simplify, modify or reconstruct the titles of articles in order to give them more sales punch. In doing this, the ad men in the circulation department are, in effect, working with headlines. They try to make a good headline better. Sometimes they do this by shortening an article title, as in the above example. Sometimes they do it by lengthening a title. Sometimes they change only a word or two. Sometimes they reconstruct the entire title.

Here are some magazine article titles that were given more impact by being shortened.

(Original title)	Hot Tips on Heating Your Home
(Revised title on cover sticker)	How to Cut Fuel Bills
(Original title)	A Smart Shopper's Guide to Bargains
(Revised title)	Shopper's Guide to Bargains
(Original title)	Three Ways to Mothproof a Marriage
(Revised title)	3 Ways to Save a Marriage
(Original title)	How to Understand the Perplexing Teen-Ager
(Revised title)	How to Understand Your Teen-Ager
(Original title)	Which Diet Tips Pay Off?
(Revised title)	Diet Tips That Pay Off

Here are some article titles that were given more sales appeal by being lengthened:

(Original title)	When Your Husband's Affection Cools

(Revised title)   When Your Husband's Affection Cools—
                   and what to do about it
(Original title)   Birth Control for Men
(Revised title)   Now—Safe, Simple Birth Control for Men
(Original title)   You Can Read Faster
(Revised title)   Read Faster—a 20-Day Plan
(Original title)   Key to Fitness at Any Age
(Revised title)   Key to Fitness at Any Age for Men and Women

Here are some article titles that were given greater interest by reconstructing:

(Original title)   The Smugglers of Misery
(Revised title)   Where All the Drugs Come From

(Original title)   Building on the Positives in Marriage
(Revised title)   4 Ways to Keep Your Marriage Young

(Original title)   High Blood Pressure—New Light on
                   a Hidden Killer
(Revised title)   New Protection Against Heart Attack

(Original title)   Backyard Gardens Are Back in Style
(Revised title)   How to Start a Backyard Garden

(Original title)   What You Can Do to Combat Inflation
(Revised title)   10 Ways to Beat the High Cost of Living

Summing Up

The next time you write a headline, don't be satisfied with your first draft. Put it aside overnight and then read it again. See if you can make it better by shortening it or by lengthening it or by reconstructing it.

Advertising is your means of public approach. If you make a product good enough, even though you live in the depths of the forest, the public will make a path to your door, says the philosopher. But if you want the public in sufficient numbers, you would better construct a highway. Advertising is that highway.

William Randolph Hearst

Hundreds Are Changing To Fragrant Frostilla

Are your hands rough, red, cracked? There's quick relief in fragrant Frostilla's soothing, softening, hand-beautifying protection.

Fragrant Frostilla is made from an old family formula beloved by women since 1873. Not just a cream, not just a liquid, it's a rich, thick *soothing* lotion that relieves sunburn, windburn, cracked lips, rough, dry skin on face, elbows, ankles, hands. Many women with sensitive skin love Frostilla as a powder base, an all-purpose protective lotion that helps keep skin soft, young, romantic.

Quick drying! Not sticky! Long lasting! Thrifty! One drop is enough!

Get acquainted offer: Tear out this advertisement and mail to Frostilla, Dept. O, 1740 Bailcy Ave., Buffalo 11, N. Y. for *free* generous trial bottle. You'll never want to be without fragrant Frostilla.

Popular Secretary Caught Red Handed

Too bad she didn't know there's quick relief for rough, red, cracked hands in Fragrant Frostilla's soothing, softening, hand-beautifying protection.

Fragrant Frostilla is made from an old family formula beloved by women since 1873. Not just a cream, not just a liquid, it's a rich, thick, *soothing* lotion that relieves sunburn, windburn, cracked lips, rough, dry skin on face, elbows, ankles, hands. Many women with sensitive skin love Frostilla as a powder base, an all-purpose protective lotion that helps keep skin soft, young, romantic.

Quick drying! Not sticky! Long lasting! Thrifty! One drop is enough!

Get acquainted offer: Tear out this advertisement and mail to Frostilla, Dept. P, 1740 Bailey Ave., Buffalo 11, N. Y. for *free* generous trial bottle. You'll never want to be without fragrant Frostilla.

Which Ad Brought the Most Replies?

Above are two ads for a hand lotion. The ads were tested two ways: (1) By opinion tests; people were asked which ad they thought would bring the greatest response, and (2) By split-run tests in newspapers, to find out which ad actually brought the greatest response. In the opinion tests, people chuckled at the clever ad "Popular Secretary Caught Red Handed" and voted it the winner. In the split-run tests the ad "Hundreds are Changing to Fragrant Frostilla" brought 89% more responses than "Popular Secretary." Be wary of clever ads, and don't rely too much on opinion tests to measure direct response.

I never stopped eating yet I lost 107 pounds.

By Catherine Gutches — as told to Ruth L. McCarthy

At 235 pounds, I looked as wide as my stove. But it didn't stop me from stirring up another batch of calories.

One thing's for sure. I didn't get up to 235 pounds by eating TV dinners. It was meals like cucumbers dipped in egg and breadcrumbs and fried in butter, served with macaroni smothered in cheese, and sweetened with a dessert - like Bundt cake or my own date and nut roll that did it. Believe me, when you eat like that, it's easy to get fat, especially when you start young.

I was raised on a produce farm in Paramus, N.J. And I grew up working side by side with the farm hands, so I learned to eat hearty as soon as I could lift and lick a cake spoon.

When I was in my teens, I'd get up at five, have breakfast of fried potatoes, ham, bread, jam and coffee. Then I'd work in the fields until seven. That would give me just enough time to take a bath, eat another snack and go off to school. When I'd get home, I'd be hungry enough to eat the icebox bare.

It's no wonder I weighed 165 pounds by the time I was 21, the year I married Ted — a six-footer who weighed three pounds less than I did. It didn't seem to bother him, though. He's Dutch and, with my German parentage, we both took to eating like there was no other reason for living.

Our friends were all 200-pounds plus, too. Why, once, when I complained about the shape I was in, one of them said: "Don't worry, Catherine, your skin is stretched to the limit. Now you can eat all you want." And I did. Then my back began to ache, my feet started to hurt from carrying all that weight, and my stomach continually got in the way. What a mess.!

Finally, a friend of mine said to me: "Catherine, let's try those reducing-plan candies, Ayds®." And she bought me a box of the vanilla caramel kind. First, I read the label on the box to check out the ingredients. When I found that Ayds contains vitamins and minerals, but no drugs — nothing harmful — I started right in on the plan with her.

Then I remembered hearing once during a physical exam that to burn up fat, you need to eat the right foods, like meat and salads and vegetables. To me it was like comparing the body to a furnace that needs proper stoking to get it to burn like it should. Well, on the Ayds plan, I began to stoke mine good. Instead of stuffing myself with starches, sweets and junk, I ate like I should. Only I ate less, because I wanted less.

I took one or two Ayds like the directions say, with a hot drink, and those candies really helped curb my appetite. Why, in six weeks, I'd lost 13 pounds on the Ayds plan. And I'll tell you, when I saw the scales going down, there was no more eating just to fill up that big cavity in front.

People really didn't take much notice, though, until I'd lost 50 pounds. That's when my clothes looked like they were designed by Omar, the Tent Maker, and everybody began remarking about my losing weight.

Sometimes, it's hard even for me to believe what's happened. Me, a grandmother who gained a girlish figure at age 55. But the best thing is how it happened. Thanks to the Ayds plan, I lost 107 pounds, yet I never stopped eating. And I've never felt better.

Now that I'm down to 128 pounds, I still like to cook and bake, but I've given up tasting what's in the pot and licking what's on the spoon.

BEFORE AND AFTER MEASUREMENTS		
	Before	After
Height	5'2"	5'2"
Weight	235 lbs.	128 lbs.
Bust	52"	39"
Waist	48"	29½"
Hips	52"	36"
Dress	52	12

(Advertisement)

Is This an Ad or an Article?

This ad for Ayds fat reducing plan is an example of how to get high readership. Make your ad look like editorial material. Other headlines in this series: "I got stuck in a church pew before I lost 70 pounds.". . ."I lost 79 pounds and turned into Casanova's dream girl." The ads show photographs of real people and tell real life stories. The copy is written in conversational style and is set in magazine article format. The ads are signed by their authors and the advertiser's logotype is omitted.

15

What Kinds of Layouts and
Illustrations Attract the Most Readers?

It has been said that the greatest crime an advertisement can commit is to remain unnoticed. Getting advertisements to be noticed is the job of the layout man and the art director. But just as the copywriter who hopes to write the Great American Novel must put away "fine writing" when he is writing copy, so must the art director put away "fine art" when he is producing an advertisement. At least fine art must be made a secondary consideration. The principal job of an advertisement is to sell goods. Therefore, you should use layouts and illustrations in which salesmanship comes first and art second.

An art director described the mental development he went through in trying to produce advertisements that sold goods. When he first started in the advertising business he tried to apply the things he learned in art school. His first consideration in making an ad layout was good taste and good design. His first consideration in selecting an illustration was that it should be as similar as possible to the painting of the old masters. The result was that his advertisements brought "Ooo's!" and "Ah's!" of delight from other art directors. His advertisements were the kind that won prizes at commercial art exhibitions.

Being a practical man and knowing that the principal job of an advertisement is to sell merchandise to the masses, this art director showed his creations to elevator men, taxi drivers, stenographers, clerks, and others not directly interested in art. He showed each of these people a group of advertisements and asked which attracted them the most. When the first elevator man showed preference for the most inartistic advertisement, the art director laughed the matter off. When a clerk did the same thing, it seemed like a coincidence.

But when dozens of people passed over the artistic creations and selected something that looked like a typical Sears Roebuck ad, the art director began to see a great light. Since then he has conducted hundreds of tests. He has found that the artistic qualities of an advertisement are not nearly as important as the ability of the advertisement to get attention and to drive home a selling point. Sometimes the rules of fine art must be completely reversed in producing an effective advertisement.

Fine Art Versus Commercial Art

Many advertising artists are still in the mental stage that this art director was in before he started showing advertisements to average people. During the next ten years the tendency in advertising layout and illustration will be more and more toward advertisements that aim primarily to sell the goods.

The trouble with applying the rules of fine art to advertising is that fine art seeks to please the senses, and to tone in with surroundings. Why are park benches usually painted green instead of orange? Because green is more artistic. Because green tones in with the surroundings. But does the advertiser want to tone in with his surroundings? Does the manufacturer want to pay $40,000 for a color page in a magazine just to soothe the artistic senses of the reader? No. He wants to jar the reader and stop him on the spot—to rouse him and stir him to action.

How to Make Type Work for You

The principal consideration in selecting the style of type for your headline is that it should be big enough and powerful enough to seize the attention of the reader.

The principal consideration in selecting type for your copy is that it should be easy to read. The easiest type for people to read is the type they read most often. Therefore, set your copy in the customary, everyday styles of type used in newspaper articles and magazine articles. Avoid fancy type. Avoid script. Avoid too many italics. Avoid type that is too faint or too bold. Avoid any style of type that calls attention to the type itself rather than to the message. Do not try to create atmosphere with type.

Some art directors use type merely as a decoration. They force the type into neat squares or oblongs or other shapes. They arrange it so that all the lines will come out of equal length, like the inscription on a memorial tablet. Sometimes they use an unusually light face type or a script so that the block of copy will not interfere with the illustration. Sometimes they use the type as part of the design by setting it in long, hard-to-read lines of fancy type with wide white spaces between the lines. Devices of this kind may make an advertisement more artistic, but they do not invite the eye to read. Remember that people buy magazines and newspapers to read stories and articles. Therefore, if you want your copy to be read, set the text like a story or an article.

In selecting type for your advertisements, you would do well to take a look at the typical mail order ads that are repeated again and again. Note the strong, black, readable type in which the headlines are set. Note the clear-cut type in which the copy is set. If you do not know the names of the various styles of type, you will not go wrong if you tear a good mail order ad out of a magazine or newspaper and say to your printer: "Please set my ad like this."

In preparing your ad layout, make your headline large enough and bold enough so that even the most careless glancer cannot help but catch your message. If your headline is a long one, set some of the more important words in extra-large type.

Large type in a headline has strong attention value. It also gives force to your message. Consider this headline in ordinary size type:

Announcing new models

Now see how much more emphatic the headline looks in larger type:

ANNOUNCING NEW MODELS

The big type adds strength and force to your announcement. It makes big news out of it instead of little news. It gives the impression that you are speaking in a strong voice instead of in a whisper. An announcement in small type suggests that you yourself do not think that the announcement is important.

Even when you have no news—no announcement to make, you can give your headline a news flavor by putting it in big type. Consider this headline in ordinary size type:

To men who want to get ahead

This is an interesting headline, but consider how much more important it becomes when it is spread clear across the page in large type:

TO MEN WHO WANT TO GET AHEAD

The big type seems to add an announcement quality, a news quality, even though the headline contains no news at all.

Featuring Important Words in Headlines

When you are dealing with a lengthy headline, you may not have room to set all the words in large type. In that case, you can set part of the headline in large type. For example, here is a long headline in which none of the words have been featured:

You can laugh at money worries
if you follow this simple financial plan

Here is the same headline with certain words featured in large type. In setting up an ad, these featured words can be made to stand out on the page and stop readers. Note that the featured words convey a complete message in themselves. This is important. Do not feature words that are meaningless by themselves.

YOU CAN LAUGH
AT MONEY WORRIES
if you follow this simple
financial plan

Here are four more headlines that have been given the same treatment. In the first version of each no words have been featured. In the second version certain meaningful words have been set in large type:

(1) To men who want to
    quit work some day

(2) To men who want to
    QUIT WORK some day

(1) Break up a cold
    this quick way

(2) BREAK UP A COLD
    this quick way

(1) Thousands now play who
    never thought they could

(2) THOUSANDS NOW PLAY
    who never thought they could

(1) Who else wants a whiter wash
    with no hard work
(2) WHO ELSE WANTS
    a WHITER WASH
    with no hard work

When you hand your typewritten ad copy to your layout man or to your art director, he will appreciate it if you will indicate which, if any, important words in your headline can be set in larger type than the rest of the headline.

If you write a long headline, it is wise to include a meaningful phrase that can be set in extra-large type. If you can do so, it is especially good to arrange your thoughts so that the meaningful phrase occurs at the beginning of your headline. This arrangement is used in three out of four of the headlines listed above. It is not used in the headline "To men who want to QUIT WORK some day."

Pictures That Get Attention

Hundreds of readership surveys have been conducted in which people have been asked which ads they noticed in various publications. As a result, it is possible to list certain types of pictures that are especially effective in getting attention. For example:

Pictures of brides
Pictures of babies
Pictures of animals
Pictures of famous people
Pictures of people in odd costumes, such as might be worn at a
    masquerade
Pictures of people in odd situations, such as a man wearing an
    eye patch
Pictures that tell a story, such as a little girl trying on her
    mother's hat
Romantic pictures, such as a man carrying a girl across a
    rushing brook
Catastrophe pictures, such as car accidents
News pictures, such as the launching of a space vehicle.
Timely pictures, such as pictures of Santa Claus at Christmas
    time and pictures of Abraham Lincoln on Lincoln's birthday

One interesting observation that has come out of readership surveys is that men tend to look at ads containing pictures of men and that women tend to look at ads containing pictures of women. Apparently the pictures act as labels. A man figures that an ad containing a picture of a man is likely to be an ad for a man's product and that an ad containing a picture of a woman is likely to be an ad for a woman's product.

Before the widespread use of readership surveys, some ad men believed that the way to stop a male reader was to show a picture of a bathing beauty. Apparently this technique stops the wrong readers or it stops them in the wrong mood. This type of picture may create desire for the girl, but it does not seem to create desire for the product being advertised. I recall the story about the Eskimo who sent $29.95 in response to a mail order catalog ad for a woman's dress. When the dress was delivered, the Eskimo complained. For $29.95 he had expected to get the woman model who had been shown wearing the dress in the catalog illustration!

Pictures That Sell

In using information gained from readership surveys, it is wise to remember that the high attention value of a picture does not necessarily mean high sales value. In order to have sales value, the picture should be related to the product.

Some ad men have wrongly used readership survey results by illustrating ads with pictures of high attention value but without relation to the product. For example, if you use a picture of a bride or a baby in order to get high attention value for an automobile ad, you will stop the wrong people in the wrong mood. On the other hand, a picture of a bride is fine for selling wedding gifts such as silverware. And a picture of a baby is fine for selling baby powder.

Based on sales tests of advertisements, following are typical examples of pictures that have sales value:

1. Picture of the product. For example, in an automobile ad, show a picture of the automobile.
2. Picture of product in use. For example, a man using a new garden tool he just bought.
3. Picture of reward of using the product. For example, a woman admiring a cake she baked, or eating a pudding she prepared.
4. Picture of attainment of ambition. For example, a boy receiving a diploma. Another example: A correspondence school ad showing a smiling man handing his wife some

money. Headline: "Here's an extra $50, Grace—I'm making real money now."

5. Picture of an enlarged detail. For example, a magnifying glass showing an enlargement of a new kind of pen point.
6. Dramatic pictures. For example, an ad for a memory course showed a picture of a blindfolded man. Headline: "A startling memory feat you can do." Another example: The famous trademark of the Victor Talking Machine Company showed a dog listening to a phonograph. Headline: "His master's voice."

An error to avoid in the choice of pictures is the use of pictures that are too far-fetched or too clever. Here is what sometimes happens. An ad man works for years preparing ads for sea-going cruises. He gets tired of pictures of happy people embarking on a ship or pictures of joyful groups playing shuffleboard on the deck of a ship. He craves something different. And so this ad man prepares a cruise ad that features a picture of a ship's compass or a picture of a ship captain's hat. This is clever, but too far-fetched. This ad man has forgotten two important truths, namely:

1. To the average person who is glancing rapidly through a publication, a picture of a compass is an ad for a compass. A picture of a hat is an ad for a hat.
2. The person who has finally saved up money enough to take a cruise is delighted with pictures of people embarking or pictures of groups playing games aboard ship. This is just what he is looking for. So don't lose him or confuse him with pictures of hats or compasses.

When you are looking for an idea for an ad illustration, you will often find that a picture of the product will produce the most sales. For example, the Book-of-the-Month Club shows pictures of books. If you look through a mail order catalogue you will find the following:

Pictures of sewing machines in sewing machine ads.
Pictures of vacuum cleaners in vacuum cleaner ads.
Pictures of dresses in ads for dresses.
Pictures of shoes in ads for shoes.

The above examples are not intended to rule out the use of dramatic and exciting illustrations. Exciting pictures are fine if you can think up a picture in which the excitement in the picture is related to the product.

Why Photographs Make Good Illustrations

After you have selected the subject matter for your illustration, it is usually better to use a photograph of the subject instead of a drawing. For believability, there is nothing as effective as a photograph. If you do use a drawing or a painting, let your drawing be as lifelike as possible—as photographic in style as possible.

The effectiveness of photographs can be illustrated by a few personal experiences. A woman friend of mine spent half an hour telling me about her little nephew, whom she adored. I didn't learn much about the child from what she said. Her description was too idealized. Then she showed me a large crayon portrait of a beautiful boy. I looked at the drawing, but there wasn't enough reality in it for me to tell what he was really like. Finally she showed me a snapshot of the youngster on roller skates. This tiny photograph told me what the boy was really like. He looked like a real boy with a character of his own and a nice smile. I could have recognized him. But I could never have recognized him from the crayon portrait. The portrait was unreal and unconvincing.

Another time I was looking through a summer resort catalogue. The advertisements of two resorts attracted me. But one advertisement had a distinct advantage over the other. It showed photographs of the resort and the surrounding country. These photographs told me exactly what the resort was like. They offered the next best thing to an actual visit of inspection. The other advertisement showed an idealized drawing of the hotel and surrounding grounds. It pictured flags flying, fountains playing, and artistic sailboats on the lake nearby. The drawing didn't prove a thing. It gave no real information. It failed to convince. It was plainly just an artist's ideal conception of a summer hotel.

At another time I wanted to buy airplane luggage. I searched through newspapers and magazines for advertisements. Some of the ads showed drawings of luggage, some showed paintings, others showed photographs. The ads with the photographs interested me most. I knew that if I went to look at that luggage, I would not be disappointed. The actual luggage would look like the photographs. On the other hand, if I went looking for luggage of which I had seen only a drawing or an idealized painting, I might be disappointed. The actual article might not look anything like its portrait.

A photograph adds real information to an advertisement. Photographs convince. Photographs are proof. Everybody knows that when you look at a photograph of a person or a piece of merchandise or a summer resort, you are looking at a real likeness. There are little details in photographs that tell so much—little details of expression or surrounding atmosphere. A glance at a photograph is the next best thing to seeing the actual object.

An old Chinese proverb says, "A good picture is worth a thousand words." If this is true, then a good photograph is worth two thousand words.

Using Heads of People in Advertisements

Why do mail order advertisers so often use men's heads and women's heads as illustrations for advertisements? The answer is that this type of illustration often brings more sales than other types.

Pictures of people's heads are good attention-getters. This is especially true when the model is looking directly at you and is related to the product or service, for example, a photo of a user of the product or a graduate of a mail order correspondence course. A photograph of a person looking you square in the eye will stop you quicker than a picture of a cake of soap or a landscape.

Pictures of people's heads are economical in the matter of space. All you need to show is the face. This means that if you have a large space reserved for your illustration, you can enlarge the face until it fills the space, thus making an illustration that simply cannot be missed.

If you are using long copy and have only a small space left for the illustration, there is nothing you can put in that space that is more eye-catching than a person's head. Many 60-line mail order advertisements are so crowded with copy that the space left for the illustration is no larger than a postage stamp. Yet this small space is big enough to carry an effective picture of a man's or woman's head.

What are the other types of illustrations used in advertisements? Outdoor scenes, groups of people, office scenes, home scenes, and landscapes are some. Illustrations of this kind are all right if you have plenty of space in which to put them. But they cannot be used to good advantage where you are using quarter-pages or where your copy is long.

Take the case of the landscape picture. You cannot crowd an effective landscape into a small space. If you show a miniature of the entire landscape, the details of the picture become unrecognizable. If you try to cut off parts of the landscape, you are likely to spoil it.

But suppose you are using a man's head. You can omit his shoulders and his collar. You can even cut off the top of his head, leaving only his face, and still have a good illustration. A person's head, especially if he is looking at you, is one of the most effective illustrations you can use in small space. It is also extremely effective when enlarged to fill a larger space.

There are other strong reasons for using people's heads as advertising illustrations. Take the case of a testimonial advertisement. If you show a photograph of the person who wrote the testimonial, the reader will feel more confidence in the message. He will feel that it must be true, or else the testimonial giver would not dare to allow his photograph to be used. Furthermore, as the reader reads the testimonial, he can glance every now and then at the person who wrote it. He can see what that person looks like. This increases reader interest and gives a more intimate touch to the message.

The Advertiser's Logotype

An important part of many advertisements is the advertiser's logotype or name of the advertiser, which is featured in large type, usually at the bottom of the ad.

Sometimes the logotype is the name of the manufacturer and sometimes it is the name of the product. For example, here are some manufacturers' names that are often used as logotypes:

General Electric
General Motors
U.S. Steel
Du Pont
Philco

Here are some product names that have frequently been used as logotypes:

Spam
Lux
Chanel
Cadillac

The manufacturer repeats the logotype over and over again in the hope that you will remember it and be favorably inclined toward his brand when you buy. This is long-haul advertising as distinguished from short-haul advertising for immediate sales.

In radio advertising, the manufacturer cannot feature a logotype in big print and so he often compensates for this by repeating his name or the name of his product over and over again. For example, in a one-minute radio commercial for Colgate Toothpaste, the name Colgate may be repeated many times.

In TV advertising, the manufacturer can get name publicity in two ways if he desires, namely, by flashing his name in big print on the screen and by having his name frequently repeated by the announcer.

The effect of the logotype on the consumer is difficult to measure because it takes months and sometimes years to produce a measurable result. Yet the effect is known to exist because tests have shown that people will buy a familiar product in preference to one that is unfamiliar. They will buy·from a known manufacturer more readily than from an unknown manufacturer. Therefore, the advertiser's logotype should not be omitted from an ad except under special conditions such as the following:

1. If the name of the product is mentioned in the headline of an ad, it need not be mentioned again in the logotype.
2. Sometimes a picture of the product with the name printed on the package takes the place of the logotype.
3. Some mail order advertisers omit the logotype because they are selling an item or service that is bought only once in a lifetime. For example, a book or a correspondence course. These advertisers are advertising for an immediate sale instead of building up name publicity over the years. By omitting the logotype, these concerns reduce their space cost.
4. Readership surveys have shown that editorial items get higher reading than ads. Therefore, some advertisers omit the logotype in order to produce ads that don't look like ads. For example, ads that look like cartoons, or ads that look like news items, articles, or stories. These ads sacrifice the advantage of a logotype in order to gain the advantage of increased readership of their complete text set in small print.

Ads Without Pictures

Some of the best-pulling mail order ads have been all-type ads with no pictures. For example, the ad for the Roth Memory Course with the headline: "How I Improved My Memory in One Evening." This ad pulled so well that it ran for years. (See illustration in back of book.) An all-type ad for Tecla Pearls was also run for years and became famous. (See illustration in back of book.)

An all-type ad selling subscriptions to a well-known newspaper was the best puller of a number of ads tested, some with illustrations, some without illustrations. The headline of this ad was: "How to Get the *Times* Delivered to Your Home." At the present writing, this ad has been running for 14 years. No other ad has equalled it in pulling power.

These examples are not intended to sell you off the idea of using pictures, but to point out that a picture is not a must in every ad. Pictures cost money, and the space they occupy costs money. Every illustration should be tested with this question: Does it add sufficient sales value to warrant its cost?

Summing Up

In choosing illustrations for your ads, you will usually get more sales if you cash in on the experience of mail order advertisers and department stores whose existence depends on ads that produce direct, traceable sales.

Avoid weird, outlandish, or far-fetched pictures that have nothing to do with the product or service you are selling. Use pictures that attract buyers, not curiosity seekers. Here are some safe bets:

1. Pictures of the product.
2. Pictures of the product in use.
3. Pictures of people who use the product.
4. Pictures showing the reward of using the product.

The American standard of living is due in no small measure to the imaginative genius of advertising, which not only creates and sharpens demand, but also, by its impact upon the competitive process, stimulates the never-ceasing quest of improvement in quality of the product.

Adlai E. Stevenson

Pictures That Get Attention

Pictures of people's heads are good attention-getters. This is especially true if the person is looking directly at you and is related to the product or service. Pictures of people's heads are economical in the matter of space. If you are using long copy and have only a small space left for the illustration, there is nothing you can put in that space that is more eye-catching than a person's head.

By JEANNETTE FRANK
Nutritionist and Author

You May Be Eating More Salt Than You Should

Nutrition authorities caution against excessive salt intake. But there is an easy and appetizing alternative.

AMERICAN eating patterns are undergoing revolutionary changes. More than ever before, people are consuming more of their meals away from home. The spectacular growth of chain restaurants is testimony to this trend. Between-meal snacking is another current phenomenon as is the popularity of pre-prepared convenience foods. It seems we are eating or snacking all day long, frequently away from home, and often on the run. Many meals are even being consumed in our cars!

The accelerating pace of modern living has certainly changed our eating habits. But it has also brought in its wake an increase in our consumption of sodium chloride, ordinary table salt. Snack foods, convenience foods, foods served in restaurants tend to be heavily seasoned with salt. And salt, that generally harmless, most common of all household staples, may not be medically indicated when consumed in excessive quantities.

What are the possible nutritional pitfalls of salt? The connection between salt intake and hypertension or high blood pressure, one of the major causes of strokes and coronaries, has been known since the beginning of the century. But there are many other reasons to avoid salt. Excess salt holds fluid in body tissues, and retained fluid may contribute to problems related to overweight. Some doctors advise reduction of salt intake to women suffering excessive discomfort and depression resulting from menstruation. Arthritis sufferers are sometimes advised to reduce sodium intake when undergoing steroid therapy. Of course, no drastic dietary changes should be undertaken without consulting your doctor.

If you want to reduce your intake of salt or if your physician specifically prescribes a low sodium diet, you should know about America's leading salt substitute, Adolph's. This product looks, sprinkles and tastes like salt and has no bitter aftertaste. That's why many doctors have been recommending it to their patients for over 15 years. You can find Adolph's Salt Substitute in the dietetic section of your food store. Available regular or seasoned.

Editorial-style Ads Get High Reading

This page appeared in *Reader's Digest*. It is an ad for Adolph's Salt Substitute. It looks like a magazine article. A split-run test of two mail order ads showed that an ad that looked like a magazine article pulled 81% more orders than the identical copy, set in ad-style. *Caution:* A disadvantage of some editorial-style ads is that people who read only the headline do not receive a sales message because they don't know what product is being advertised.

Wanted Girl Scout Leaders

Assistant Leaders Wanted, Too.

Why be a Girl Scout Leader? Because you care about girls, and girls care about you. You want to share good things with them.

If you are a Leader, what do you do? You work with girls – little girls and big girls. You show them the many things you know. They learn from you, and you learn from them.

You have ideas. The girls have ideas. You make plans, and the girls make plans. The plans turn into action. You work on projects. You go places and see things. You have troop meetings and meetings with other Leaders. You make friends. And you receive help whenever you need it.

Thousands of men and women have brightened their lives as well as the lives of others by becoming Girl Scout Leaders.

About the Girl Scout Movement

The Girl Scouts of the U.S.A. is open to all girls 7 through 17 who subscribe to its ideals as expressed in the Girl Scout Promise and Law. Founded in 1912 and incorporated in Washington, D.C., in 1915, it was chartered by the Congress of the United States in 1950.

Be a Leader

If you can spare the time, you can become a Girl Scout Leader or Assistant Leader. Helpers wanted, too.

To find out more, just mail the coupon below. You will receive by mail, and without obligation, a 50-page, illustrated magazine entitled: "Girl Scout Leader." This magazine tells you about adults in Girl Scouting today. Send for it now.

— — — — — — — — — —

Girl Scouts of the U.S.A.
830 Third Avenue
New York, N.Y. 10022

Without obligation, please send me free literature telling how I can become a Girl Scout Leader, Assistant or Helper.

Name

Address

City_____State____Zip____

Telephone

Wanted Girl Scout Leaders

Assistants Wanted, Too.

Thousands of men and women have brightened their lives as well as the lives of others by becoming Girl Scout Leaders.

The Girl Scouts of the U.S.A. is open to all girls 7 through 17 who subscribe to its ideals as expressed in the Girl Scout Promise and Law. Founded in 1912 and incorporated in Washington, D.C., in 1915, it was chartered by the Congress of the United States in 1950.

If you can spare the time, you can become a Girl Scout Leader or Assistant Leader. Helpers wanted, too. Send this ad with your name and address and telephone number to Jane Underwood, Girl Scouts of the U.S.A., 830 Third Avenue, New York, N.Y. 10022. You will receive by mail, and without obligation, a 50-page, illustrated magazine entitled: "Girl Scout Leader." This magazine tells you about adults in Girl Scouting today. Send for it now.

Girl Scout Leaders Wanted

Assistants wanted, too. For information, without obligation, on how you can become a Girl Scout Leader, send this ad with your name and address and telephone number to Girl Scouts of the U.S.A., 830 Third Ave., N.Y., N.Y. 10022.

Girl Scout Leaders Wanted

Thousands of men and women have brightened their lives and the lives of others by becoming Girl Scout Leaders. Assistant Leaders and Helpers are wanted, too. For information, without obligation, on how you can become a Girl Scout Leader, send this ad with your name and address and telephone number to Girl Scouts of the U.S.A., 830 Third Avenue, New York, N.Y. 10022.

Wanted...Girl Scout Leaders
Assistant Leaders Wanted, Too.

Why be a Girl Scout Leader? Because you care about girls, and girls care about you. You want to share good things with them.

If you are a Leader, what do you do? You work with girls – little girls and big girls. You show them the many things you know. They learn from you, and you learn from them.

You have ideas. The girls have ideas. You make plans, and the girls make plans. The plans turn into action. You work on projects. You go places and see things. You have troop meetings and meetings with other Leaders. You make friends. And you receive help whenever you need it.

Thousands of men and women have brightened their lives as well as the lives of others by becoming Girl Scout Leaders.

The Girl Scouts of the U.S.A. is open to all girls 7 through 17 who subscribe to its ideals as expressed in the Girl Scout Promise and Law. Founded in 1912 and incorporated in Washington, D.C., in 1915, it was chartered by the Congress of the U.S. in 1950.

If you can spare the time, you can become a Girl Scout Leader or an Assistant Leader. Helpers are also needed.

To find out more, just mail the coupon below. You will receive by mail, and without obligation, a 50-page, illustrated magazine entitled: "Girl Scout Leader." This magazine tells you about adults in Girl Scouting today. Send for it now.

— — — — — — — — — —

Girl Scouts of the U.S.A.
830 Third Avenue
New York, N.Y. 10022

Without obligation, please send me free literature telling how I can become a Girl Scout Leader, Assistant or Helper.

Name

Address

City_____State____Zip____

Telephone

How to Prepare an Ad in Various Sizes

First you should write the full-length version of the ad. Then make some cuts such as omitting paragraphs, subheads, and coupon. Then reduce the copy to the essentials. Then cut the copy to 40 or 50 words. In the above example, a ten-inch, single column ad has been reduced, step by step, to a single inch.

page 4   page 1

center spread

Featuring Important Words

This ad is a 4-page insert in *TV Guide*. Notice how the words in big print convey a quick message to glancers. If the message is meaningful, some of the glancers will be converted into readers. Care should be taken in selecting words to be featured. The featured words must get attention and create desire to read more.

WHY WALL STREET JOURNAL READERS LIVE BETTER

By a Subscriber

I work in a large city. Over a period of time I noticed that men who read The Wall Street Journal are better dressed, drive better cars, have better homes and eat in better restaurants.

I said to myself, "Which came first, the hen or the egg? Do they read The Journal because they have more money, or do they have more money because they read The Journal?"

I started asking discreet questions. I found that it works both ways. Men who are well off have to have the information in The Journal. And average fellows like me can actually win advancement and build up increased incomes by reading The Journal. How do I know? Because not long ago I subscribed to The Wall Street Journal and it has put me ahead already.

This story is typical. Because the reports in The Wall Street Journal come to you daily, you get quick warning of any new trend that may affect your income. You get the facts in time to protect your interests or seize a profit. The Journal is a wonderful aid to salaried men making $7,500 to $30,000 a year. It is valuable to owners of small business concerns. It can be of priceless benefit to ambitious young men.

The Wall Street Journal is the complete business DAILY. Has largest staff of writers on business and finance. The only business paper served by all three big press associations. It costs $24 a year, but you can get a Trial Subscription for three months for $7. Just tear out this ad and attach check for $7 and mail. Or tell us to bill you.   NYT 0-00

Address: The Wall Street Journal, 44 Broad St., New York 4, N. Y.

This Ad Needs No Logotype

When you mention the name of the product in the headline, you do not need to repeat the name in the form of a logotype at the bottom of the ad. The above ad layout has two advantages. The headline conveys a sales message to glancers who read only headlines. The ad looks like a news item. This increases readership of the copy.

SIMULATED SITUATION BASED ON ACTUAL INCIDENT.

"Dear American Tourister: You saved my life."

On October 20, 1969, Charles Pendley and his American Tourister were hit by a car going 40 miles an hour.

Luckily for Mr. Pendley, the American Tourister absorbed the force of the blow. If it hadn't, the doctor later told him, he probably wouldn't be alive.

Mr. Pendley suffered a broken wrist. The American Tourister suffered some too. But the locks, which weren't even locked, stayed shut. Nothing inside (including a bottle of after-shave lotion and a camera) got hurt.

Now, while we don't build an American Tourister to withstand things like speeding cars and onrushing trains, we do build an American Tourister well.

We mold every piece out of sixteen different strong materials, and wrap it all up with a tough stainless steel frame. Instead of putting reinforcement at the corners, we reinforce it with fiberglass all over. We give each bag nonspring locks, designed not to spring open on impact.

Maybe American Tourister can't promise to save your life. But think what we do to save your underwear.

How to Get Attention

This dramatic photo gets attention and arouses curiosity. The reader wants to know more. So he reads the copy: "Charles Pendley and his American Tourister were hit by a car going 40 miles an hour. The American Tourister absorbed the force of the blow. If it hadn't, the doctor later told him, he probably wouldn't be alive." The rest of the copy is a sales talk for the sturdily built American Tourister travel case. Under the picture, in tiny type, is this line: "Simulated situation based on actual incident."

16

How to Make Small Ads Pay

One of my earliest discoveries in mail order advertising was that dif ferent products have different space size requirements.

For example, a reducing belt was sold at a profit by using smal. mail order ads (60 lines by single column) with the headline FAT MEN. The illustration showed a fat man being pulled in at the midsection by a broad belt around his waist. When full-page ads were used to advertise this product, the selling cost was increased. In other words, the full-page ads did not bring in enough extra orders to pay for the extra space.

On the other hand, a treatment for growing hair was sold profitably by mail order by using full-page magazine ads. We tested some 60-line ads for this product, but these small ads failed to bring in enough mail order sales to make a profit.

What is the reason for this situation? The copy chief of the agency that handled this advertising said:

> The small ads worked well in the case of the reducing belt because a reducing belt is easy to explain. A picture of a man being pulled in at the waistline and a few lines of copy are all that is needed to make clear how the product works. On the other hand, there is a lot of skepticism in men's minds regarding hair growing treatments. It requires a long, scientific explanation to make clear how the product works and a lot of testimonials from satisfied customers to prove that the treatment really does work. Therefore, full-page ads are required. A small ad does not give you enough room to do a convincing selling job for a hair growing treatment.

A third class of products are those that can be sold profitably in both small- and large-size ads. For example, in writing mail order ads for the U.S. School of Music Correspondence Course, we found that various sizes of space were profitable, from full pages down to one-inch, single-column ads.

In considering the question of whether to use small ads or large ads, there are arguments for and against both. There are limitations of small ads and there are also advantages. You should bear in mind the limitations and advantages listed below:

Ten Limitations of Small Ads

1. Small ads don't impress your dealers as much as large ads.
2. You can't include a long list of names and addresses of your dealers.
3. You can't use color in small ads. It would be too expensive.
4. You can't show an appetite-arousing picture of a lemon pie or a chocolate cake.
5. You can't create a large volume of sales quickly.
6. You can't create the impression of importance or bigness as well as you can with large ads.
7. You can't show a landscape picture or a family group admiring the new living room furniture.
8. You can't show an effective picture of your new model car or refrigerator.
9. You can't use certain effective editorial techniques, such as comic strips or ads that look like magazine articles.
10. You can't get the best positions for your small ads in magazines or in newspapers.

Ten Advantages of Small Ads

1. You can run a whole series of small ads for the price of a single full page. Thus, small ads enable you to advertise frequently at low cost.
2. If you make a variety of products, you can feature a different product in each ad in a series of small ads.
3. If your product has a variety of uses, you can feature different uses in different ads.
4. Instead of running a series of pages in a single publication, you can advertise in six or more publications by using small ads.
5. You can gain flexibility by putting part of your appropriation into big ads and part into small ads.

6. You can offer free booklets, literature, samples, and catalogues. You can make mail order sales.
7. You can get leads for salesmen.
8. In newspapers you can get special paid position, such as running your wedding ring ad alongside the engagement notices, your baby carriage ad alongside the birth notices.
9. You can get high readership by using such editorial techniques as small cartoons, news items and picture-caption ads.
10. You can profitably advertise so-called limited-market products or services as illustrated by headlines such as these: Accounting, Corns, Drafting, False Teeth, Feet Hurt, Hearing Aids, Kill Rats, Loans, Maternity Dresses, Shorthand, Stenotype, Toothache. The reason is this: There is not enough profit in corn remedies, for example, to support full-page ads. Furthermore, if the reader of a publication does not have a corn, your full-page ad, no matter how attractive, will not sell him a corn remedy. On the other hand, if the reader does have a corn that is bothering him, he will be stopped by the one-word headline, Corns, in a small ad. Since you cannot predict when the reader's corns will be troublesome, you are better off with a small ad in every issue of a publication than with a big ad once in a while.

Suggestions for Making Small Ads Pay

Use telegraphic language, as if you were sending a cablegram and you had to pay fifty cents a word. For example, the sentence, "We will be glad to mail you a copy of our free booklet on request," can be condensed to two words, "Free Booklet." Sometimes a single word "Booklet" is used. A classified ad describing farms for sale ended with the terse offer, "Bklt."

One way to produce a good small ad is to take a big ad and boil down the copy. Cut out the introduction. Cut out the sentences with the least selling power. Omit all unnecessary words. Use short words in place of long words. This is often done with mail order ads. By the time a page ad is cut down to a half-column there is not an ounce of fat left in the ad. It is all bone and muscle, and it frequently pulls several times its weight in sales.

But suppose you don't have a big ad to cut down. Then write a long piece of copy today and cut it down tomorrow.

Headlines of Small Ads

If you can find a one-word headline that will attract the right prospects, such as "Accounting," "Deaf," or "Loans," it will probably be your best headline. The reason is because it can be set in big type without taking up much room. However, never feature a meaningless word such as "If" or "Because" just in order to get a one-word headline. It is more important for your headline to mean something than it is for it to be brief. If your product doesn't lend itself to a one-word stopper headline, try to write a headline in two, three, or five words.

Good phrases to use in small ad copy are those that condense a lot of meaning into brief space. Examples:

$100 a Week	Anybody Can Learn
Learn in 6 Weeks	Amaze Your Friends
Our 36th Year	Money Back if Not Delighted
Since 1893	Equipment Included
New	100,000 Users
Fun-packed	Trial Plan
Now You Can	Test Yourself
15 Minutes a Day	Free 48-page Book
Mrs. E. C. Made $65	No Obligation
No Special Talent Needed	Send No Money
Age No Obstacle	Write TODAY

Illustrations for Small Ads

Question: Should you use an illustration? If you are using a cartoon ad or a picture-caption ad, your ad will be mostly illustration. However, in the standard type of ad, an illustration should be weighed carefully before using. *Reason*: You can put a whale of a lot of selling copy into the space usually occupied by an illustration. If a picture is needed to show the product or to make clear the use of the product, put it in. If the illustration is appropriate and compact, such as the head of a nurse for a course in nursing, put it in. Otherwise omit the illustration to make the ad smaller or to allow more room for copy.

Ad Style vs. Editorial Style

There are two opposite techniques you can use to prepare small ads. You can use either one, but not both at the same time. Technique Number One is to make your ad look like an ad. Use all the ad man's tricks—stopper headline, long copy, small print, jam-packed layout. But use these tricks so effectively that prospects will be stopped and sold in spite of the fact it is obviously an ad.

Technique Number Two is to make your ad look like editorial material, such as a cartoon or a picture-caption item, or like a news item. This technique will get you a higher readership rating. But you have to omit all your standard ad tricks such as one-word headlines or coupons. If you use ad tricks in an editorial ad, you will simply be telling people, "This is an ad." You will let the cat out of the bag before the cat is in the bag.

Checking Results from Small Ads

Key your ads by telling readers to write to a certain department number to obtain a booklet or sample, or offer to sell the product by mail at full price. By keying your ads, you can tell which ads, which publications, and which seasons of the year are most resultful for you. Then after a while you can stop spending money on the less successful ads and spend that money running your best ads in the most responsive publications.

Test Your Ads

Prepare several different ads and run them with a keyed offer in one of the publications on your list in order to find out which ad brings the most replies. Better still, do a split-run test so that two ads can be tested on the same day, under identical conditions. Newspapers in many cities offer split-run testing. Some magazines offer split-run testing, for example, *TV Guide*. See chapter 18 for a detailed explanation of split-run testing.

One final word: Publications and agencies should not fear that the use of small ads will reduce advertising appropriations. You can spend just as much on small ads as on large ads. You simply run the small ads more often and in more publications. One advertiser who recently shifted to small ads said, "These little ads are making our sales go up faster than the big ads did. If this continues, we will be able to spend more money on advertising."

Small ads enable small concerns to advertise who otherwise could not afford to advertise at all. These small advertisers sometimes become big advertisers.

So do not underestimate the power of small ads. Remember that David slew Goliath with a small pebble. Two speeches were made at Gettysburg, but the short one was remembered longer.

Getting Results from Classified Ads

All over the U.S. in the classified ad departments of newspapers, men and women ad takers sit at telephones and write insertion orders for ads that come in by phone. Sometimes an advertiser will specify that his ad is to run three times or five times, thereby earning a lower rate. And sometimes an advertiser will telephone and cancel the ad after one or two appearances because the merchandise, or whatever, has been sold. It is then that the ad takers get stories of the results produced by classified ads. These result stories are often published in the papers.

For example, here is a classified ad that ran in *The New York Times*:

```
         PARTNER WANTED
I have just obtained the exciting MRS.
AMERICA FRANCHISE for N.J. Already
showing extraordinary potential income. My
partner could not raise his $10,000. Can
YOU? Mr. Richard Stockton at Mrs. America
Headquarters will handle interviews. Phone
NYC 212 MU 2-9160
```

Regarding this ad *The Times* reported the results as follows:

The advertisement for Mrs. America Productions, Inc.—a firm that produces pageants and license rights to the Mrs. America name in each state—appeared in the "Business Opportunities" columns of *The New York Times*. Only two days after it ran—even before a contract was signed—the advertiser had the $10,000 he had asked for.

Here are result stories that were published by newspapers in other cities:

A man who ran a "House for Sale" ad in the Baltimore News-American said: "I had a full house. Over 40 prospects called."

A sailboat owner ran this ad in the *Philadelphia Bulletin:* "PENGUIN with trailer. Exc. cond. $50." ..."I was swamped with offers," he said.

A Norfolk woman ran this ad in the *Virginian-Pilot:* "Seven months old male, half German Shepherd, all shots, Va. license, rabies tag; $25." ... "Sold my dog to the first person who came by," she said.

A Montana rancher ran this ad in the *Rapid City, S.D. Journal:* "Married man for year 'round job on southeastern Montana cattle ranch." The rancher said, "We had very good results—six or seven responses."

A coffee shop owner said he got 60 calls from this ad in the *Washington, D.C. Post:* "COOK—For a small downtown cafeteria, 5 days a wk., gd salary & benefits for the right man."

To promote the use of classified advertising the *Buffalo Courier Express* reprints successful ads and tells readers the results obtained and the low cost of the advertising. Examples:

"SNOW TIRES, 2 Atlas Weatherguard 815x15 on Ford wheels, used 1 season, $40 pair." ... 5 calls first day. Ad cost $1.35.

"FRANCISCAN china, Desert Rose pattern, matching crystal, service for 8. Bargain price." ... 22 calls first day. Ad cost $1.35.

"RUGS, 1 each: 14x12 and 9x15. Reasonable." ... 15 calls first day. Ad cost 90¢.

The *Baltimore News American* promoted the use of tiny classified ads using abbreviated copy and occupying only a single line of space in the newspaper. The paper reported that all of the following ads were successful.

BIKE—Boys, 24" $10.
PIANO—Upright, rea.
WIG—Champagne beige, $20.
14' Boat, trailer. $40.

Classified advertising has a long history of success. Today this form of communication is bigger than ever. A recent issue of the daily *New York Times* carried 18 pages of classified ads; and on Sunday over 100 pages. Another stronghold of classified ads is the *Los Angeles Times*. A newspaper man figured that it would take an average reader more than twenty-four hours to read all the classified ads in a single daily issue of that paper.

Classified advertising offers the advantages of low cost, flexibility, and selectivity. You can run your ad in the city where your prospects are located and you can run it under the classified heading that selects the buyers of your product or service.

The prosperity of every country in the world is directly in relation to the amount of advertising.

Col. Robert R. McCormick

A Formula for Writing a Successful Small Ad

Shown here are four small mail order ads that have been repeated again and again. Notice how simple and direct they are. Here is their formula: The picture shows the product, and the headline tells what the product does for you. The picture-headline technique has been used successfully for many years. This method will not fit all goods and services, but it is effective in cases where it does fit.

Note the hail marks which have caused minor skin blemishes on some of these apples. These are proof of their growth at a high mountain altitude, where the sudden chills from hail storms help firm the flesh and develop the natural fruit sugars which give these apples their incomparable flavor.

This Ad Saved a Crop

Jim Young, a member of the Copywriters Hall of Fame, and part-time apple grower, named this ad his favorite. He said: "A few years ago there was a hail storm just before harvest. I had thousands of mail orders and checks, and almost every apple hail-pocked. Problem: Should I send the checks back—or risk dissatisfied customers? Actually these apples were damaged only in appearance. They were better eating than ever. Cold weather, when apples are ripening, improves their flavor. So I filled the orders. In every carton I put a printed card [shown above]. Not one customer complained. Next year I received orders which said: 'Hail-marked apples, if available; otherwise the ordinary kind.' "

How to Increase Magazine Circulation

Here is an effective way to increase magazine newsstand sales. Run small newspaper ads in which each ad features a popular article. The four ads shown here all feature articles contained in a single issue of *Reader's Digest*—in this case, a May issue. These ads, which look like news items, were repeated again and again in newspapers during the period when the May issue was on sale.

SAVE ONE GALLON OF GAS IN EVERY TEN

Sluggish motors get a new lease on life with Wynn's Friction Proofing Oil. This new chemical compound added to your present brand of motor oil every 1000 miles, bonds a super-slick surface to engine parts. This virtually eliminates the friction drag that wastes up to half your car's power, and gives you so much extra mileage from gasoline that it's like getting one gallon free with every ten you buy. Besides paying for itself in gasoline savings, Wynn's cuts carbon and sludge, frees sticky valves. reduces wear and repairs. Try Wynn's for new pep, power, economy from your car. We're so sure you'll continue to use it that we make this special introductory offer of a regular 1000-mile size 95¢ can of Wynn's for only 10¢. Just send your name and address, enclosing 10¢ in coin or stamps. By return mail you'll get a certificate entitling you to a 95¢ can of Wynn's without additional charge at any Wynn dealer. Limit one. Offer expires April 30. Write today—Wynn Oil Company, Dept. C-12, Azusa, California.

AT SERVICE STATIONS, GARAGES, NEW CAR DEALERS

CAR OWNERS! SAVE ONE GALLON OF GAS IN EVERY TEN

Sluggish motors get a new lease on life with Wynn's Friction Proofing Oil. This new chemical compound added to your present brand of motor oil every 1000 miles, bonds a super-slick surface to engine parts. This virtually eliminates the friction drag that wastes up to half your car's power, and gives you so much extra mileage from gasoline that it's like getting one gallon free with every ten you buy. Besides paying for itself in gasoline savings, Wynn's cuts carbon and sludge, frees sticky valves. reduces wear and repairs. Try Wynn's for new pep, power, economy from your car. We're so sure you'll continue to use it that we make this special introductory offer of a regular 1000-mile size 95¢ can of Wynn's for only 10¢. Just send your name and address, enclosing 10¢ in coin or stamps. By return mail you'll get a certificate entitling you to a 95¢ can of Wynn's without additional charge at any Wynn dealer. Limit one. Offer expires April 30. Write today—Wynn Oil Company, Dept. C-12, Azusa, California.

AT SERVICE STATIONS, GARAGES, NEW CAR DEALERS

How Two Words Added 20% to Pulling Power

Here are two ads for a gasoline additive. Each offers a sample of the product. The ads are identical except that one contains the words "Car Owners" in the headline. The ads were split-run tested in newspapers. The ad beginning with the words "Car Owners" pulled 20% more responses than the other. This experience is typical. Words that select prospects often add pulling power. Examples: Boys, Girls, Young Men, Students, Teachers, Fat Men, Wine Lovers, Home Owners, Mothers, Brides, Sportsmen, Dog Owners.

"Imagine him threatening to knock my block off if I didn't use enough Angostura* in his Old Fashioned!"

*Angostura sharpens your taste so that your Old Fashioned seems zestier and richer It does the same for your favorite cola drink, too! Use 5 or 6 dashes for a "Navy cola."

I said "DON'T FORGET THE ANGOSTURA* IN MY MANHATTAN!"

MAKES BETTER DRINKS

*Everyone knows how Angostura rounds-out the taste of a Manhattan! But do you know how frequently fine chefs use Angostura on roasts and other meat dishes for extra-piquant flavor?

"Notice how mad he was when I forgot Angostura* in his Manhattan?"

AROMATIC BITTERS

MAKES BETTER DRINKS

*It's the zesty tang of Angostura that gives a lift and a lilt to Manhattans. But don't overlook Angostura's spicy contribution to soups, salads and desserts!

A Famous Cartoon Series

Not everybody should try to write cartoon ads. Success in this endeavor requires the happy combination of two rare talents—a writer with a keen sense of humor and an artist who can draw genuinely funny pictures. These ads for Angostura Bitters are typical of a famous series that got high readership and a reported increase of 42% in sales in six months.

sea story

We probably shouldn't be telling this story because it isn't very dignified. But it's true and we can't resist it.

A man came into our Murray Street store some time back and asked to see a suit in a rather old-fashioned pattern that was no longer in stock. We suggested that he might like to see some of the newer patterns and he was more than agreeable. He said, in fact, that he would take *any* Hart Schaffner & Marx suit in the store. When the fitting was completed the Wallachs salesman asked him why he had shown so little interest in the model and so much concern with the label.

"Well, it's like this," he answered. "My ship is docked down the street. Just got in. We sailors are not always what you might call careful with our money. Sometimes we're flush. Sometimes we're flat and need cash. It's a well-known fact that there is only one suit of clothes that you can hock in any port in the world and that's a Hart Schaffner & Marx."

That's what the man said. We trust you will never have reason to prove the truth of his statement.

One of a Famous Series

The purpose of this series of editorial-style ads is to make friends for Wallachs' chain of men's-wear stores in and around New York City. The campaign started in 1948 in New York newspapers and has been running ever since. Said copywriter Leslie Pearl, the originator and author of the series: "The ads that get the most comment are those based on incidents that happen in the stores. These little stories are contributed by Wallach's salesmen. They sound true because they are true."

How to give
QUICK REST
to tired eyes
MAKE THIS SIMPLE TEST TODAY

EYES OVERWORKED? Put two drops of gentle, safe Murine in each eye. Then feel that refreshing, soothing sensation that comes instantly. You get—

QUICK RELIEF from the discomfort of tired eyes. Murine's seven important ingredients are scientifically blended to cleanse and refresh overworked, tired eyes. Use Murine morning and night and whenever your eyes tell you to.

MURINE
FOR YOUR EYES

A series of copy tests for Murine determined the best appeals and the most effective headlines and layouts. As a result of a campaign of frequently repeated small ads, Murine became the best-selling eye preparation in the U.S.

DU PONT SPONGES are soft when wet—hold lots of water—float in the pan—can be sterilized by boiling. They're excellent for washing dishes, windows, walls, autos . . . and bath.

Guaranteed by Good Housekeeping

Better Things for Better Living . . . Through Chemistry

DU PONT SPONGES

The various uses of Du Pont sponges have been popularized by means of small ads, each featuring a different use.

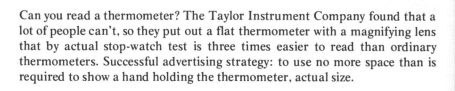

Can you read a thermometer? The Taylor Instrument Company found that a lot of people can't, so they put out a flat thermometer with a magnifying lens that by actual stop-watch test is three times easier to read than ordinary thermometers. Successful advertising strategy: to use no more space than is required to show a hand holding the thermometer, actual size.

It pays to do business in New York State!

World's richest markets in your own backyard. New York State's retail market totals 14,750,000 people, who earn $27,107,000,000 annually, and have accumulated savings of $28,691,000,000. Industry-wise, the Empire State has 59,400 factories which produce each year goods valued at over 20 billion dollars. A New York State location for your business puts you in the center of this concentration of buying power. For full market data, write: N. Y. State Dept. of Commerce, Room 134, 112 State St., Albany 7, New York.

FREE SKI GUIDE

Complete data on 58 New York State ski centers . . . vertical drop and length of trails and slopes . . . locations and rates of all ski tows . . . detailed maps to help you get there. Just mail a postcard requesting SKI NEW YORK to New York State Dept. of Commerce, room 3-2, 112 State St., Albany 7, N.Y.

This Free Ski Guide offer ran only 13 times in New York City newspapers; it produced 6,146 replies.

This ad is one of a "family" that ran in every issue of a sizable list of business magazines to help mold top management opinion for the New York State Department of Commerce. Each headline stated the basic theme of the campaign. The supporting facts in the text were varied from ad to ad.

In addition to promoting the Gold Bond line in large space, the National Gypsum Company wanted to make a special appeal to men who like to do remodeling work themselves. Small-space ads that were run in *Popular Mechanics, Popular Science*, and other men's and farm magazines brought an unusually high response.

MAKES FALSE TEETH FIT

for the life of your plates

EASY TO USE STRIPS

If your plates are loose and slip or hurt, refit them for instant, permanent comfort with soft Plasti-Liner strips. Lay strip on upper or lower plate...bite and it molds perfectly. *Hardens for lasting fit and comfort.* Even on old rubber plates Plasti-Liner gives you good results six months to a year or longer. Ends forever mess and bother of temporary applications that last a few hours or days. Stops slipping, rocking plates and sore gums. Eat anything. Talk freely. Enjoy the comfort thousands of people all over the country now get with Plasti-Liner.

Easy to Re-fit or Tighten False Teeth Permanently
Tasteless, odorless, harmless to you and your plates. Can be removed as per directions. Users say: *"Now I can eat anything."* Satisfaction guaranteed or your money back.

SEND NO MONEY Just order a $2.25 package of PLASTI-LINER to reline both upper and lower plates, or $1.25 to reline one plate. Deposit money with your postman when he delivers. **Or send the money now, and save C. O. D. charges.** Generous sample of special plate cleaner supplied free.

PLASTI-LINER COMPANY, 1740 Bailey Avenue Buffalo 11, N. Y., Dept. OOO

BRIMMS PLASTI-LINER

If you have artificial dentures and they bother you, a full-page ad in four colors is not necessary to get you to read about something that promises relief. The words "False Teeth" or a picture of false teeth will leap out at you from a small space ad.

Frequent small-space ads are ideal for a company manufacturing many thousands of small products. Dennison's paper and other specialties have thus been able to appear in over fifty magazines, with excellent trade and consumer response.

NEXT 90 DAYS CAN CHANGE YOUR LIFE

A Warning from
The Wall Street Journal

You are living in a period of rapid changes. The next 90 days will be filled with opportunities and dangers.

Fortune will smile on some men. Disaster will dog the footsteps of others.

Because reports in The Wall Street Journal come to you DAILY, you get fastest possible warning of any new trend affecting your business and personal income. You get facts in time to protect your interests or seize a profit.

If you think The Journal is just for millionaires, you are WRONG! It is a wonderful aid to salaried men making $7,500 to $25,000 a year. It is valuable to owners of small businesses. Read it 90 days and see what it can do for YOU.

To assure speedy delivery to you anywhere in the U.S., The Journal is printed daily in seven cities from coast to coast. It costs $24 a year, but in order to acquaint you with The Journal, we make this offer: You can get a Trial Subscription for 3 months for $7. Just send this ad with check for $7. Or tell us to bill you. Address: The Wall Street Journal, 44 Broad Street, New York 4, New York.

TM-10-12

Also provides permanent chain link protection for children and property.

● **EASY TERMS**

● **EXPERT ERECTION SERVICE**

Cyclone is the trade-mark name of fence made only by Cyclone Fence Division. Accept no substitute.

For Free Estimate
CYCLONE FENCE DIVISION

NO JOB TOO LARGE — NO JOB TOO SMALL FOR CYCLONE

Note the key number "TM-10-12" at the bottom of this advertisement. This means that the ad appeared in *Time* magazine, October 12th issue. Note also the line in the last paragraph, "Just send this ad with check for $7." Each ad in this series carried an identifying key number. The traceable sales from these ads were tabulated. Thus it was possible to discover just which advertisements produced the most sales and which publications were most resultful.

Residential Cyclone Fence is a high-cost purchase. The market is limited, compared with that for many consumer items bought daily in retail stores. Therefore, no large budget for local advertising is practical. For fifteen years small newspaper ads like this one (with the local dealer's address filled in) proved successful on the garden page or building page of Sunday newspapers.

17

Ten Brain Teasers

Twenty tested advertisements are described in this chapter. Ten were successful in getting sales. Ten were unsuccessful. See if you can pick the successes. Correct answers can be found on pages 251-253.

Imagine for the next ten minutes that you are the creative director of an advertising agency specializing in tested advertising. Your agency has ten accounts, and each account needs new copy. You have called your copy staff into conference and you have asked them to submit ideas. You have received twenty advertising suggestions— two on each account. It is now up to you to decide which ideas you will use and which you will discard.

The twenty suggestions are arranged in pairs below. Each pair consists of a success and a failure. Headline, illustration, and offer are included in every case. Where it is not obvious, the copy plot is explained.

Out of each pair of suggestions, you are to check mentally the one suggestion you believe would bring the best results. Then turn to pages 251-253 where the headlines of the successful advertisements are listed, and see how many you got right.

There are no catch questions in this test—no large displays of the word "Free." No extra prominence has been given to the offer in one advertisement and not to the other. Each pair of advertisements was tested in magazines or newspapers under conditions as nearly similar as possible. The inquiries were followed up by direct mail or by a salesman's call. The pulling power or lack of pulling power of each advertisement rests mainly on its headline and illustration.

Bear in mind also that in every case the pulling power of the two advertisements differed, not by a narrow margin, but by a wide margin. The advertisements that failed were bad failures. They were used only once. The advertisements that were successful were highly successful. They were repeated again and again before their effectiveness wore out.

(1) SUGGESTIONS FOR ADVERTISING A HOME-STUDY COURSE IN BUSINESS

Suggestion Number One

Illustration: [No illustration]

Headline: To a $15,000 man who would like to be making $25,000

Offer: Free booklet: "What an Executive Should Know."

Suggestion Number Two

Illustration:

Picture of man reading booklet

Headline: Here's proof that this training pays financially

Offer: Free booklet: "What an Executive Should Know."

(2) SUGGESTIONS FOR ADVERTISING A HAIR-GROWING REMEDY

Suggestion Number One

Illustration:

> Man pointing his finger at another man's bald head

Headline: "60 days ago they called me 'Baldy' "

Copy Plot: The copy tells the story of a man who got excellent results from the hair-growing remedy.

Offer: Free book, "The New Way to Grow Hair."

Suggestion Number Two

Illustration:

> Hair specialist offering a bank check to the reader

Headline: If I can't grow hair for you in 30 days you get this check

Copy Plot: The copy explains that the check you get is your money back refund in case you are not satisfied with the results from the hair-growing treatments.

Offer: Free book, "The New Way to Grow Hair."

(3) SUGGESTIONS FOR ADVERTISING
LIFE INSURANCE

Suggestion Number One

Illustration:

Picture of man and wife

Headline: Here's one question you shouldn't ask your wife

Copy Plot: "I want to talk It over with my wife," is what some men say when a salesman urges them to buy life insurance. This is wrong. A husband should buy life insurance without asking his wife.

Offer: Free book: "How to Get the Things You Want."

Suggestion Number Two

Illustration:

Miniature picture of family standing at one end of a life insurance policy; miniature picture of home at other end of policy

Headline: Get rid of money worries for good

Copy Plot: This life insurance plan can provide money to take care of a man's family, pay off a mortgage, and pay a disability income if needed.

Offer: Free book: "How to Get the Things You Want."

(4) SUGGESTIONS FOR ADVERTISING A COURSE IN PIANO INSTRUCTION

Suggestion Number One

Illustration:

```
Picture of man playing piano
```

Headline: "A few months ago I couldn't play a note"

Offer: Free book: "Music Lessons in Your Own Home."

Suggestion Number Two

Illustration:

```
Picture of group of people playing musical
instruments. Panel shows method of in-
struction and displays the words "Easy as A B
C"
```

Headline: Here's a strange way to learn music

Offer: Free book: "Music Lessons in Your Own Home."

(5) SUGGESTIONS FOR ADVERTISING A RETIREMENT INCOME PLAN

Suggestion Number One

Illustration:

Picture of happy couple starting on an automobile trip

Headline: A vacation that lasts the rest of your life

Offer: Free booklet: "Retirement Income Plan."

Suggestion Number Two

Illustration: [No illustration]

Headline: How you can retire on a guaranteed income for life

Offer: Free booklet: "Retirement Income Plan."

(6) SUGGESTIONS FOR ADVERTISING THE WALL STREET JOURNAL

Suggestion Number One

Illustration: [No illustration]

Headline: "How $7 started me on the road to $20,000 a year"

Copy Plot: The story of a man who sent $7 for a trial subscription to *The Wall Street Journal.* Later he became a regular subscriber. Reading the *Journal* helped him get an income of $20,000.

Offer: Send $7 for a trial subscription.'

Suggestion Number Two

Illustration: [No illustration]

Headline: Some $20,000 jobs are looking for applicants

Copy Plot: There are a number of jobs paying $20,000 or more that are available to trained men. Reading *The Wall Street Journal* will help you train for one of these jobs.

Offer: Send $7 for a trial subscription.

(7) SUGGESTIONS FOR ADVERTISING A WEEKLY BOOK REVIEW MAGAZINE

Suggestion Number One

Illustration:

Group of men and women chatting in living room

Headline: This fascinating literary circle now open to you

Copy Plot: This magazine keeps you up to date on the latest books.

Offer: Send for a free copy of the magazine.

Suggestion Number Two

Illustration:

Photograph of famous contributor to the Book Review Magazine

Headline: Can you talk about books with the rest of them?

Copy Plot: This magazine keeps you up to date on the latest books.

Offer: Send for a free copy of the magazine.

(8) SUGGESTIONS FOR ADVERTISING A COURSE IN DANCING

Suggestion Number One

Illustration:

Picture of dancing instructor dancing with young lady

Headline: Why good dancers are more popular than "Walk-Arounds"

Offer: Free Test Lesson and beautifully illustrated 32-page book that tells all about Arthur Murray's course in dancing.

Suggestion Number Two

Illustration:

Picture of couple dancing with masks on at a masquerade

Headline: "How a *faux pas* made me popular"

Copy Plot: A story about a young man who is embarrassed by his poor dancing. He takes the course in dancing and soon becomes popular.

Offer: Free Test Lesson and beautifully illustrated 32-page book that tells all about Arthur Murray's course in dancing.

(9) SUGGESTIONS FOR ADVERTISING A COURSE
OF TREATMENTS FOR PEOPLE WITH
NERVOUS AILMENTS

Suggestion Number One

Illustration:

> Panel containing list of symptoms of nervous
> troubles

Headline: Thousands suffer from sick nerves and don't
know it

Offer: Please send me a copy of your book, "New
Nerves for Old." I am enclosing 25 cents in
coin or stamps.

Suggestion Number Two

Illustration:

> Photograph of nerve specialist

Headline: Have you these symptoms of nerve
exhaustion?

Offer: Please send me a copy of your book, "New
Nerves for Old." I am enclosing 25 cents in
coin or stamps.

(10) SUGGESTIONS FOR ADVERTISING A SET OF BOOKS CONTAINING THE WORLD'S GREAT LITERATURE

Suggestion Number One

Illustration:

```
┌─────────────────────────────────────────────┐
│                                             │
│          Picture of set of books            │
│                                             │
└─────────────────────────────────────────────┘
```

Headline: How to Get Rid of an "Inferiority Complex"

Copy Plot: Reading this set of books will improve your education, and your conversation and help you in business and in social life.

Offer: Free "Guide Book" to books

Suggestion Number Two

Illustration:

```
┌─────────────────────────────────────────────┐
│                                             │
│  Picture of Joan of Arc at the siege of a walled │
│  city                                       │
└─────────────────────────────────────────────┘
```

Headline: The writings in these immortal books are as stirring as the mightiest deeds of history

Offer: Free "Guide Book" to books

Answers to Brain Teasers

Below are the headlines of the twenty keyed advertisements that were tested by actual sales response. Each headline is marked successful or unsuccessful. See how many you guessed right.

(1) (a) To a $15,000 man who would like to be making $25,000 [successful]
(b) Here's proof that this training pays financially [unsuccessful]

The headline of the successful ad is specific, mentions money twice, and contains a strong indication of increased earnings. The headline of the losing ad features the word "financially," which is not as effective as specific dollar figures.

(2) (a) "60 days ago they called me 'Baldy' " [successful]
(b) If I can't grow hair for you in 30 days you get this check [unsuccessful]

In the successful ad, the picture of the bald-headed man and the word "Baldy" selected the right audience at a glance. The copy contains evidence of results. In the losing ad, the picture does not select the audience and the headline suggests that the remedy may not work.

(3) (a) Get rid of money worries for good [successful]
(b) Here's one question you shouldn't ask your wife [unsuccessful]

The headline of the successful ad contains a promise of a benefit. The other headline is purely a curiosity headline and fails to promise a benefit.

(4) (a) Here's a strange way to learn music [successful]
(b) "A few months ago I couldn't play a note" [unsuccessful]

The successful headline promises a benefit ("learn music") and arouses curiosity with the words "strange way."

(5) (a) How you can retire on a guaranteed income for life [successful]
(b) A vacation that lasts the rest of your life [unsuccessful]

The successful headline selects the right audience and promises a benefit. The other headline lacks clarity and is misleading. It attempts to be clever by describing retirement as a vacation that lasts the rest of your life.

> (6) (a) "How $7 started me on the road to $20,000"
> [successful]
> (b) Some $20,000 jobs are looking for applicants
> [unsuccessful]

The successful headline selects the right audience and offers a specific benefit. The other headline reads like a help-wanted ad and selects the wrong audience.

> (7) (a) Can you talk about books with the rest of them?
> [successful]
> (b) This fascinating literary circle now open to you
> [unsuccessful]

The successful headline selects the right audience for a book review magazine and implies a promise—namely, that you will be able to talk about books if you read the magazine. The other headline is not entirely clear and is misleading. It suggests that you are being invited to join a literary club.

> (8) (a) "How a *faux pas* made me popular" [successful]
> (b) Why good dancers are more popular than "Walk-Arounds" [unsuccessful]

The words "made me popular" imply a promise of a benefit. The French phrase, *faux pas*, arouses curiosity, which is increased by the picture of the masked couple. The unsuccessful headline does not promise a benefit.

> (9) (a) Have you these symptoms of nerve exhaustion?
> [successful]
> (b) Thousands suffer from sick nerves and don't know it [unsuccessful]

The successful headline contains the word "you," and arouses curiosity. It also implies the promise of a remedy for nervous ailments. The other headline is simply a statement of a fact.

> (10) (a) How to Get Rid of an "Inferiority Complex"
> [successful]

(b) The writings in these immortal books are as stirring as the mightiest deeds of history [unsuccessful]

The successful headline contains a specific promise of a personal benefit.

Perhaps you scored 100 per cent correct answers on this test. If so, you are to be congratulated. You are a better judge of pulling power than some men who have spent years in advertising. Perhaps you scored 50 per cent or less. If so, don't be discouraged, because all ten of the advertisements that failed were considered good enough to test by the men working on these accounts. If the advertisements had not been considered good, no money would have been spent to test them. It is this difficulty of judging results in advance that makes advertising, as one advertising man said, "The hardest, most interesting, most exasperating, satisfying, worthwhile, and exciting business that ever engaged the talents of a group of people."

Advertising can never be an exact science, like mathematics or chemistry, but it can become more accurate and more scientific than it is today. The purpose of this book is to help make advertising more scientific. Advertising can never become completely accurate, however, because of the human element involved—in advertising you are dealing with the minds and the emotions of human beings, and these will always be, to a certain extent, unstable and unmeasurable. That is why it is necessary to test, test, test—to test copy, media, position in publications, seasonal variation, and time of day in broadcast advertising. Test everything on a small scale before you spend money on a large scale.

Mail order advertisers have learned this lesson over and over again. For example, a new mail order advertisement is prepared. The copywriter is enthusiastic about it, the copy chief thinks it is good, the account executive is sure it will pull, and the client rubs his hands in expectation of the orders he is going to get. The advertisement runs. The orders fail to come in. The experts were wrong—all wrong. Yet they have been working on mail order copy for years. They are close students of what pays and what does not pay. If anybody should be able to judge in advance the pulling power of a piece of copy, mail order men should. Yet they were all completely mistaken. It is experiences like this that teach scientific-minded advertisers to beware of theories and stick to facts.

The reverse of the above experience sometimes happens. A new advertisement runs in which few have confidence. And the orders pour in. That's what makes tested advertising one of the most exciting and challenging fields in this exciting business. The rules are hard to learn. Sometimes it seems as if there are no rules. But at least there is this one great rule:

Test everything. Doubt everything. Be interested in theories, but don't spend a large sum of money on a theory without spending a little money to test it first.

I know that half of my advertising is wasted but I do not know which half.

William Wrigley

18

Seventeen Ways to Test Your Advertising

What kind of headlines attract the most readers? What kind of pictures get the most attention? What sales appeals sell the most merchandise? What kind of copy will be most successful in persuading people to buy your product or service?

This book has given you the findings of years of experience and the results of millions of dollars spent in discovering answers to these questions. But there will always be new questions coming up. You will write new headlines and new copy. You will think up new sales appeals and new illustration ideas.

Which of your new ideas will be the most effective? There will be times when you will want to subject your ideas to some sort of testing, in order to make sure that the dollars you spend in advertising will bring the best possible results.

On the following pages there are described seventeen different kinds of advertising tests you can use. Included are detailed descriptions of certain tests that have been briefly mentioned before. Which of these tests you should select will depend on the nature of your problem and the amount of time and money you can afford to devote to testing.

1. Put your newly written ad aside until the next day

The simplest way to test a piece of advertising copy you have just written is to put it aside and read it the next day. In rereading your own copy a day later, you can approach it with a cold, analytical mind, almost as if you were an outsider reading somebody else's copy. Certain errors that were not apparent to you when you were writing with speed and enthusiasm may become clear to you as you read calmly and objectively.

Also, you may be able to improve the style of the piece you have written. You may think of short words that can replace long words. You may find unnecessary phrases that can be omitted. You may find long sentences that can be broken up into short sentences. You may find that your message can be speeded up by omitting the first paragraph. You may discover that your copy should have an action paragraph added at the end.

Your chances of producing a good ad will be improved if you will write several ads instead of just one. Your chances of finding a good headline will be increased if you will write many headlines. Then you can select the best copy and the best headline.

2. Ask somebody to read your ad copy aloud to you

Some writers test their copy by reading it aloud to another person. This method has advantages, but it is not as good a test as having another person read your copy aloud to you.

The trouble with reading your own copy to another person is that you know in advance what message you want to convey. You know what words to emphasize in order to bring out your meaning. You know how to make a long sentence sound simple by pausing at the proper places. Another reader does not know these things. He approaches your copy with a cold mind. It is up to your copy to warm him up. You can tell by his tone whether your copy has interest or emotion or humor. You can tell by the smoothness of his reading whether your copy is clear.

While the other person is reading your copy aloud, you should sit with pad and pencil and make notes. If he stumbles over a sentence, you should assume that this is your fault, not his. You should rewrite the sentence. If an idea is not clear to him, you should assume that it will not be clear to other people. You should make your idea clear or omit it.

By asking somebody else to read your copy aloud, you can get a quicker reaction to it than by putting it aside to reread yourself the next day. The reader you choose can be your boss, your spouse, your associate, your assistant, or the person in the next office.

3. Opinion test by interview

An opinion test consists of showing another person some ad layouts or a list of headlines or some samples of copy and saying, "Which do you like best?" or "Which ad would you be most likely to read?" Experiments have shown that it doesn't matter how you phrase the question.

The important thing is to give your respondent at least two things to choose from. The reason is that since most people want to please, they are likely to respond favorably to the ad. If you show just one ad and say, "Here is an ad I wrote . . . please tell me what you think of it," most people will reply, "I think it's good." This gets you nowhere. You should hand your respondent two or more ads and say, "Which do you like best?"

If you are testing a list of headlines on several people, it is good to hand each person a clean carbon copy or photocopy of the headlines and say, "Please check with pencil the headlines you like best." Don't let one person see the check marks made by another person. His judgment may be swayed in favor of a headline that other people have previously checked.

Opinion tests can be refined by talking only to prospects. You can show food ads to housewives, pipe tobacco ads to pipe smokers, dog food ads to dog owners.

Opinion tests can be extended to any degree you choose. You can interview five, ten, or twenty people. You can hire survey reporters who will show your ad layouts to a hundred people. You can conduct opinion tests in several cities.

No matter how much you refine an opinion test, you should remember that it is subject to error because it is based on opinions. It is not a sales test. In those cases where it has been possible to apply both opinion testing and sales testing to the same set of ads, it has been found that the two methods do not always obtain the same results. Here are some of the reasons for this:

1. People avoid voting for an ad that reflects discredit on themselves. For example, suppose you want to test the following appeals for toothpaste:
   a) How to avoid tooth decay
   b) How to get rid of bad breath
   The appeal "bad breath" will not win in an opinion test, but it might win in a sales test.
2. Most people believe that an ad has to have a picture in it in order to be a good ad. Therefore an all-type ad will not win in an opinion test. However an all-type ad will sometimes beat an illustrated ad in a sales test.
3. People tend to vote for so-called "clever" ads in an opinion test. However, simple ads usually beat "clever" ads in a sales test.
4. An opinion test can be upset by a split vote.

Here is how a split-vote error can occur. Suppose housewives are asked to select the better of two ad layouts, namely (1) layout with picture of a child versus (2) layout with picture of a home. Let us say that the score is 60 per cent for the child picture and 40 per cent for the home picture. *Result*: Child picture wins.

However, suppose you decide to "refine" the test by substituting two layouts with child pictures in place of one layout with a child picture because you want to try a boy picture versus a girl picture. The layout with the home picture remains the same.

You now show the housewives three layouts and ask which they like best. The 60 per cent of the housewives who previously voted for the child picture will now split their votes and you will get a result like this:

30 per cent for boy picture
30 per cent for girl picture
40 per cent for home picture

Result: Home picture wins. Note that the result of the three-way test reverses the result of the previous two-way test.

The proper way to do the above test is in two stages, as follows:

1. First you should test a home picture versus a child picture.
2. Then, in a separate set of interviews, you should test a boy picture versus a girl picture.

You may say at this point, "Why should I do an opinion test if it can sometimes produce a wrong answer?"

There are several things to consider in this regard. Here they are:

1. An opinion test is quick and easy and frequently gives you the right answer.
2. An opinion test is inexpensive.
3. Due to pressure of closing dates, an opinion test is sometimes the only testing method you will have time for.
4. Some ad men claim that only an actual sales test is worthwhile. However, even a sales test can sometimes produce a wrong answer due to hidden factors you do not know about.
5. An opinion test gives you a chance to talk to the people who are voting on your ads. You may learn things you didn't suspect. You may uncover new copy ideas you forgot to include.

The value of opinion testing can be summed up as follows: An opinion test, if properly handled, can help you get nearer to the truth although it may not always give you the absolute truth.

One company president used an opinion test as a sales device. He wanted to reach certain influential executives with his sales message so he prepared several ads and mailed sets of proofs to a list of prospects. In an accompanying letter, the president said, "Will you please look at the enclosed ads and then check on the enclosed postcard the headline of the ad you think I should run in the trade press?"

In this way, the president induced a number of his best prospects to read several of his ads even before the ads were published.

4. Mail order sales test

A national advertiser recently asked this question: "In testing ads by mail response, when should you use a coupon and when should you use a hidden offer?"

Answer: You should use a hidden offer when you don't want too many replies and when you want to avoid replies from curiosity seekers.

You should use a coupon when you want a lot of replies and when the replies are of real value to you. For example:

1. When the coupon is an order blank and represents an actual mail order sale.
2. When the coupon secures a lead for a salesman.
3. When you want to distribute a large number of booklets or samples.
4. When the coupon is a questionnaire and you want to find out the age or business position or other information about your readers.

The coupon stimulates replies as follows:

1 By calling attention to your offer.
2. By making it easy for the reader to reply.
3. By giving the reader a reminder he can tear out and put into his pocket.

Among the most frequent users of testing via coupons are the mail order advertisers who sell books, novelties, phonograph records, or other merchandise by including a coupon order form in each ad.

In the case of these advertisers, every ad is a sales test. The testing method consists of trying several different ads and then repeating over and over the ads that bring the most sales per dollar of space cost.

Mail order advertisers test not only copy, but media, various positions in media, space size, and seasonal variation.

Here are examples of some of the selling devices included in the coupons of mail order ads:

Send check or money order.
Charge my credit card.
Bill me.
Enroll me as a member.
Send me booklet, sample or catalog—free or for 10¢ or 25¢.
(Sales are made by direct mail follow-up letters.)

5. Testing ads with coupons plus calls by salesmen

Some items are too high in price to be sold via mail order coupons. For example, office machines, home improvements, life insurance policies, mutual funds, and correspondence courses. In such cases the coupons offer free literature and the prospect is called on by a salesman. Here are typical coupon offers.

Please send free book, "How to Succeed."
Without obligation, send booklet "How to Fence
   Your Home."
Send information on Life Insurance.

This plan gives you a double check on the selling power of each ad you test. First you count the number of coupons each ad produces, and second, you count the number of sales resulting from each ad.

Over a period of time, you can also determine the quality of the coupons you receive. You may find that certain publications bring higher quality leads than others. You may discover that ads featuring a free offer in the headline will bring lower quality leads than ads that subordinate the free offer.

6. Testing ads with coupons that offer samples or literature

There are many advertisers who do not wish to follow up coupon leads with a call by a salesman. For example, advertisers of beauty products, household products, drug products, or vacation trips. However, these concerns do have an interest in distributing literature or samples and in checking up on the pulling power of their copy. There are two approaches to this type of testing:

1. You can use a copy testing plan where you select a publication that is typical of your entire list of publications and pretest all

new ads in that publication. After tabulating results, you can run the best-pulling ads in your entire list of publications.

2. You can use a less specialized approach where you simply key all of your coupons and keep a record of coupon returns and cost per coupon. You can study these records from time to time in order to learn which ads and which publications are getting the highest response.

Here are sample offers taken from magazines. Note that they have a cash requirement in order to screen out curiosity seekers.

Please send free 30-day supply of vitamins. I enclose 50¢ for packing and postage.

Free ... terry-cloth apron with purchase of sponge mop. A $1.95 value, it's yours by sending a paid receipt (or sales slip) with 25¢ to cover mailing.

Enclosed is 25¢ for custom-made drapery swatches and directions for measuring.

Here are some typical offers of literature. Some have a cash requirement and some are free.

Send for Free Vacation Guide.

Free! Travel Planning Map of America.

Please send your book, "How to Build a Flexboard Garage."
I enclose 25¢ in coin.

Enclosed is 25¢ for my copy of "Planning and Decorating Your Dream Bathroom."

7. Testing ads with hidden offers

Question: When should you test your copy with a hidden offer instead of featuring your offer in a coupon?

Answer: (1) When you do not want too many replies, and (2) When you want to avoid replies from professional coupon-clippers.

The first matter to be decided when you are going to test a series of ads is what offer to use. One advertiser said, "I'd like to test my copy, but I don't know what to offer."

The fact is that on almost all propositions you can use one of the following offers:

1. A sample of the product.
2. A booklet about the product or service.

On certain propositions it is difficult to get sufficient replies. On others, it is so easy to get replies that you have to take steps to reduce their number.

Hard-to-Get Replies

An advertising agency copywriter wanted to test a lot of different selling appeals for a headache remedy. He put together some small all-type ads measuring 75 lines by two columns. Each appeal to be tested was featured in the headline of one of these ads. For example:

Ad No. 1. Quick Relief for Nervous Headache
Ad No. 2. Why Thousands Use this Headache Remedy

The agency man wanted to get at least a hundred replies from each test ad. Experience shows that a hundred replies is about right. If you average only ten replies per test ad, the results may not be dependable. On the other hand, if you average a thousand replies per test ad, you may find that the cost of mailing out samples is unnecessarily high.

The ad manager was dubious about including an offer of a free bottle of the headache remedy. He said, "We may be swamped with requests for free bottles. Let's offer a free booklet instead."

The agency man preferred to offer a sample of the product so that the test would approach the characteristics of an actual sales test. He prevailed on the ad manager to permit a test of a low-pressure offer in a single ad. The pulling power of the offer was reduced in three ways as follows:

1. Instead of offering a full-size bottle, the ad offered a sample bottle.
2. Instead of offering the sample bottle free, the copy required the reader to send 25¢.
3. The offer was completely hidden in the last paragraph of the copy. There was no subhead featuring the offer.

An all-type ad containing this offer was run in a single newspaper with half a million circulation. The copywriter waited nervously for results. He feared that his client, the ad manager, would be annoyed if the ad brought too many replies.
Result: The ad brought only two replies.

The next step was to run an ad containing the following offer: "Just tear out this ad and send it with your name and address and we will mail you a regular 35¢ size bottle absolutely FREE." *Result*: The ad brought slightly over a hundred replies, which was about the amount desired. The ad agency then proceeded to run other ads with different headlines in order to test the comparative pulling power of various sales appeals.

Regarding this test, one man said: "Hidden offers of food samples or soap samples sometimes pull hundreds or even thousands of replies. Why is it so difficult to get people to write for a headache remedy?"

Answer: A headache remedy appeals to a narrower audience than an offer of food or soap. Also, if a man does not have a headache, he may not bother to read a headache ad. And if he does have a headache, he will probably go to a drugstore and buy a remedy. He will not wait several days to have the remedy delivered by mail.

On the other hand, the desire for food and soap is universal and continuous. Every reader knows that he will be able to use a sample of these items regardless of whether the sample arrives in three days or in three weeks.

How to Get More Replies from Hidden Offers

If your booklet or sample offer does not pull sufficient inquiries, you can sweeten the offer by including the promise of a free gift.

In testing lamp bulb ads, it was found that a hidden offer of a booklet did not pull a sufficient number of requests. Therefore the offer was made more attractive by including a free gift. This method worked well. Here is the offer:

> A handsome, double-action automatic pencil and extra leads . . . and an interesting booklet about light and seeing . . . will be sent to you free if you tear out this ad and send it to us with your name and address.

In another case, an airline wanted to test a series of 100-line, all-type ads for airplane trips to Bermuda. The ads were tested in a single newspaper of 600,000 circulation. The advertiser found that a hidden offer of a booklet pulled less than fifty replies per ad. This was not considered sufficient.

The advertiser sweetened the offer by including an offer of a free pair of sunglasses and a free map of Bermuda in addition to the free booklet. The offer was described as a "Free Bermuda Vacation Kit." This offer brought more than enough replies for a copy test—over 400 replies per ad.

The "free kit" idea was also used successfully in copy tests for other limited appeal propositions. For example, a "Free Painter's Kit" brought plenty of replies in testing house paint ads. A "Homeowner's Kit" had good pulling power in testing ads for building materials.

How to Describe a Booklet Attractively

In testing ads for an investment service, it was found that the line "Send for free booklet" did not pull sufficient replies. By including the following attractive description of the booklet, the number of requests was increased more than 500 per cent:

> Where can I find out about investments that pay dividends? What do they pay? Where can I get facts?
>
> An 18-page booklet has been prepared to answer such questions. This free booklet gives you facts in simple language.
>
> It tells you what you own when you own stock. It tells you what dividends are ... and how often you may expect to receive them.
>
> Did you know there is a way to reduce investment risks? That's in this booklet, too. Plus a list of companies whose stocks have paid a cash dividend every year for 20 to 103 years. The booklet includes some stocks that sell for less than $20 a share.
>
> If you are interested in extra income, send for this booklet—whether you have $200 or $5,000 to invest. Write for your free copy today. Booklet will be sent by mail. No obligation.

Other Ways to Increase Replies

Use a Sunday newspaper: If you are testing ads in a daily paper and you do not get enough replies, you can switch to a Sunday paper. Sunday papers pull better because people have more time to answer ads on Sunday.

Use more circulation: If you are testing your ads in a paper with 250,000 circulation, you can switch to a paper with 500,000 circulation. This will double the number of your replies.

Use additional newspapers: If you are testing your ads in a single newspaper, you can add additional newspapers to bring the number of replies up to a sufficient quantity.

Use bigger ads: If you are testing ads of 100-line size, you can increase the size of your ads to 200 lines or to 500 lines. Bigger ads bring more replies.

Of course, in any ad, you can increase replies by featuring the offer in a headline or in a subhead. However, that method is not recommended because the featuring of the offer tends to invalidate a copy test by focusing attention on the offer instead of on the sales appeal you are testing.

Summary: Briefly stated below are the recommended methods for increasing hard-to-get replies in a hidden offer copy test:

1. Offer the sample or booklet free instead of for 25¢.
2. Set a value on the offer, such as "regular 50¢ size."
3. Sweeten the offer by adding a free gift.
4. Describe the offer attractively by listing its good features.
5. Run your test ads in a Sunday newspaper instead of in a daily.
6. Run your test ads in a publication with larger circulation.
7. Run your test ads in additional publications.
8. Increase the size of your test ads.

8. A continuing sales test by mail

Some advertisers make a continuing, year-round sales test of their advertising by including a mail order offer in every ad and in every publication. A key number is included in each ad so that the advertiser can trace the source of every mail order that comes in.

As a rule, the mail orders received by this method do not pay the cost of the space, but they do give the advertiser a chance to make comparisons. For example:

1. You can compare the pulling power of one ad versus another.
2. You can compare the pulling power of one publication versus another.
3. You can keep records that will tell you in which months of the year your ads pull best.
4. You can find out in which positions in publications your ads do best.

Here is the last paragraph of a *Wall Street Journal* ad using this method. Note the key number at the end of the ad. This particular key number (NYT 1-10) stands for *New York Times*, January 10.

The *Wall Street Journal* is the complete business DAILY. Has largest staff of writers on business and finance. The only business paper served by all three big press associations. It costs $35 a year, but you can get a Trial Subscription for three months for $13. Just tear out this ad and attach check for $13 and mail. Or tell us to bill you. Address: The *Wall Street Journal,* 200 Burnett Road, Chicopee, Mass. 01021   NYT 1-10

9. Testing ads by telephone response

The following story illustrates how to handle this type of test:

"I talked with our chief engineer and he says the best feature of our new air conditioner is that it gets rid of humidity," said the sales manager of an appliance company. "If the air in a room is kept dry, the human body cools itself."

"I see," said the ad manager.

"Maybe we should talk about getting rid of humidity in our ads. I remember an old saying—It isn't the heat, it's the humidity."

"That doesn't sound like a very exciting ad campaign."

"Well, I must admit that our salesmen do not use the humidity appeal very much. They talk about cooling the air. They tell customers how to keep a room cool in hot weather. I wonder which appeal we should use in our ads, coolness or humidity?"

"We can try both appeals. We can run an ad on humidity and put in a telephone number and ask people to telephone for information. We can keep track of how many telephone calls we get. Then we can run an ad on coolness and keep a record of how many telephone calls that ad brings."

"Where will you run the ads?"

"In a daily newspaper."

"The ad that runs on the hottest day will be the winner. You know how people crowd into our showrooms on hot days."

"All right, we'll run each ad several times. We'll alternate the ads—first an ad on coolness, then an ad on humidity. Then coolness, then humidity. That will average out the weather factor."

"Good idea. Now, how about having the phone calls switched to our showroom? Then when somebody telephones we can have the call handled by one of our salesmen. We can make some sales and test the ads at the same time."

"Fine," said the ad manager.

Results of this Test

Two ads were prepared. The ads were set in type in editorial style with no pictures. Each ad measured two columns by 100 lines. In the last paragraph of each ad was a telephone number and a sentence urging the reader to telephone for further information.

Here are the headlines of the two ads. See if you can guess which ad brought the most telephone calls.

> *No. 1.* Get rid of that humidity with a new room cooler that also dries the air.
>
> *No. 2.* How to have a cool, quiet bedroom—even on hot nights.

These ads were run alternately, about once a week, in a newspaper with half a million circulation. A record was kept of the number of telephone calls produced by each ad.

It was not long before the pattern of results became apparent. The second headline, "How to have a cool, quiet bedroom—even on hot nights," averaged two and a half times as many calls as the first one, "Get rid of that humidity."

As a result of this test, the humidity appeal was dropped from the ad headlines and the coolness appeal was featured in all ads during the rest of the summer. Sales results were excellent. (These ads are reproduced on page 288.)

Other Examples

A finance company wanted to test "hard-sell" ads versus "soft-sell" ads. Here are examples of the two different campaigns:

Hard-Sell:
Headline: How You can Get a Loan of $100
Copy: The copy stressed quick, private service and no inquiries of friends, relatives, or employer. A list of figures showed the various amounts you could borrow and a monthly pay-back plan.

Soft-Sell:
Headline: When can a Loan Help You?
Copy: The copy employed a philosophical approach and presented arguments like these: "Sometimes a loan proves helpful. Sometimes it only gets one in deeper. Don't borrow unless a loan will improve your position. We make loans to those who can use funds constructively."

These ads were tested in newspapers. One ad contained a panel of copy that said: "For quick information on loans, simply telephone [telephone number] and ask for Miss Miller." All telephone calls to Miss Miller were credited to that ad. The other ad contained an identical panel of copy except that the line "Ask for Miss Miller" was changed to read "Ask for Miss Johnson." All telephone calls to Miss Johnson were credited to the ad containing the name Miss Johnson.

In this test, the ad with the headline "How you can get a loan of $100" brought two and a half times as many telephone calls as the other ad.

In commenting on the results of this test, the account executive said: "The headline 'When can a loan help you?' is a philosophical headline. When a man is in trouble, he doesn't want philosophy—he wants money! And so he responds better to the ad, 'How you can get a loan of $100.'" (These ads are reproduced on page 385B.)

Here are some other situations in which ads were tested by including an urge to telephone for information and by keeping records of which ads produced the most telephone calls.

An engineering concern ran help-wanted ads in the classified section of newspapers and included a telephone number in the copy. Each ad urged the job applicant to telephone for information and told the name of a certain individual to ask for. For example: Ask for Mr. Digby, Ask for Mr. Thompson, etc. This method was used to test the pulling power of different copy approaches and also to test the pulling power of different newspapers.

A private school used the same method to test which ads were most effective in getting phone calls from prospective students. The school also used this method to determine which day of the week was best. *Result*: Sunday was found to be better than weekdays.

A typewriter manufacturer used this method, not only to test copy, but as a productive source of leads for salesmen to call on.

10. Testing advertising appeals by mail

"How can we keep our competitors from learning about our new campaign if we run a copy test in newspapers?" said the advertising manager of a soap company.

"We can avoid testing in big cities. We can run our test ads in a small city like Peoria," said the account executive.

"I'm afraid of that. This new X-appeal has never been used to sell soap. I don't want it to leak out in advance of our national campaign. You know, our business is very competitive. If we run X-appeal ads in Peoria, our competitors will know about it in a few days."

"We can skip the copy test," said the account man.

"No, I want to get a comparison of the pulling power of the X-appeal ads versus our current Y-appeal ads. I want some evidence to show to our management."

"We can do an opinion test among housewives. We can have interviewers shows X-layouts and Y-layouts and ask women to vote for their preference."

"No, a lot of women might be embarrassed to vote for the X-appeal ads. The ads are a bit shocking. But I think they have sales appeal."

"We could do a copy test by mail."

"How would that work?"

"We would buy a list of names and addresses of typical housewives from a mail order list broker," said the account executive. "We could buy a good-sized list—10,000 names. We could get up mailing pieces based on our ads. Or we might mail actual proofs of ads. We could include an offer in the ads—and a reply card. We would mail X-appeal ads to half of the women on the list and Y-appeal ads to the other half. The reply cards would be keyed—Dept. X and Dept. Y—so that we could tell which appeal pulled best."

"What should we offer?"

"A sample of the soap."

"Free or for money?"

"Either way. If we charge 25¢ for the sample we would have to enclose return envelopes instead of postcards. And we would have to mail a larger number of letters in order to get sufficient replies. On the other hand, if the sample is offered free, we could use a smaller mailing and enclose postcards for reply."

"Should the postcards have the offer printed on them?"

"No, because some women might read the offer before reading the ad. They might even send for the offer without reading the ad. That would upset our test. The postcards should merely have blank spaces for the housewife to write in her name and address. Then the copy test would operate in proper sequence. There would be a hidden offer in the copy in the ads. Only those women who were sufficiently interested in the ads would read the copy and discover the hidden offer."

"How much would a copy test like that cost?"

"About two thousand dollars."

"How long would it take?"

"About two weeks."

Typical Examples

The above incident illustrates a method of copy testing that has been used from time to time over the years.

One example is the case of a cigar manufacturer who wanted to test six different appeals. Six headlines were written and each headline featured a different appeal. To save on mailing costs, double postcards were used instead of letters. Headlines and appropriate copy messages (containing a hidden offer) were printed on one side of the card and the attached business reply card contained the manufacturer's name and address and space for the recipient's name and address. Here is the hidden offer:

> Sign your name on the attached postcard, mail it now, and we will send you three cigars with our compliments. We want you to know how good they are. And if you want more later—and we feel sure you will—your nearest cigar store has them.

One of the cards containing a new appeal in the headline pulled nearly 50 per cent more replies than any of the other cards. This appeal was used subsequently as the basic theme of a successful ad campaign.

A package goods manufacturer also used mailings to test the pulling power of several different appeals. Five appeals were tested. Each appeal was featured in the headline on 2,000 postcards making a total mailing of 10,000 postcards to housewives. Under each headline appeared three paragraphs of copy about the product. This was followed by a final paragraph containing the hidden offer, as follows:

> To get your free package, simply sign the attached card with your name and address and drop it in the mail. No stamp is needed. There is no obligation, of course. But don't delay. Put the attached card in the mail now.

Food manufacturers, drug manufacturers, and correspondence school advertisers have also used this method of pretesting basic appeals or proofs of ads before running the ads in publications. The offers used have been samples of the product or booklets about the product or service.

11. Opinion tests by mail

If your copy testing problem is one that can be helped by an opinion test, you can, if you wish, do your opinion test by mail instead of by personal interview. For example, you can send out two thousand letters printed on a special letterhead with some such heading as the words "Research Bureau." Here is a typical letter:

RESEARCH BUREAU
Room 1891
590 Lexington Ave., New York, N.Y. 10017

Dear Friend:

The other day I made a statement that I was immediately challenged to prove.

I said that it wasn't necessary to go and see people in order to ask them questions. I claimed that if you wrote to them in the right sort of way, they would be glad to answer.

Will you help me prove that I am right? All you need do is compare the six roughly sketched advertisements attached to this letter and decide which one of them would be most likely to interest you.

Then enter your choice at the bottom of this sheet, using the initial that appears under the ad. After you have chosen number one, decide which ad is second, which third, and so on until you have entered all six in the spaces provided.

Do not return the ads' themselves. Just enclose this letter containing your vote in the attached stamped and addressed envelope.

Gratefully yours,
Jane Thompson

My first choice is advt_____   My fourth choice is advt_____
My second choice is advt_____   My fifth choice is advt_____
My third choice is advt_____   My sixth choice is advt_____
Please indicate whether you are male____or female_____

12. Testing bus cards

A cosmetic manufacturer prepared two different bus cards featuring two different sales appeals. Let us designate these as Card A and Card B.

Card A featured the social popularity the user of the product would gain by using the cosmetic. At the bottom of the card was printed a line in small type that said, "For a trial bottle, send 25¢ to Dept. A." Below this line was printed the address of the manufacturer.

Card B featured a specific skin ailment the cosmetic would help to relieve. At the bottom of the card was printed the offer of a trial bottle for 25¢. The only difference was that the reader was instructed to write to Dept. B instead of to Dept. A.

As you may know, in buying showings of bus cards or subway cards, it is possible to buy small showings or large showings, as follows:

1. If you buy a half-showing, your bus card will be placed in every other bus on a certain bus line. In other words your card will appear in half the buses (or in half the subway cars, in the case of subway advertising).
2. If you buy a full showing, your card will appear in every bus or in every subway car.

The cosmetic advertiser bought two half-showings on a certain bus line. In one of the half-showings he placed Card A. In the other half-showing he placed Card B. In this way, each card received identical exposure under identical conditions. The test was continued for two months and during that period this advertiser received 65 per cent more replies from one card than from the other card. Incidentally, the results of this test agreed with a mail order test in newspapers in which this manufacturer tested the same two appeals.

13. Sales testing in selected cities

A question sometimes asked by students of advertising in regard to testing ads is: "Why don't you just publish in newspapers in a single city the ad or ads you wish to test and measure the sales results?" The answer is that this method sounds simple, but in actual practice may be expensive, time-consuming, and subject to errors. For example:

1. If you are selling an old and established product, the sales of your product will continue to a certain extent with or without additional advertising.
2. If you sell through wholesalers, it may be a long time before any extra sales (resulting from your newspaper ads) will be reflected in your factory shipments to wholesalers. Housewives won't buy your household cleanser, for example, until their present supply is used up. The corner grocer or supermarket manager won't reorder until his stock runs low. The wholesaler won't send an order to your factory until his inventory is nearly exhausted. Hence, an ad campaign in Peoria might be successful in making housewives want your product, but you would not know about it until months later.
3. It is difficult to measure one advertising appeal against another by this method because both appeals will probably sell some merchandise. You have to find two equally matched cities so that you can advertise one appeal in one city and another appeal in another city and compare the difference in

sales results. No matter how carefully you try to match two cities, you may find that your test is adversely affected by conditions you cannot control, or even by hidden conditions you are unaware of at the time.

In spite of the difficulties of sales testing in selected cities, this method has been used for many years and will continue to be used because the results are measured in actual sales.

If you wish to test two different advertising appeals in selected cities, here are some precautions that may help to give you an accurate measurement.

1. Don't just test one ad (Ad A) versus another ad (Ad B). The difference in sales results would probably be too small to measure. You should prepare two campaigns, namely Campaign A and Campaign B. Run Campaign A for a long time (two to six months) in one city or in a selected group of cities. Run Campaign B for the same length of time in a different city or in a selected group of cities.

2. Instead of running small ads once in a while, you can speed up results by running big ads frequently. In other words, during the test period you can overadvertise in order to accentuate the difference in the selling power of Campaign A versus Campaign B.

3. You should try to find a quicker and more sensitive measure of sales results than your factory shipments to wholesalers. For example, you can send out survey reporters at regular intervals to visit certain typical stores. By arrangement with store owners these survey reporters should count the packages of your product on shelves and keep running inventories that will reflect sales results quickly and accurately.

Sales Testing a New Product

If you are launching a new product, you may find that sales testing is more practical than it would be in a case where you are trying to increase the sales of an established product. For example, one man who invented a new patent medicine started sales testing in his hometown by running a new and different ad each week in the daily newspaper. The ad directed prospects to buy at the local drugstore.

Each week this man personally visited the drugstores in his town and counted the packages of his product on the shelves. During some weeks he found that he made no sales and during other weeks he made a few sales.

Then one day he ran a newspaper ad based on an entirely different sales appeal. As a result, he discovered that during that particular week the supply of his product was entirely sold out.

This discovery, in a single city, of an effective sales appeal was the beginning of a patent medicine advertising campaign that later became well-known throughout the United States.

14. Department store sales test

In trying to discover a method for sales testing some ads, a manufacturer said to himself, "If I owned a department store, I could easily test the selling power of various different ads for my product. I would simply run the ads, one each week, in a daily newspaper in my city and keep a record of the sales resulting from each ad.

"Of course, there might be a few inaccuracies in this method. For example, one ad might run in a better position than another ad. And there might be some cumulative sales effect of a whole series of ads. Nevertheless, if one of my ads made an outstanding sales record, I would know it. And I could double-check the results by repeating that same outstanding ad at a later date."

While thinking about this problem, the manufacturer had this idea: "Perhaps I don't need to own a department store in order to use this method. Maybe I can induce a department store manager to cooperate with me in testing the selling power of some ads. I will tell him that I will pay the cost of running some ads in the daily newspaper if he will do me the favor of reporting to me the sales results from each ad. The ads will feature my merchandise and will be signed with the name of his store."

This method was tried and found to be successful. Department store managers were approached on the basis of "I'll do a favor for you (pay for some ads urging people to go to your store) if you will do a favor for me (tell me the sales results)."

The same method has been used with chain drugstores in large cities in order to test the selling power of various ads for drugstore items. Ads are run in newspapers once a week. Each week's ad features a different selling appeal in the headline. And each ad is signed with the name of a certain drugstore chain. This causes the sales results to be concentrated in stores owned by that particular drug chain. This concentration of sales in a few stores owned by the same chain makes the sales results easier to measure than if the sales results were scattered through dozens of independent stores.

15. Readership tests by interview

Suppose you ran an ad in the daily newspaper in your city and you wanted to find out how many people saw your ad. Suppose that the day after your ad appeared you decided to call on your friends and neighbors and ask them if they saw your ad.

Let us say that you had to call on ten neighbors before you found one who had noticed your ad. You would then say to yourself "One out of ten is 10 per cent. The newspaper in which my ad appeared has 20,000 circulation. Therefore, my ad was noticed by 10 per cent of 20,000 people or a total of 2,000 people."

This method is the readership method of testing the effectiveness of advertising. The above example is, of course, an oversimplification of the method. In actual practice you have to improve the efficiency of a readership test by using refinements such as the following:

1. Don't call on friends. They are likely to try to please you by saying that they noticed your ad even though they did not actually notice it.
2. In interviewing people, don't point to a particular ad. It is better to turn the pages of the newspaper and say, "Did you notice anything on page 2? Did you notice anything on page 3? As I turn the pages of the newspaper, please point out anything you may have noticed." You can go through the entire newspaper in this way or you can save time by confining your interview to a few pages. In any event, you will get an idea of how your ad compares in attention value with other ads in the newspaper.
3. If you wish, you can ask additional questions. If a person says he saw a certain ad, you can then say, "Did you read any of it?" If the person says yes, you can ask further questions such as, "What part of the ad did you read? Did you buy the product advertised? Do you intend to buy the product? Did the ad make you want to buy the product?"
4. To increase the reliability of a readership test, it will be necessary for you to interview many more than ten people. It will be necessary to interview hundreds of people and this will require the hiring of a staff of survey reporters—men or women who will go from house to house and ask the questions you want asked.

In actual practice, the readership method of ad testing is usually done by hiring the services of a professional organization specializing in this work. These specialized companies make readership tests of ads in both magazines and newspapers and prepare printed reports showing the per cent of readers who said they saw or read various advertisements. You can buy these readership reports and have them mailed to you at regular intervals. This type of service is usually too expensive for an individual to buy. It is usually bought by advertising agencies or by large companies that invest millions of dollars in advertising.

The readership method of measuring the effectiveness of advertising has advantages and disadvantages. For example, one advantage is that you can get reports on the readership of all the ads in a publication including your competitors' advertising. A disadvantage is that an ad that gets a high rating by this method may not necessarily produce many sales. It may be an attention-getting ad without being a selling ad.

16. Readership tests by mail

Sometimes readership tests are done by mail instead of by personal interview. For example, here is an extract from a letter that was sent out by the publisher of a magazine:

> Your regular copy, Mr. Caples, of our July issue was mailed to you several weeks ago. You have undoubtedly had an opportunity to read it by this time.
>
> We will be sincerely grateful if you will cooperate with us in a study we are making among a few selected readers.
>
> What we would like to know particularly is which advertisements interested you when you went through this issue. We are also interested in your reading of editorial material. An extra copy of the July issue is enclosed. You will also find enclosed a special editor's pencil and a postage-paid return envelope.
>
> Will you kindly draw a line down the middle of each ad and each editorial item that interested you?
>
> If you have not seen this issue at all, please mark a large X on the front cover and return it anyway. The editor's pencil is yours to keep as a souvenir.
>
> We will also welcome any comments you wish to make on specific editorial items or advertisements.
>
> Thank you very much for cooperating with us in this study. Your help will be of great value to us and to our advertisers.

17. Split-run copy testing in publications

"Here are two mail order ads I'd like to test," said an advertising manager to his assistant. "I'd like to find out which ad is the better puller."

"Where shall we test them?" asked the assistant. "In a magazine?"

"No, let's test them in a daily newspaper. That way we can get a quick test. Magazines have longer closing dates."

"Which ad shall we run first?"

"That's a problem. I'm afraid that the ad we run first may have an unfair advantage. The first ad may grab the easy-to-get customers. The second ad will be left with slim pickings. The first ad may look like the winner on sales. But the second ad, although it gets fewer sales, may be the better of the two ads."

"I could argue the other way," said the assistant. "I've always heard that the effect of advertising is cumulative. Therefore, the first ad that appears will warm up the customers, but the second ad will get the most sales."

"H'm," said the ad manager. "I wish this advertising business were not so complicated! Isn't it almost time to go to lunch?"

Variables in Copy Testing

The above story illustrates one of the variables that may affect a copy test, namely, the order of appearance of the ads. Some advertisers try to compensate for this variable by testing ads in two newspapers and by reversing the order of appearance of the ads in the second newspaper. In the first newspaper, for example, Ad A runs on Monday and Ad B on Tuesday. In the second newspaper, Ad B runs on Monday and Ad A runs on Tuesday. Returns from the two sets of ads are averaged.

The position of an ad in a newspaper is another variable that affects copy testing. One ad may get top-of-page position on the women's page while another ad gets bottom-of-page position on the society page. To avoid this variable, you can ask newspaper make-up men to cooperate by placing test ads in similar positions. For example, you can include in your insertion orders this instruction: "Both of these ads are to appear in the upper right-hand corner of the women's page."

The weather can affect a copy test, too. One ad may have the advantage of appearing on a rainy day when a lot of people stay home and have more time to answer ads. This variable can be compensated for by running your test ads in several widely separated cities.

How Split-run Copy Testing Works

The advent of split-run copy testing put an end to these troublesome variables. By means of split-run testing, it became possible to test two different advertisements on the same day and in the same position by running each ad in one-half of the circulation of a newspaper. How this is possible is explained below.

The presses that print certain newspapers print from metal cylinders on which each page of the newspaper is etched twice on each cylinder. Hence, a complete revolution of the cylinder prints two copies of a single page.

When an advertiser wants to use split-run testing in the newspaper, he provides the paper with two advertisements of the same size. One advertisement (A) is etched on one side of the cylinder, the other advertisement (B) is etched on the other side. Thus, a complete revolution of this cylinder prints two copies of the same page, a different advertisement occupying the same space on each page.

Each newsdealer, no matter where he is located, receives a supply of newspapers in which Advertisement A and Advertisement B are equally divided. Thus, in every locality and neighborhood into which the newspaper goes, exactly the same number of newspapers containing Advertisement A and Advertisement B reach the newspaper readers.

The importance of this in testing is immediately apparent. Every variable that might affect the result of the test is removed. Each advertisement is tested under conditions exactly alike. Both advertisements reach readers simultaneously in the same geographical areas and under the same weather conditions. Both advertisements occupy the same position in the newspaper and are surrounded by the same editorial matter. Absolutely the only variable to which the advertisements are subjected is the one the advertiser himself puts in for the purpose of testing one against the other.

Various Uses of Split-run Testing

Split-run copy testing in newspapers in one of the greatest inventions ever devised for the benefit of scientific-minded advertisers. Here are three reasons why:

1. The method is quick. You can test two ads on a Monday, for

example, and in most cases you will know as early as Tuesday or Wednesday which is the winner.

2. The method is accurate. No longer do you need to say, as a result of a test, "Ad A is about twice as good as Ad B" (or about half again as good as Ad B, whichever the case may be). You can now say, for example, that "Ad A is 43 per cent better than Ad B."

3. You can test fine points. This method is so accurate that you can test small differences between ads. For example, the following small differences between ads were tested.

Test No. 1. Two drug product ads were tested that were identical except that in Ad A the headline was printed above the picture and in Ad B the headline was printed below the picture. Ad B pulled 8 per cent more replies.

Test No. 2. Two beauty product ads using pictures of the same girl model were tested. The ads were identical except that in Ad A the girl was smiling and in Ad B the girl had a serious expression. Ad A pulled 25 per cent more replies.

Test No. 3. Two all-type automotive ads were tested. The copy was identical in both ads except for a change in headline wording as follows:

Headline of Ad A: Save one gallon of gas in every ten
Headline of Ad B: Car Owners! Save one gallon of gas in every ten

Ad B pulled 20 per cent more replies.

Test No. 4. Two financial ads were tested that were identical except that Ad A contained the subhead "Send for Free Booklet" above the coupon and Ad B omitted the subhead. The ad with the subhead above the coupon pulled 5 per cent more replies than the other ad.

Split-run copy testing can be used for mail order tests, coupon tests, hidden offer tests, readership tests, layout tests, illustration tests, and store sales tests. Advertisers have only scratched the surface of the possibilities of split-run testing. Just think, in a single day in a typical large city, you can put a certain ad (Ad A) into the hands of 250,000 people and you can put a different ad (Ad B) into the hands of another 250,000 people under identical conditions. This is accurate sampling on a massive scale and at low cost. To do large-scale sampling of this kind by other research methods would present enormous difficulties and cost staggering sums of money.

There are more than 1,600 split-run newspapers in the United States, listed by the Standard Rate and Data Service. You can do split-run copy testing in any of these papers. You encounter no more difficulty than the scheduling of ads, the answering of replies, and the tabulating of results. And the cost is merely the cost of the newspaper ads plus a small mechanical fee charged by newspapers for split-run testing.

Many magazines also offer split-run testing. *TV Guide* has more than 80 editions in which copy can be split-run tested. Due to long closing dates (a month or two in advance of publication date), you cannot get a quick split-run test in magazines, but you can make copy testing a regular part of your advertising campaign.

How to Test a Whole Series of Ads by Split-run

An advertising manager was talking to an agency man about split-run copy testing. "I can see how you are able to test two ads by split-run. You just run each ad in half the circulation of a newspaper on the same day and count the replies," said the advertising manager. "But can you test more than two ads—for example four ads or ten ads?"

"Yes, you can test four ads by doing three split-run tests a week apart," said the advertising agency man. "For example, let's say that during the first week you do a split-run test in a daily newspaper and Ad A gets 100 replies and Ad B gets 150 replies. The next week you can test two more ads, for example, Ad C versus Ad D. Let's say that Ad C is the winner. Now you have two winners—Ad B is the winner of the first test and Ad C is the winner of the second test. During the following week you can split-run test the two winners against each other and find out which ad is the best of the entire series of four ads."

"How would you test ten ads?" said the ad manager.

"You can divide the ten ads into groups—four ads plus four ads plus two ads—and test the groups separately. Then you can test the winners of the groups against each other. It's the same plan as they use in intercollegiate track meets where a lot of athletes are competing. First you have preliminary contests to weed out the obviously hopeless contestants. Then you have the semifinals and then the finals.

"A slightly different plan can be used if desired. Suppose you have ten ads, numbered from one to ten. Let's say that on a certain Monday you split-run test Ad Number One versus Ad Number Two. You count the replies and by Thursday you find that Ad Number One is the winner. Now, thanks to short newspaper closing dates, you have time to schedule your winning Ad Number One versus Ad Number Three on the following Monday. Again you count replies and you find out which ad is the winner of this second split-run test. You then schedule the winner of the second test against a new, untested ad on the third Monday. You can continue this process every Monday until all of your ads have been tested and you emerge with an overall winner."

"It takes a lot of time, doesn't it?" said the ad manager.

"Well, it takes ten weeks to test ten ads. And the process can go on indefinitely. This plan has the advantage that it gives the copywriter time to study the results as the test progresses. If the writer finds that a certain appeal is doing well, he can create and test new ads that accentuate that appeal. In other words, as the test progresses, the writer is given a sense of direction in which to travel."

A Quick Way to Test Ads by Split-run

"Is there any faster way to test a series of, say ten ads?"

"Yes, there is a plan that lets you test ten ads in ten days instead of ten weeks."

"How does it work?"

"You select one of your ads and use it as a Control Ad or measuring stick. Every day you run your Control Ad in half the circulation of a split-run newspaper, and every day you run one of the ads you want to test in the other half of the circulation. For example, your schedule might start off like this:

Monday: Ad Number One versus Control Ad
Tuesday: Ad Number Two versus Control Ad
Wednesday: Ad Number Three versus Control Ad

"You can continue this process until you have split-run tested all ten ads against the same Control Ad."

"How do you tabulate the results in order to select the winning ad?"

"Well, as a rule, some ads pull more replies than the Control Ad and some pull fewer replies than the Control Ad. The winning ad is the one that exceeds the Control Ad by the greatest percentage. Your tabulation of results might look like this:

Ad Number One is 20 per cent better than the Control Ad
Ad Number Two is 35 per cent poorer than the Control Ad

Ad Number Three is 60 per cent better than the Control Ad

And so on.

"Obviously, Ad Number Three is the best up to this point and Ad Number One is the second best. After all ten ads in the series have been tested against the Control Ad, you can rank the entire series in order of merit, from one to ten. In some tests it has been found that the best-pulling ad will outrank the Control Ad by several hundred per cent."

"Doesn't a test of this kind tend to wear down the pulling power of the ads as the test progresses?"

"Sometimes it does. Sometimes the tenth pair of ads in a series will pull only half the total of the first pair. You can help to avoid this wearing down of pulling power by using small-sized test ads, for example, 100 lines each. Small-sized ads do not wear out their pulling power as fast."

"Does this wearing down of pulling power upset the test?"

"No, it doesn't. Many times we have repeated, at the end of a series of test ads, the same pair of test ads that we ran at the beginning, in order to double-check the results. The percentage of difference between the two repeated ads has been approximately the same as at the beginning of the test. In other words, you get the same results no matter at what point in the series a certain pair of ads appears."

How Thirty-six Headlines Were Tested

"What is the largest number of ads you have tested in a short time by this method?" said the ad manager.

"In one instance we tested thirty-six ads in two weeks. We wrote a piece of patent medicine copy containing two elements: (1) a complete sales talk for the medicine, and (2) a hidden offer of a sample bottle of the medicine for 25¢," said the agency man.

"Then the copy department wrote thirty-six different headlines for this single piece of copy. We wanted to know which headline would induce the most people to read the ad. The copy was set in type—no pictures—in single-column size and 75 lines deep. We then set the thirty-six headlines in type. We got thirty-six proofs of the test matter of the ad and pasted a different headline on each proof. This gave us a total of thirty-six ads to test.

"Four newspapers that offer split-run testing were selected. Let us call them Newspapers A, B, C, and D.

"We picked a single Control Ad (any ad in the series can be used as a control) and scheduled this Control Ad to run in half the circulation of Newspaper A on ten different days—Monday through Friday, for two weeks. Each day, in the other half of the circulation of Newspaper A, we ran one of the thirty-six ads we wanted to test. In this way we tested ten ads in two weeks. Likewise, during the same two weeks, we tested ten different ads in Newspaper B using the same Control Ad as a measuring stick. In Newspaper C we tested ten more ads using the Same Control Ad, and in Newspaper D we tested in the same way the remaining six ads in our total of thirty-six ads.

"The net result was that in a period of two weeks we tested thirty-six different headlines against the same Control Ad and then ranked the entire list in order of pulling power. One of the headlines exceeded the Control Ad by 300 per cent and another by 200 per cent. The selling appeals contained in these two winning headlines were used as the basis of a successful national campaign."

General Comments on Testing

As previously stated, advertising is not an exact science like chemistry. If you tell a chemist that you are going to mix certain chemicals in certain proportions, he can predict the result accurately. However, if you tell an advertising man that you are going to run a certain advertisement in a certain publication, he cannot tell you exactly what results you will get. He can only give you an approximate opinion based on his own past experience.

Of all branches of advertising, mail order advertising comes the nearest to being a science. Given a tested piece of copy and a tested publication, an experienced mail order man can often predict results surprisingly well. It is for this reason that a study of mail order methods is valuable to the general advertiser.

Compare for a moment the present-day situation in advertising with the manufacturing situation. Would a manufacturer of electronic products install a new type of insulation without first subjecting it to all sorts of tests? Certainly not. Would an automobile manufacturer buy a trainload of new axles or enamel or fabric without pretesting? The answer is no. Yet scores of manufacturers are buying trainloads of advertising, and the only test to which the advertising is submitted is their own personal opinion or the opinion of a subordinate. Advertising will never produce the results it can produce until some sort of testing is brought into the picture.

Four important factors in every advertising campaign are:

1. Copy—what you say in your advertisements. This includes the appeal used and the method of expressing that appeal.
2. Media—which magazines, newspapers, broadcasting facilities, or other media you select to carry your message to the public.
3. Position—what position your advertisements occupy in publications; which day of the week or what time of day you select for your broadcast messages.
4. Season—in which months of the year you run most of your advertising.

Any one of these factors can cause a wide difference in results from advertising. As mentioned before, the author once saw one ad bring in 19 1/2 times as much business as another ad. Yet both advertisements appeared under similar conditions and both cost the manufacturer the same amount of money. This is an extreme case. Let us be conservative and say that in an average advertising campaign consisting of a dozen advertisements, some of the advertisements will produce two or three times as much business as others.

Certain publications will do the same, that is, produce several times as much business as others. As for the position of your ad in a publication, certain special positions often add 50 per cent to 100 per cent to inquiries and sales. And as for season, it is not unusual for a mail order advertiser to receive twice as many orders from a January advertisement as from an August advertisement, both advertisements costing the manufacturer the same.

Consider the tremendous effectiveness of an advertising campaign that gets all these factors right—copy, media, position, and season. The manufacturer who gets these factors right is multiplying the effect of his advertising dollar. He makes one dollar do the work of ten dollars.

The manufacturer who gets these factors wrong—especially copy and media—is throwing a large part of his advertising appropriation away.

Regardless of what method of testing you use, the important thing is to have some method of testing. Testing enables you to throw opinions overboard and get down to facts. Perhaps there is some particularly effective appeal in your sales story. Perhaps you do not realize how effective this appeal would be if featured in advertising. Testing will enable you to find out. Perhaps you are spending money on some hopeless appeal. Testing will point the way to the discarding of this appeal.

Testing enables you to guard against an advertising manager whose pet ideas may be hurting your advertising. Testing enables you to guard against an advertising agency whose idea of agency service is merely to turn out pretty layouts and stereotyped copy. Testing enables you to guard against mistaken ideas that you yourself may have in regard to advertising. And finally, testing enables you to keep in touch with trends in advertising. What was good advertising a few years ago may not always be good advertising today.

Trends change. Sometimes the attitude of the public changes, When an advertiser comes out with a new idea, he may be able to cash in on it for a while. Then other advertisers copy his method. His idea is no longer new. It becomes common. The public gets used to it and tires of it.

However, there is one rule that never changes: Test everything on a small scale before you spend money on a large scale. Testing enables you to keep your finger on the public pulse. It enables you to sense trends in advance. It enables you to separate the wheat from the chaff, the sheep from the goats, the winning ideas from the duds. It enables you to multiply the results you get from the dollars you spend in advertising.

If I were starting life over again, I am inclined to think that I would go into the advertising business. Advertising covers the whole range of human needs. It brings to the greatest number of people actual knowledge concerning useful things. It is essentially a form of education. It has risen with ever-growing rapidity to the dignity of an art.

Franklin D. Roosevelt

Does he still say..."You're lovely"?

E YES light on lovely hair and linger there when it shines in all its natural beauty. *Your* hair will be soft, sparkling, and lustrous when you do it at home with new different Wildroot Hair Set that replaces old-fashioned thick gummy wave sets. Does all they do and more! Light bodied. Faster drying. And because it contains processed Lanolin, leaves your hair soft, natural, and at its lovely best. Style your own distinctive hair-do quickly, without fuss or disappointment! And watch those admiring glances! For regular 25c bottle free, mail this ad with your name and address to Wildroot, Buffalo 8, N. Y., Dept. H4.

GIRLS! Want quick curls?

E YES light on lovely hair and linger there when it shines in all its natural beauty. *Your* hair will be soft, sparkling, and lustrous when you do it at home with new different Wildroot Hair Set that replaces old-fashioned thick gummy wave sets. Does all they do and more! Light bodied. Faster drying. And because it contains processed Lanolin, leaves your hair soft, natural, and at its lovely best. Style your own distinctive hair-do quickly, without fuss or disappointment! And watch those admiring glances! For regular 25c bottle free, mail this ad with your name and address to Wildroot, Buffalo 8, N. Y., Dept. H3.

Can You Guess the Winner?

These ads were split-run tested in newspapers. Each ad offers a free bottle of Wildroot Hair Set. The ad with the headline "Girls! Want Quick Curls?" brought two and a half times as many replies as the other ad. This test ran 25 years ago. A recent test for a Home Permanent showed the same result. An

New Home Permanent Conditions Hair As It Curls

Today's woman often finds herself too busy to spend valuable time at the beauty parlor. If you're constantly on the go, you'll be glad to know that now you can give yourself a professional-looking wave at home in remarkably little time. Think of the time and money you'll save! Rexall Fast Home Permanent is really fast! It makes all other home permanents old-fashioned, and here's why. No pre-shampooing is necessary, thanks to a new miracle cleansing ingredient right in the neutralizer. Secondly, the neutralizer is pre-mixed, ready to apply right from its own handy plastic squeeze-bottle. And the neutralizer is specially formulated to act as a foaming shampoo-conditioner. You get soft, natural-looking curls, clean and lustrous without a trace of wave odor. There's a Fast Permanent for every type of hair: Regular for normal hair; Gentle for easy-to-wave hair; Super for hard-to-wave hair. There are also Fast Permanents for Little Girls' and Silver hair. Make your next home permanent a Fast permanent and you'll see why it's the favorite of women from coast to coast. Get acquainted offer: For a $1.00* Fast Home Permanent outfit absolutely Free, mail this ad to Rexall, Dept. H9, Box 36222, Los Angeles, Calif. Choose the type of permanent you desire by placing a check mark in the proper box... ☐ Regular... Gentle... ☐ Super... ☐ Little Girls'... ☐ Silver. Limit: ONE to a family. Offer good for 30 days only.
*Suggested minimum retail price

Girls...Want a Fast Permanent?

Today's woman often finds herself too busy to spend valuable time at the beauty parlor. If you're constantly on the go, you'll be glad to know that now you can give yourself a professional-looking wave at home in remarkably little time. Think of the time and money you'll save! Rexall Fast Home Permanent is really fast! It makes all other home permanents old-fashioned, and here's why. No pre-shampooing is necessary, thanks to a new miracle cleansing ingredient right in the neutralizer. Secondly, the neutralizer is pre-mixed, ready to apply right from its own handy plastic squeeze-bottle. And the neutralizer is specially formulated to act as a foaming shampoo-conditioner. You get soft, natural-looking curls, clean and lustrous without a trace of wave odor. There's a Fast Permanent for every type of hair: Regular for normal hair; Gentle for easy-to-wave hair; Super for hard-to-wave hair. There are also Fast Permanents for Little Girls' and Silver hair. Get acquainted offer: For a $1.00* Fast Home Permanent outfit absolutely Free, mail this ad to Rexall, Dept. H16, Box 36222, Los Angeles, Calif. Choose the type of permanent you desire by placing a check mark in the proper box... ☐ Regular... ☐ Gentle... ☐ Super... ☐ Little Girls'... ☐ Silver. Limit: ONE to a family. Offer good for 30 days only.
*Suggested minimum retail price.

ad with the headline "Girls ... Want a Fast Permanent?" outpulled all other ads tested. This is an example of how certain basic appeals go on forever.

HOW TO HAVE A
COOL, QUIET BEDROOM
EVEN ON HOT NIGHTS

Don't toss and turn in a hot, stuffy bedroom. Find out today how you can be cool and comfortable the rest of the summer—the rest of your life. A low-cost Air Pilot room conditioner makes your bedroom as comfortable as an outdoor sleeping porch. The Air Pilot brings into your hot bedroom the cooler, fresher outdoor air. It shuts out honking automobile horns, next-door radios, and noises that steal away rest and sleep. It filters out dust, dirt, and irritating pollen. And it is as easy to install as a radio.

TRY IT FOR 7 DAYS

Take advantage of this wonderful offer today. You can get an Air Pilot in your home and keep it for ONE ENTIRE WEEK.

Under our trial plan, at a small installation charge, you can prove how the Air Pilot fills your room with cool, clean, filtered air . . . how it shuts out disturbing noises. YOU CAN DO ALL OF THIS BEFORE YOU BUY . . . without any obligation.

Don't put off this trial. For full information tear out this ad and send it with your name and address to Dept. K, Standard Air Conditioning Inc., 50 West 40th Street, New York City. But it will be much quicker to telephone PEnnsylvania 6-9616 now and say: "Tell me how I can try air conditioning without obligation." Standard Air Conditioning Inc., is a subsidiary of American Radiator and Standard Sanitary Corporation.

GET RID OF
THAT HUMIDITY
with New Room Cooler that also dries the air!

It's not the heat, it's the humidity that makes you uncomfortable in this weather. So this new machine not only *cools* the air. It actually wrings moisture from it! This means you can have dry, cool, moving air without dampness or chill.

Don't buy any air conditioning unit until you try this one . . . developed by a division of American Radiator & Standard Sanitary Corporation.

SPECIAL 7-DAY TRIAL

For a small charge you can try it for one week. See how it cools you off, not just with refrigeration, not just with healthful, circulating fresh air, but with *controlled humidity!* That means comfortable cooling . . . not chilling.

Only an expert knows the exact air conditioner that is *right for you.* So we prefer you to try what we recommend on an inexpensive 7-day trial plan. If you like it, you buy it. If you don't, you pay a small installation cost only. For details of this try-out plan, phone PEnnsylvania 6-9616, Department G. Or see our complete line of portable air conditioning at our showroom, 50 West 40th Street, New York City. Standard Air Conditioning Inc., a division of American Radiator & Standard Sanitary Corporation.

FOR DETAILS CALL PEnn. 6-9616

This Copy Test Settled an Argument

This copy test was run in the early days of air conditioning. The sales manager thought the ad on the left would sell more air conditioners. The engineer in charge of production disagreed. He said: "It's not the heat, it's the humidity that makes people uncomfortable. The humidity ad will win." The ads were tested in *The New York Times*. Each ad invited phone calls, and the calls were turned over to salesmen. The ad on the left "How to have a cool, quiet bedroom" produced two and a half times as many sales as the other ad.

When should I get a Loan?

BEFORE you borrow, it's a mighty good idea to make sure that a loan will solve your money problem. Sometimes a loan does more harm than good. Instead of helping the borrower out of his difficulty it gets him in deeper.

But often a loan provides the one way out. If you are troubled by overdue bills, for instance, a loan can supply the cash you need to get rid of worry. If you need medical or dental service, a loan can help to protect your health. When taxes or insurance must be paid, a loan may prevent serious loss. In all these situations, as in many others, a loan can help you to help yourself.

Household Finance makes loans that help. Anyone may apply for $20 to $300. You will not be urged to borrow.

The manager of your local Household Finance office has had years of experience in dealing with all kinds of family money problems. You can freely discuss your needs with him in confidence and in privacy. You will find him a friendly, considerate "Doctor of Family Finances." If a loan is the answer to your problem, he will arrange it for you promptly and simply.

Why don't you phone or visit the nearest Household office?

Don't get a Loan until you read about these features of the Household Plan

1. Anyone may apply to Household Finance for a loan of $20 to $300 on furniture, car or note.
2. Small monthly payments. Example: $15.00 first month decreasing each month to $10.25.
3. You do NOT need co-makers or endorsers. No salary or wage assignment required.
4. Prompt action. Money usually the next day.
5. Household Finance's rate is 2½% per month on your unpaid balance. Charges on all Household loans are substantially less than the lawful maximum.
6. Loan may be repaid ahead of schedule to reduce cost. Charge made on unpaid balance only.
7. No credit inquiries made of friends or relatives.

FOR QUICK INFORMATION ON LOANS TELEPHONE
LAckawanna 4-0346
Ask for Miss Gill
and say "What do I have to do to get a loan?" The information you want will be cheerfully given.

HOUSEHOLD FINANCE
CORPORATION... "Doctor of Family Finances"

HOW YOU CAN GET A LOAN OF $100–
If you can pay back $7.50 a month

Read how Household Finance makes loans in strict privacy, without embarrassing inquiries, at reasonable rates, with repayment in small monthly installments

If you need money to clean up overdue bills, get dental or medical service, meet an emergency, or for any other worthy purpose, this information will be important to you.

All you do to apply for a Household Finance loan is give us a few facts about yourself. You need no stocks or bonds, no bankable security. You don't have to ask anyone to sign the loan papers with

you (married couples sign together). No credit inquiries are made of your friends or relatives. Getting a loan from Household is a simple, private transaction promptly completed without embarrassment to you.

You may repay your loan in 10 to 20 monthly installments which decrease each month. On a $100 loan repaid in 20 months, for instance, your first

monthly payment would be $7.50, your last payment, $5.13. These payments include Household's reasonable charge for the use of the money you borrow.

Borrow for less

Efficient operation has permitted Household to reduce its charges below the lawful maximum. You get the advantage of Household's favorable rate whatever the amount of your loan.

Every day this simple loan plan helps hundreds of people to solve urgent money problems. Why don't you learn more about Household's helpful money service today? Come to the nearest office and discuss your problem with the friendly, understanding manager without obligation.

Answering 7 questions most people ask about making a Household Loan

1. Anyone may apply to Household Finance for a loan of $20 to $300 on furniture.
2. Small monthly payments. Example: $15.00 first month decreasing each month to $10.25 last month, repays a $200 loan in 20 months including charges.
3. You do NOT need co-makers or endorsers. No salary or wage assignment required.
4. Prompt action. Money usually the next day.
5. Household Finance's rate is 2½% per month on your unpaid balance. Charges on

all Household loans are substantially less than the lawful maximum.
6. Loan may be repaid ahead of schedule to reduce cost. Charge made on unpaid balance only.
7. No credit inquiries made of friends or relatives.

FOR QUICK INFORMATION ON LOANS TELEPHONE
LAckawanna 4-0346
Ask for Miss Baker
and say "What do I have to do to get a loan?" The information you want will be cheerfully given.

HOUSEHOLD FINANCE
CORPORATION... "Doctor of Family Finances"

How to Test Ads by Telephone Calls

Above are two ads for a finance company. In the lower right corner of the top ad is a panel that says:

> For quick information on loans telephone LAckawanna 4-0346.
> Ask for Miss Gill, and say: "What do I have to do to get a loan?"
> The information you want will be cheerfully given.

In the lower right corner of the bottom ad is a panel with the same copy, except that the respondent is told to ask for Miss Baker. By comparing the number of customers obtained by Miss Gill with the number obtained by Miss Baker, the advertiser can tell which ad is more effective.

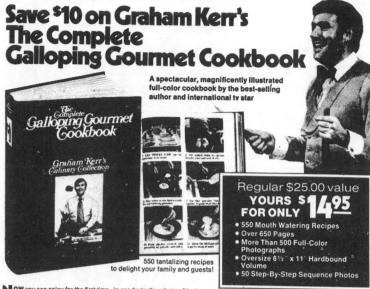
How a Publisher Tested Two Different Payment Plans

These two ads for Graham Kerr's cookbook were split-run tested in the *National Observer.* The ads are identical except for the payment plan. The price panel in one ad offers the cookbook for $14.95. The coupon says: . . . "bill me just $14.95 plus shipping and handling charges." The price panel in the other ad offers the cookbook for $5.30 per month. The coupon says: "I

will pay just $5.30 a month until the complete price of $14.95 (plus shipping and handling) is paid." This test enabled the advertiser to find out which payment plan sold the most books, and more importantly, which payment plan was more profitable in the long run.

Choose 3
of these advance
magazine articles—FREE

HERE'S HOW TO GET THEM. To acquaint you with the wide variety of interesting articles appearing in today's leading magazines, we make this special offer.

From the descriptions of articles below, pick the three you would most like to read. Circle with pencil the numbers of these three articles on the coupon below. Then clip the coupon and mail it to us with your name and address. We'll send you *free* copies of the three articles you choose—without any obligation to you whatsoever.

This offer is good for *only seven days*, so send us the coupon TODAY.

1 TV Violence Is Harmful. Tests show that children exposed to TV violence become strikingly more aggressive, some even tripling their capacity for antisocial behavior. *And Saturday morning cartoons are among the worst offenders.* Here are the facts, along with 4 positive steps we must take now.

2 Home Improvements That Pay Off. Many homeowners assume that money spent on improvements will be returned when they sell their house. But this is not always the case. Here's a basic guide to home improvements — including storm windows, patios, pools, kitchen remodeling, etc., etc. — showing you how each one rates as a cash investment.

3 I Am Joe's Hair. Here's what you—and everyone—should know about hair, including no-nonsense facts about hair "strengtheners", conditioning", the dangers of vitamin A, and a certain kind of baldness that cures itself automatically!

4 Cooking to Cut Calories. The way you choose and prepare foods can make a big difference in their caloric value—and your weight. Read what to look for in the supermarket, how to extract unwanted calories from meat, *how to keep low-calorie meals appetizing without any change in the size of your usual portions.*

5 The Power of Shared Feelings. The ability to reach out to others is not only a cure for loneliness, it can give you an exhilarating sense of new-found freedom. How does it work? Here are helpful clues, along with specific suggestions to help you make this rewarding e*xperience a habit.

6 At Last: A Blood Test for Cancer. This new diagnostic test, called the "radio immune assay", is something doctors have been searching for. Read how it is already being used in medical centers across the country, how it can "catch" cancer before the symptoms are apparent, and how it can prolong the life of cancer patients whose condition is already known.

7 What to Do When They Audit Your Tax Return. What are your chances of being audited? Which deductions are most likely to be challenged? (And what sort of proof should you have?) You'll find the answers here—together with 5 basic rules to help you get through any audit painlessly.

8 $6.95 Book Condensed: "Women's Doctor". A prominent obstetrician and gynecologist re-creates a typical year in his life, showing you what-his profession is really like. Read how he feels about his patients and discover his (sometimes unorthodox) views on abortion, cancer, the Pap smear, episiotomy, and hormone therapy in menopause.

9 The Miracle of Personal Resurrection. Christians tend to think of resurrection as something that happened 2,000 years ago. Few are aware that they themselves, in small yet significant ways, can be "raised to newness of life". Read how it happens—in your work, in your marriage, in your daily routine.

10 Father: The Forgotten Man. Is the man in your family a "computer", a "pawn", a "good citizen", or a "moonlighter"? All four have a tendency to fail as parents. Read why fathers are crucial to a child's academic success and to his (or her) sexual development. And read how any man can become a *better* father.

11 How Car Dealers Set Their Prices. It's surprisingly easy to figure out how much a new car costs the dealer, just by looking at the "sticker" price. But how much will he settle for? And what about your trade-in? You'll find the basics you need to know to make the best deal possible.

12 Redbook's Survey: How Women Really Feel About the "New Feminism". A recent survey of 120,000 American women reveals some surprising shifts in popular opinion. Discover how women *really* feel about equality in marriage, day-care centers, job discrimination, and militant feminism.

CIRCLE NUMBERS OF 3 ARTICLES YOU WANT*

Cut out coupon and mail today!

*Note: Only one set to a reader

To: TBS Computer Centers Corporation
1212 Avenue of the Americas, New York, N.Y. 10036

Gentlemen: Please send me FREE the 3 articles I have circled below by number.

1	2	3
4	5	6
7	8	9
10	11	12

Mr.
Miss
Name Mrs.
(Please Print) Age
Address
City State Zip

AAP0

How to Test the Promotability of Magazine Articles

An item by Philip H. Dougherty in the Ad News section of *The New York Times* explained this ad as follows: "A reader has sent in an ad from *The Albany Times-Union* with the comment 'Looks like something new in magazine solicitations to me.' ... The titles all strongly suggest *Reader's Digest* fare and a call to that publication confirmed this. What is the *Digest* doing? They are finding out in advance of publication which articles are the most promotable."

A Split-run Copy Test in TV Guide

At the top is the center spread of a four-page insert that ran in half the circulation of the New York Metropolitan Edition of *TV Guide*. At the bottom is the center spread of a different four-page insert that ran in the other half of the circulation. This is a split-run test to find out which ad produced the most sales. At the present writing, *TV Guide* has 89 editions. You can do a split-run test in any one or all of the editions. If you want a low-cost test, you can use a small city edition with 100,000 circulation. If you want a large-scale test, you can use New York with 2 million circulation.

WO?? OUT?

Nervous? Run Down?

This message may change your whole life

If, day after day, you find yourself waking up tired, having to drag yourself through the day, you probably charge it up to "getting older," or overwork, or maybe "nerves." And probably you feel "that's life"—there's nothing much you can do about it. This is not necessarily so.

For your tired, worn out feeling may have a simple, easily correctable cause. You may simply not be getting enough of the essential B-Complex vitamins, thiamin and riboflavin. When you lack these vital elements, your blood cells start to wear out faster than your body can replace them. And when this is happening to you, *naturally* you feel tired, weak, irritable — thoroughly miserable.

But here is good news! If this is your trouble, we can promise you will get a new lease on life with Rybutol. Because, penny for penny, ounce for ounce, Rybutol is the highest-potency B-Complex formula advertised anywhere. It is the largest-selling B-Complex formula of its kind in America. And so you, too, can discover the remarkable difference between Rybutol and any other formula you *ever* tried, we make you this unusual offer:

We will send you a generous 7-day maintenance supply of high-potency Rybutol (49¢ value) *free*. Simply send your name and address with this ad and 10¢ to help cover mailing to: Rybutol, Dept. E27, Box 657, Grand Central Annex, New York 17, N.Y. Offer good for 10 days only.

HO?? TO ?ET MORE E?E?Y FROM THE FOOD YOU EAT

If you lack thiamin and riboflavin

If, day after day, you find yourself waking up tired, having to drag yourself through the day, you probably charge it up to "getting older," or overwork, or maybe "nerves." And probably you feel "that's life"—there's nothing much you can do about it. This is not necessarily so.

For your tired, worn out feeling may have a simple, easily correctable cause. You may simply not be getting enough of the essential B-Complex vitamins, thiamin and riboflavin. When you lack these vital elements, your blood cells start to wear out faster than your body can replace them. And when this is happening to you, *naturally* you feel tired, weak, irritable — thoroughly miserable.

But here is good news! If this is your trouble, we can promise you will get a new lease on life with Rybutol. Because, penny for penny, ounce for ounce, Rybutol is the highest-potency B-Complex formula advertised anywhere. It is the largest-selling B-Complex formula of its kind in America. And so you, too, can discover the remarkable difference between Rybutol and any other formula you *ever* tried, we make you this unusual offer:

We will send you a generous 7-day maintenance supply of high-potency Rybutol (49¢ value) *free*. Simply send your name and address with this ad and 10¢ to help cover mailing to: Rybutol, Dept. E28, Box 657, Grand Central Annex, New York 17, N.Y. Offer good for 10 days only. E-38

Nov. 1

WORN OUT?

Nervous? Run Down?

This message may change your whole life

If, day after day, you find yourself waking up tired, having to drag yourself through the day, you probably charge it up to "getting older," or overwork, or maybe "nerves." And probably you feel "that's life"—there's nothing much you can do about it. This is not necessarily so.

For your tired, worn out feeling may have a simple, easily correctable cause. You may simply not be getting enough of the essential B-Complex vitamins, thiamin and riboflavin. When you lack these vital elements, your blood cells start to wear out faster than your body can replace them. And when this is happening to you, *naturally* you feel tired, weak, irritable — thoroughly miserable.

But here is good news! If this is your trouble, we can promise you will get a new lease on life with Rybutol. Because, penny for penny, ounce for ounce, Rybutol is the highest potency B-Complex formula advertised anywhere. It is the largest-selling B-Complex formula of its kind in America. And so you, too, can discover the remarkable difference between Rybutol and any other formula you *ever* tried, we make you this unusual offer.

We will send you a generous 7-day maintenance supply of high-potency Rybutol (49¢ value) *free*. Simply send your name and address with this ad and 10¢ to help cover mailing to: Rybutol, Dept. E27, Box 657, Grand Central Annex, New York 17, N.Y. Offer good for 10 days only.

WHY RYBUTOL CAN MAKE YOU FEEL PEPPIER

WHERE OTHER VITAMINS FAIL

If, day after day, you find yourself waking up tired, having to drag yourself through the day, you probably charge it up to "getting older," or overwork, or maybe "nerves." And probably you feel "that's life"—there's nothing much you can do about it. This is not necessarily so.

For your tired, worn out feeling may have a simple, easily correctable cause. You may simply not be getting enough of the essential B-Complex vitamins, thiamin and riboflavin. When you lack these vital elements, your blood cells start to wear out faster than your body can replace them. And when this is happening to you, *naturally* you feel tired, weak, irritable — thoroughly miserable.

But here is good news! If this is your trouble, we can promise you will get a new lease on life with Rybutol. Because, penny for penny, ounce for ounce, Rybutol is the highest-potency B-Complex formula advertised anywhere. It is the largest-selling B-Complex formula of its kind in America. And so you, too, can discover the remarkable difference between Rybutol and any other formula you *ever* tried, we make you this unusual offer:

We will send you a generous 7-day maintenance supply of high-potency Rybutol (49¢ value) *free*. Simply send your name and address with this ad and 10¢ to help cover mailing to: Rybutol, Dept. E70, Box 657, Grand Central Annex, New York 17, N.Y. Offer good for 10 days only.

Nov. 2

Testing a Series of Ads by Split-run

On this page, and continued on the following pages, is a series of ten ads that were tested in ten days by split-run in a daily newspaper. The ad with the headline "Worn out" was selected as the Control Ad or measuring stick. (Any ad in a series may be used as the control.)

On Monday, November 1, the ad with the headline "How to get more energy from the food you eat" was split-run tested against the Control Ad. On Tuesday, November 2, the ad "How Rybutol can make you feel peppier" was tested against the Control Ad.

Every day, for ten days, omitting Saturday and Sunday, this process was continued. (At first glance, the November 1 ads look the same as the November 3 ads. However, different subheads were used.)

This series is a test of the various appeals contained in the headlines and subheads. The copy is identical in all the ads. The last paragraph of every ad

WORN OUT?

Nervous? Run Down?

This message may change your whole life

If day after day, you find yourself waking up tired, having to drag yourself through the day, you probably charge it up to "getting older," or overwork, or maybe "nerves." And probably you feel "that's life"— there's nothing much you can do about it. This is not necessarily so.

For your tired, worn out feeling may have a simple, easily correctable cause. You may simply not be getting enough of the essential B-Complex vitamins, thiamin and riboflavin. When you lack these vital elements, your blood cells start to wear out faster than your body can replace them. And when this is happening to you, naturally you feel tired, weak, irritable — thoroughly miserable. But here is good news! If this

is your trouble, we can promise you will get a new lease on life with Rybutol. Because, penny for penny, ounce for ounce, Rybutol is the highest potency B-Complex formula advertised anywhere. It is the largest selling B-Complex formula of its kind in America. And so you, too, can discover the remarkable difference between Rybutol and any other formula you ever tried, we make you this unusual offer:

We will send you a generous 7-day maintenance supply of high-potency Rybutol (49¢ value) free. Simply send your name and address with this ad and 10¢ to help cover mailing to: Rybutol, Dept. E27, Box 657, Grand Central Annex, New York 17, N.Y. Offer good for 10 days only.

HOW TO GET MORE ENERGY FROM THE FOOD YOU EAT

If you lack Vitamin B₁ & B₂

If, day after day, you find yourself waking up tired, having to drag yourself through the day, you probably charge it up to "getting older," or overwork, or maybe "nerves." And probably you feel "that's life"— there's nothing much you can do about it. This is not necessarily so.

For your tired, worn out feeling may have a simple, easily correctable cause. You may simply not be getting enough of the essential B-Complex vitamins, thiamin and riboflavin. When you lack these vital elements, your blood cells start to wear out faster than your body can replace them. And when this is happening to you, naturally you feel tired, weak, irritable — thoroughly miserable. But here is good news! If this

is your trouble, we can promise you will get a new lease on life with Rybutol. Because, penny for penny, ounce for ounce, Rybutol is the highest-potency B-Complex formula advertised anywhere. It is the largest-selling B-Complex formula of its kind in America. And so you, too, can discover the remarkable difference between Rybutol and any other formula you ever tried, we make you this unusual offer:

We will send you a generous 7-day maintenance supply of high-potency Rybutol (49¢ value) free. Simply send your name and address with this ad and 10¢ to help cover mailing to: Rybutol, Dept. E30, Box 657, Grand Central Annex, New York 17, N.Y. Offer good for 10 days only.

Nov. 3

WORN OUT?

Nervous? Run Down?

This message may change your whole life

If day after day, you find yourself waking up tired, having to drag yourself through the day, you probably charge it up to "getting older," or overwork, or maybe "nerves." And probably you feel "that's life"— there's nothing much you can do about it. This is not necessarily so.

For your tired, worn out feeling may have a simple, easily correctable cause. You may simply not be getting enough of the essential B-Complex vitamins, thiamin and riboflavin. When you lack these vital elements, your blood cells start to wear out faster than your body can replace them. And when this is happening to you, naturally you feel tired, weak, irritable — thoroughly miserable. But here is good news! If this

is your trouble, we can promise you will get a new lease on life with Rybutol. Because, penny for penny, ounce for ounce, Rybutol is the highest potency B-Complex formula advertised anywhere. It is the largest selling B-Complex formula of its kind in America. And so you, too, can discover the remarkable difference between Rybutol and any other formula you ever tried, we make you this unusual offer:

We will send you a generous 7-day maintenance supply of high-potency Rybutol (49¢ value) free. Simply send your name and address with this ad and 10¢ to help cover mailing to: Rybutol, Dept. E27, Box 657, Grand Central Annex, New York 17, N.Y. Offer good for 10 days only.

SHOULD YOU BE TAKING VITAMINS?

If, day after day, you find yourself waking up tired, having to drag yourself through the day, you probably charge it up to "getting older," or overwork, or maybe "nerves." And probably you feel "that's life"— there's nothing much you can do about it. This is not necessarily so.

For your tired, worn out feeling may have a simple, easily correctable cause. You may simply not be getting enough of the essential B-Complex vitamins, thiamin and riboflavin. When you lack these vital elements, your blood cells start to wear out faster than your body can replace them. And when this is happening to you, naturally you feel tired, weak, irritable — thoroughly miserable. But here is good news! If this

is your trouble, we can promise you will get a new lease on life with Rybutol. Because, penny for penny, ounce for ounce, Rybutol is the highest-potency B-Complex formula advertised anywhere. It is the largest-selling B-Complex formula of its kind in America. And so you, too, can discover the remarkable difference between Rybutol and any other formula you ever tried, we make you this unusual offer:

We will send you a generous 7-day maintenance supply of high-potency Rybutol (49¢ value) free. Simply send your name and address with this ad and 10¢ to help cover mailing to: Rybutol, Dept. E10, Box 657, Grand Central Annex, New York 17, N.Y. Offer good for 10 days only.

Nov. 4

contains this offer: "We will send you a generous 7-day maintenance supply of high-potency Rybutol (49¢ value) free. Simply send your name and address with this ad and 10¢ to help cover mailing to: Rybutol, Dept. 000, Box 657 Grand Central Annex, New York, N.Y. Offer good for 10 days only." (The numerals 000 were replaced by a different key number in each ad, such as Dept. E10, E11, etc.)

When the results of this test were tabulated, it was found that some ads pulled more replies than the Control Ad and some ads pulled fewer replies than the Control Ad. For example, the winning ad pulled 235% more replies than the Control Ad, and the poorest ad pulled 24% fewer replies than the Control Ad. The other ads were ranked in the same manner, namely, by the percentage points by which they were better or poorer than the Control Ad. A successful advertising and sales campaign was based on the winning appeal.

WORN OUT?

Nervous? Run Down?

This message may change your whole life

If, day after day, you find yourself waking up tired, having to drag yourself through the day, you probably charge it up to "getting older," or overwork, or maybe "nerves." And probably you feel "that's life"—there's nothing much you can do about it. This is not necessarily so.

For your tired, worn out feeling may have a simple, easily correctable cause. You may simply not be getting enough of the essential B-Complex vitamins, thiamin and riboflavin. When you lack these vital elements, your blood cells start to wear out faster than your body can replace them. And when this is happening to you, *naturally* you feel tired, weak, irritable – thoroughly miserable.

But here is good news! If this is your trouble, we can promise you will get a new lease on life with Rybutol. Because, penny for penny, ounce for ounce, Rybutol is the highest potency B-Complex formula advertised anywhere. It is the largest-selling B-Complex formula of its kind in America. And so you, too, can discover the remarkable difference between Rybutol and any other formula you *ever* tried, we make you this unusual offer:

We will send you a generous 7-day maintenance supply of high-potency Rybutol (49¢ value) *free.* Simply send your name and address with this ad and 10¢ to help cover mailing to: Rybutol, Dept. E27, Box 657, Grand Central Annex, New York 17, N. Y. Offer good for 10 days only.

NOW! FEEL PEPPIER, STRONGER IN JUST 7 DAYS

If, day after day, you find yourself waking up tired, having to drag yourself through the day, you probably charge it up to "getting older," or overwork, or maybe "nerves." And probably you feel "that's life"—there's nothing much you can do about it. This is not necessarily so.

For your tired, worn out feeling may have a simple, easily correctable cause. You may simply not be getting enough of the essential B-Complex vitamins, thiamin and riboflavin. When you lack these vital elements, your blood cells start to wear out faster than your body can replace them. And when this is happening to you, *naturally* you feel tired, weak, irritable – thoroughly miserable.

But here is good news! If this is your trouble, we can promise you will get a new lease on life with Rybutol. Because, penny for penny, ounce for ounce, Rybutol is the highest potency B-Complex formula advertised anywhere. It is the largest-selling B-Complex formula of its kind in America. And so you, too, can discover the remarkable difference between Rybutol and any other formula we make you this unusual offer:

We will send you a generous 7-day maintenance supply of high-potency Rybutol (49¢ value) *free.* Simply send your name and address with this ad and 10¢ to help cover mailing to: Rybutol, Dept. E16, Box 657, Grand Central Annex, New York 17, N.Y. Offer good for 10 days only.

Nov. 5

WORN OUT?

Nervous? Run Down?

This message may change your whole life

If, day after day, you find yourself waking up tired, having to drag yourself through the day, you probably charge it up to "getting older," or overwork, or maybe "nerves." And probably you feel "that's life"—there's nothing much you can do about it. This is not necessarily so.

For your tired, worn out feeling may have a simple, easily correctable cause. You may simply not be getting enough of the essential B-Complex vitamins, thiamin and riboflavin. When you lack these vital elements, your blood cells start to wear out faster than your body can replace them. And when this is happening to you, *naturally* you feel tired, weak, irritable – thoroughly miserable.

But here is good news! If this is your trouble, we can promise you will get a new lease on life with Rybutol. Because, penny for penny, ounce for ounce, Rybutol is the highest potency B-Complex formula advertised anywhere. It is the largest-selling B-Complex formula of its kind in America. And so you, too, can discover the remarkable difference between Rybutol and any other formula you *ever* tried, we make you this unusual offer:

We will send you a generous 7-day maintenance supply of high-potency Rybutol (49¢ value) *free.* Simply send your name and address with this ad and 10¢ to help cover mailing to: Rybutol, Dept. E27, Box 657, Grand Central Annex, New York 17, N. Y. Offer good for 10 days only.

FEEL OVER 35?

If, day after day, you find yourself waking up tired, having to drag yourself through the day, you probably charge it up to "getting older," or overwork, or maybe "nerves." And probably you feel "that's life"—there's nothing much you can do about it. This is not necessarily so.

For your tired, worn out feeling may have a simple, easily correctable cause. You may simply not be getting enough of the essential B-Complex vitamins, thiamin and riboflavin. When you lack these vital elements, your blood cells start to wear out faster than your body can replace them. And when this is happening to you, *naturally* you feel tired, weak, irritable – thoroughly miserable.

But here is good news! If this is your trouble, we can promise you will get a new lease on life with Rybutol. Because, penny for penny, ounce for ounce, Rybutol is the highest-potency B-Complex formula advertised anywhere. It is the largest-selling B-Complex formula of its kind in America. And so you, too, can discover the remarkable difference between Rybutol and any other formula you *ever* tried, we make you this unusual offer:

We will send you a generous 7-day maintenance supply of high-potency Rybutol (49¢ value) *free.* Simply send your name and address with this ad and 10¢ to help cover mailing to: Rybutol, Dept. E22, Box 657, Grand Central Annex, New York 17, N. Y. Offer good for 10 days only.

Nov. 8

WORN OUT?

Nervous? Run Down?

This message may change your whole life

If, day after day, you find yourself waking up tired, having to drag yourself through the day, you probably charge it up to "getting older," or overwork, or maybe "nerves." And probably you feel "that's life"—there's nothing much you can do about it. This is not necessarily so.

For your tired, worn out feeling may have a simple, easily correctable cause. You may simply not be getting enough of the essential B-Complex vitamins, thiamin and riboflavin. When you lack these vital elements, your blood cells start to wear out faster than your body can replace them. And when this is happening to you, *naturally* you feel tired, weak, irritable – thoroughly miserable.

But here is good news! If this is your trouble, we can promise you will get a new lease on life with Rybutol. Because, penny for penny, ounce for ounce, Rybutol is the highest potency B-Complex formula advertised anywhere. It is the largest-selling B-Complex formula of its kind in America. And so you, too, can discover the remarkable difference between Rybutol and any other formula you *ever* tried, we make you this unusual offer:

We will send you a generous 7-day maintenance supply of high-potency Rybutol (49¢ value) *free.* Simply send your name and address with this ad and 10¢ to help cover mailing to: Rybutol, Dept. E27, Box 657, Grand Central Annex, New York 17, N. Y. Offer good for 10 days only.

NOW! Extra-High Potency Vitamin Formula

contains 22 vital elements

If, day after day, you find yourself waking up tired, having to drag yourself through the day, you probably charge it up to "getting older," or overwork, or maybe "nerves." And probably you feel "that's life"—there's nothing much you can do about it. This is not necessarily so.

For your tired, worn out feeling may have a simple, easily correctable cause. You may simply not be getting enough of the essential B-Complex vitamins, thiamin and riboflavin. When you lack these vital elements, your blood cells start to wear out faster than your body can replace them. And when this is happening to you, *naturally* you feel tired, weak, irritable – thoroughly miserable.

But here is good news! If this is your trouble, we can promise you will get a new lease on life with Rybutol. Because, penny for penny, ounce for ounce, Rybutol is the highest-potency B-Complex formula advertised anywhere. It is the largest-selling B-Complex formula of its kind in America. And so you, too, can discover the remarkable difference between Rybutol and any other formula you *ever* tried, we make you this unusual offer:

We will send you a generous 7-day maintenance supply of high-potency Rybutol (49¢ value) *free.* Simply send your name and address with this ad and 10¢ to help cover mailing to: Rybutol, Dept. E36, Box 657, Grand Central Annex, New York 17, N. Y. Offer good for 10 days only.

Nov. 9

Nov. 10

Nov. 11

Nov. 12

15 Famous Ads

On the following pages are reproductions of historic ads that have appeared during the last sixty years. These ads are examples of printed messages that proved to have unusual attention-value and selling power. These ads sold millions of dollars worth of goods and services and made lasting impressions on the minds of Americans. Many of today's great ads reflect these tested techniques. Perhaps you can find in these ad classics some ideas that will spark your imagination and help you to produce some of the great ads of the future.

"Here's an Extra $50, Grace
—I'm making **real** money now!"

"Yes, I've been keeping it a secret until pay day came. I've been promoted with an increase of $50 a month. And the first extra money is yours. Just a little reward for urging me to study at home. The boss says my spare time training has made me a valuable man to the firm and there's more money coming soon. We're starting up easy street, Grace, thanks to you and the I. C. S.!"

Today more than ever before, money is what counts. The cost of living is mounting month by month. You can't get along on what you have been making. Somehow, you've simply got to increase your earnings.

Fortunately for you hundreds of thousands of other men have proved there is an unfailing way to do it. Train yourself for bigger work, learn to do some one thing well and employers will be glad to pay you real money for your special knowledge.

You can get the training that will prepare you for the position you want in the work you like best, whatever it may be. You can get it without sacrificing a day or a dollar from your present occupation. You can get it at home, in spare time, through the International Correspondence Schools.

It is the *business* of the I. C. S. to prepare men in just your circumstances for better positions at better pay. They have been doing it for 28 years. They have helped two million other men and women. They are training over 100,000 now. Every day many students write to tell of advancements and increased salaries already won.

You have the same chance they had. What are you going to do with it? Can you afford to let a single priceless hour pass without at least finding out what the I. C. S. can do for you? Here is all we ask—without cost, without obligating yourself in any way, simply mark and mail this coupon.

---- TEAR OUT HERE ----

INTERNATIONAL CORRESPONDENCE SCHOOLS
BOX , SCRANTON, PA.

Explain, without obligating me, how I can qualify for the position, or in the subject, before which I mark X.

☐ ELECTRICAL ENGINEER	☐ SALESMANSHIP
☐ Electric Lighting and Railways	☐ ADVERTISING
☐ Electric Wiring	☐ Window Trimmer
☐ Telegraph Engineer	☐ Show Card Writer
☐ Telephone Work	☐ Sign Painter
☐ MECHANICAL ENGINEER	☐ Railroad Trainman
☐ Mechanical Draftsman	☐ ILLUSTRATING
☐ Machine Shop Practice	☐ Cartooning
☐ Toolmaker	☐ BOOKKEEPER
☐ Gas Engine Operating	☐ Stenographer and Typist
☐ CIVIL ENGINEER	☐ Cert. Public Accountant
☐ Surveying and Mapping	☐ TRAFFIC MANAGER
☐ MINE FOREMAN OR ENGINEER	☐ Railway Accountant
☐ STATIONARY ENGINEER	☐ Commercial Law
☐ Marine Engineer	☐ GOOD ENGLISH
☐ Ship Draftsman	☐ Teacher
☐ ARCHITECT	☐ Common School Subjects
☐ Contractor and Builder	☐ Mathematics
☐ Architectural Draftsman	☐ CIVIL SERVICE
☐ Concrete Builder	☐ Railway Mail Clerk
☐ Structural Engineer	☐ AUTOMOBILE OPERATING
☐ PLUMBING AND HEATING	☐ Auto Repairing
☐ Sheet Metal Worker	☐ Navigation ☐ Spanish
☐ Textile Overseer or Supt.	☐ AGRICULTURE ☐ French
☐ CHEMIST	☐ Poultry Raising ☐ Italian

Name_____

Present
Occupation_____

Street
and No._____

City_____ State_____

Canadians may send this coupon to
International Correspondence Schools, Montreal, Canada

One of the All-time Greats

This ad first appeared in 1919. It is typical of a famous series that built the International Correspondence Schools into the largest in the world. The appeal is as valid today as ever. For example, the copy says: "The cost of living is mounting month by month. You can't get along on what you have been making. Somehow you've simply got to increase your earnings."

A wonderful two years' trip at full pay—
but only men with imagination can take it

ABOUT one man in ten will be appealed to by this page. The other nine will be hard workers, earnest, ambitious in their way, but to them a coupon is a coupon; a book is a book; a Course is a Course. The one man in ten has imagination.

And imagination rules the world. Let us put it this way. An automobile is at your door; you are invited to pack your bag and step in. You will travel by limited train to New York. You will go directly to the office of the president of one of the biggest banks. You will spend hours with him, and with other bank presidents.

Each one will take you personally thru his institution. He will explain clearly the operations of his bank; he will answer any question that comes to your mind. In intimate personal conversation he will tell you what he has learned from his own experience. He will give you at first hand the things you need to know about the financial side of business. You will not leave these bankers until you have a thoro understanding of our great banking system.

When you have finished with them the car will be waiting. It will take you to the offices of men who direct great selling organizations. They will be waiting for you: their time will be at your disposal—all the time you want until you know all you can learn about marketing, selling and advertising.

Again you will travel. You will visit the principal industries of the country. The men who have devoted their lives to production will be your guides thru these plants in Detroit, Cleveland, Chicago and in every great industrial center.

Thru other days the heads of accounting departments will guide you. On others, men who have made their mark in office management; on others, traffic experts, and authorities in commercial law and credits. Great economists and teachers and business leaders will be your companions.

The whole journey will occupy two years. It will cost you nothing in income, for your salary will go right along. Every single day you will be in contact with men whose authority is proved by incomes of $50,000, $100,000, or even more.

Do you think that any man with imagination could spend two years like that without being bigger at the end? Is it humanly possible for a mind to come in contact with the biggest minds in business without growing more self-reliant, more active, more able?

Is it worth a few pennies a day to have such an experience? Do you wonder that the men who have had it — who have made this two years' journey — are holding positions of executive responsibility in business everywhere?

This wonderful two years' trip is what the Alexander Hamilton Institute offers you. Not merely a set of books (tho you *do* receive a business library

which will be a source of guidance and inspiration thruout your business life). Not merely a set of lectures (tho the lectures parallel what is offered in the leading university schools of business). Not merely business problems which you solve, and from which you gain definite practical experience and self-confidence.

All these—books, lectures, problems, reports, bulletins—come to you, but they are not the real Course. The real Course is the experience of the most successful business men in the country. For two years you live with them. In two years you gain what they have had to work out for themselves thru a lifetime of practical effort.

"Forging Ahead in Business"

If you are the one man in ten to whom this page is directed, there is a book which you will be glad to own. It is called "Forging Ahead in Business." It costs you nothing, yet it is permanently valuable.

If you have read this far, and if you are at least 21 years of age, you are one of the men who ought to clip the coupon and receive it with our compliments.

The car is waiting; step in

Alexander Hamilton Institute
Executive Training for Business Men

In CANADA, address the Alexander Hamilton Institute, Limited, C. P. R. Bldg., Toronto   In ENGLAND, 67 Great Russell St., London. In AUSTRALIA, 11c Castlereagh St., Sydney

ALEXANDER HAMILTON INSTITUTE
685 Astor Place   New York City

Send me the new, revised edition of "Forging Ahead in Business," which I may keep without charge.

Name ....
Please write plainly

Business
Address ....

....

Business
Position ....

An Ad That Ran for Seven Years

This ad for a two-year correspondence course in business training was written by Bruce Barton, former chairman of BBDO, Inc. The ad brought so many coupon returns that it was run again and again in magazines and newspapers for seven years. The coupons were turned over to salesmen. General advertisers sometimes ask, "Is it profitable to repeat a good ad?" Based on the experience of mail order advertisers, the answer is yes.

The man in the Hathaway shirt

AMERICAN MEN are beginning to realize that it is ridiculous to buy good suits and then spoil the effect by wearing an ordinary, mass-produced shirt. Hence the growing popularity of HATHAWAY shirts, which are in a class by themselves.

HATHAWAY shirts wear infinitely longer—a matter of years. They make you look younger and more distinguished, because of the subtle way HATHAWAY cut collars. The whole shirt is tailored more generously, and is therefore more comfortable. The tails are longer, and stay in your

trousers. The buttons are mother-of-pearl. Even the stitching has an ante-bellum elegance about it.

Above all, HATHAWAY make their shirts of remarkable *fabrics*, collected from the four corners of the earth—Viyella and Aertex from England, woolen taffeta from Scotland, Sea Island cotton from the West Indies, hand-woven madras from India, broadcloth from Manchester, linen batiste from Paris, hand-blocked silks from England, exclusive cottons from the best weavers in America. You will get a

great deal of quiet satisfaction out of wearing shirts which are in such impeccable taste.

HATHAWAY shirts are made by a small company of dedicated craftsmen in the little town of Waterville, Maine. They have been at it, man and boy, for one hundred and fifteen years.

At better stores everywhere, or write C. F. HATHAWAY, Waterville, Maine, for the name of your nearest store. In New York, telephone MU 9-4157. Prices from $5.95 to $25.00.

How to Sell Shirts

"Why is the man wearing an eye patch?" is the question nearly everybody asked on seeing this ad. And apparently, nearly everybody read the copy. The sales of Hathaway shirts were phenomenal. This ad is one of a famous series originated and written by David Ogilvy. Other ads showed the man with the eye patch pursuing various activities such as fencing, sailing, buying a painting, and conducting an orchestra. In one memorable ad, he was shown writing his will. Headline: "To my son Benjamin: one million dollars and all my Hathaway shirts."

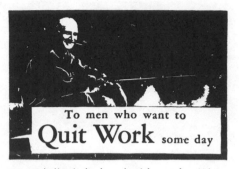

To men who want to
Quit Work some day

THIS PAGE is addressed to those thousands of earnest, hard-working men who want to take things easier some day.

It tells how these men, by following a simple, definite plan, can provide for themselves in later years a *guaranteed income they cannot outlive.*

How the Plan Works

It doesn't matter whether your present income is large or merely average. It doesn't matter whether you are making fifty dollars a week or five hundred. If you follow this plan you will some day have an income upon which to retire.

The plan calls for the deposit of only a few dollars each month—the exact amount depending on your age. The minute you make your first deposit, your biggest money worries begin to disappear.

Even if you should become totally and permanently disabled, you would not need to worry. Shortly thereafter, we would mail you a check every month so long as your disability continued, even if it lasted for many, many years—the remainder of your natural life.

And not only that. Your monthly payments would

be made for you out of a special fund provided by the company for that purpose.

Get this free book

The Phoenix Mutual Company, which offers you this opportunity, is a 135 million dollar company. For over three-quarters of a century it has been helping thousands of men and women to end money worries.

But you're not interested in us. You are interested in what we can do for *you.* An illustrated, 28-page book called "How to Get the Things You Want" tells you exactly that. It tells how you can become financially independent—how you can retire on an income—how you can provide money for emergencies—money to leave your home free of debt—money for other needs.

This financial plan is simple, reasonable, and logical. The minute you read about it you will realize why it accomplishes such desirable results — not for failures, not for people who can't make ends meet, but for hard-working, forward-looking people who know what they want and are ready to make definite plans to get it. No obligation. Get your copy of the book now.

> ### NEW RETIREMENT INCOME PLAN
> Here is what a dividend-paying $10,000 policy will do for you:
>
> *It guarantees when you are 65*
> A Monthly Income for life of $100 which assures a return of at least $10,000, and perhaps much more, depending upon how long you live.
> Or, if you prefer,
> A Cash Settlement of $12,000.
>
> *It guarantees upon death from any cause before age 65*
> A Cash Payment to your beneficiary of $10,000. Or $50 a month for at least 24 years and 8 months.
> Total $14,823
>
> *It guarantees upon death from accidental means before age 60*
> A Cash Payment to your beneficiary of $20,000. Or $100 a month for at least 24 years and 8 months.
> Total $29,646
>
> *It guarantees in event of permanent total disability before age 60.*
> A Monthly Disability Income of $100 and payment of your premiums while you are disabled.
> Plans for women or for retirement at ages 55 or 60 are also available.

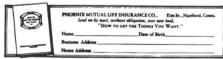

PHOENIX MUTUAL
LIFE INSURANCE COMPANY
Home Office: Hartford, Conn.   First Policy Issued 1851

PHOENIX MUTUAL LIFE INSURANCE CO.,   Elm St., Hartford, Conn.
Send me by mail, without obligation, your new book,
"HOW TO GET THE THINGS YOU WANT."

Name_____ Date of Birth_____

Business Address_____

Home Address_____

The First of a Time-honored Series

This ad is the first of a series showing men and women happily retired on a guaranteed income. The series ran for 38 years. The purpose of the ads was: (1) To get leads for salesmen, and (2) To make the name Phoenix Mutual known. Editor's note: This ad, written by John Caples, was included in *The 100 Greatest Advertisements.*

Film—the robber

of all tooth beauty. Learn how millions now combat it

It is Free

This ten-day test.
Simply send coupon.

Pepsodent multiplies the alkalinity of the saliva. That is there to neutralize mouth acids, the cause of tooth decay. It multiplies the starch digestant in saliva. That is there to digest starch deposits on teeth.

Every use of Pepsodent brings these combined effects. Together they bring a new conception of what clean teeth mean. You will be amazed and delighted.

That cloudy coat on teeth is film. At first the film is viscous—you can feel it now.

That film is clinging. No ordinary tooth paste effectively combats it. So, in old-way brushing, much of it clings and stays. Food stains, etc., discolor it, then it forms dingy coats. That is why so many teeth are clouded.

Film is unclean

Film is unclean. When it lingers on or between the teeth it threatens constant damage.

Film holds food substance which ferments and forms acid. It holds the acid in contact with the teeth to cause decay. Germs breed by millions in it. They, with tartar, are the chief cause of pyorrhea.

These film-caused troubles became almost universal. They were constantly increasing. So dental investigators started out to find ways to fight film.

Two methods found

In this research two methods were discovered. One disintegrates the film at all stages of formation. One removes it without harmful scouring.

Able authorities have proved these methods effective, by many careful tests. A new-type tooth paste was created to apply them daily. The name is Pepsodent.

Leading dentists everywhere began to advise it. The use fast spread the world over. Now careful people of some 50 nations have adopted this modern tooth paste.

Two other needs discovered

Two other essentials were revealed by research. So

Protect the Enamel

Pepsodent disintegrates the film, then removes it with an agent far softer than enamel. Never use a film combatant which contains harsh grit.

You see the results at once

The Pepsodent results are quick and apparent. Some are seen and felt at once. You can have no doubt about them.

Send the coupon for a 10-Day Tube. Note how clean the teeth feel after using. Mark the absence of the viscous film. See how teeth become whiter as the film-coats disappear.

Compare this new way with the old. Then you will know what method should be used by you and yours. Cut out coupon now.

Pepsodent

REG. U. S.

The New-Day Dentifrice

A scientific tooth paste based on modern research, made to meet modern requirements. Now advised by leading dentists the world over.

10-Day Tube Free

THE PEPSODENT COMPANY,
Dept. J, 1104 S. Wabash Ave., Chicago, Ill.

Mail 10-Day Tube of Pepsodent to

....

....

Only one tube to a family

Written by the World's Most Famous Copywriter

Ad writer Claude Hopkins was famous for his ability to write good headlines and powerful "reason-why" copy. His copy sold millions of dollars worth of merchandise. Here is a typical example of his style of writing. Note the short paragraphs, short sentences and simple language. Said Hopkins: "People will not be bored in print. They want economy, beauty, labor saving, good things to eat and wear. They will never know it unless the headline or the picture tells them."

A $10,000 Mistake

A CLIENT for whom we had copied a necklace of Oriental Pearls, seeing both necklaces before her, said: *Well, the resemblance is remarkable, but this is mine!*

Then she picked up ours!

TÉCLA

398 Fifth Avenue, New York
10 Rue de la Paix, Paris

Written by the World's Highest Paid Copywriter

Frank Irving Fletcher, the highest-paid ad writer of his time, was famous for his ability to tell a story in a few words. Above is an example. "But brevity is not desirable in all cases," he said. "If a man is interested in buying what you have to sell, you can't tell him too much."

HOW TO WIN FRIENDS AND INFLUENCE PEOPLE

JOHN D. ROCKEFELLER, SR. once said: "The ability to deal with people is as purchasable a commodity as sugar or coffee. And I will pay more for that ability than for any other under the sun."

Wouldn't you suppose every college would conduct practical courses to develop the "highest-priced ability under the sun"? To our knowledge, none has.

How to develop that ability is the subject of Dale Carnegie's book.

A few years ago Chicago University and the United Y.M.C.A. Schools made a survey to find out the prime interest of adults. The survey took two years, cost $25,000. It indicated that their first interest is health—and their second, how to understand and get along with people; how to make people like you, how to win others to your way of thinking.

Wouldn't you suppose that after the members of this survey committee had decided to gate such a course, they could readily have found a practical textbook? They searched diligently—yet could find none suitable.

The book they were looking for was published not long ago. Almost overnight it became a best seller. It is one of the fastest-selling books published in the twentieth century. More than 805,000 copies have been sold to date! It is outselling any other non-fiction book in America!

The Man Behind the Book

This book is called *How to Win Friends and Influence People*—and is written by the one man who is perhaps better qualified to write it than anyone else.

Dale Carnegie is the man to whom the big men of business come for practical education on the subject of getting along with people, dealing with them successfully, winning others to their own way of thinking. During the last 26 years he has trained more than 22,000 business and professional men and women—among them some of the most famous in the country.

When he conducts his course on Public Speaking and How to Influence People in the ballroom of the Hotel Commodore, or The Pennsylvania, or the Hotel Astor (the second largest hall in New York) the place is packed to capacity. Large organizations—such as The New York Telephone Co., Westinghouse Electric and Manufacturing Company, and many others listed elsewhere on this page—have had this training conducted by Mr. Carnegie in their own offices for their executives and executives.

This book, *How to Win Friends and Influence People*, grew and developed out of that laboratory of experience. As you can judge from the panel at the top of this 'advertisement,' it is as practical as 26 years of actual successful experience with the problems of thousands of people in all walks of life can make it.

Consider the Case of Michael O'Neil

Michael O'Neil lives in New York City. He first got

a job as an automobile mechanic, then as a chauffeur. When he got married he needed more money. So he tried to sell automobile trucks. But he was a terrible flop. He suffered from an inferiority complex that was eating his heart out.

On his way to see any prospect he broke out into a cold sweat. Then, before he could get up enough courage to open the door, he often had to walk up and down in front of an office half a dozen times.

When he finally got in he would invariably find himself antagonizing, arguing. Then he would get kicked out—never knowing quite why.

He was such a failure he decided to go back to work as a machine shop. Then one day he received a letter inviting him to attend the opening session of a Dale Carnegie course.

"It may do you some good, Mike, God knows you need it."

He didn't want to go—he was afraid that he would be out of place—that there would be a lot of college men there. But his despairing wife made him, saying, "It may do you some good, Mike, God knows you need it."

He went to the meeting, and other meetings of the course. He lost his fear. He learned how to talk effectively and convincingly; how to make people like him at once, how to win friends and influence others.

Today Michael O'Neil is a star salesman for one of the country's largest manufacturers of motor trucks. His income has mounted and skyrocketed. Last year at the Hotel Astor he stood in front of 3,800 people and told a rollicking story of his achievements. Few professional speakers could have equalled his confidence—or his success.

Michael O'Neil is a salesman—but his problem was exactly the same as that of thousands in other fields—the fundamental one of getting along with people. The way it was solved is just one example of what Dale Carnegie's help has meant to more than 22,000 others of his students in all types of endeavor. What Dale Carnegie has done for them he can do for you. Look at the chapter headings. They indicate the amount of hard-hitting, priceless information Dale Carnegie's book contains. But the subject is so intensely important that we say, look at this book without obligation. Then decide whether or not you want to own it.

THIS IS A BIG BOOK OF THIRTY-SEVEN CHAPTERS, INCLUDING:

The Big Secret of Dealing with People
Six Ways to Make People Like You Instantly
An Easy Way to Become a Good Conversationalist
A Simple Way to Make a Good First Impression
How to Interest People
Twelve Ways to Win People to Your Way of Thinking
A Sure Way of Making Enemies—and How to Avoid It
The Safety Valve in Handling Complaints
Do This and You'll Be Welcome Anywhere
How to Get Cooperation
A Formula That Will Work Wonders for You
The Movies Do It. Radio Does It. Why Don't You Do It?
How Ways to Change People Without Giving Offense or Arousing Resentment
How to Criticize—and Not Be Hated for It
How to Spur Men on to Success
Making People Glad to Do What You Want
Letters That Produced Miraculous Results
If You Don't Do This, You Are Headed for Trouble
Seven Rules for Making Your Home Life Happier

DALE CARNEGIE

Dale Carnegie is the man the men of business come to for practical instruction on getting along with people. During the last 26 years he has trained more than 22,000 business and professional men—more than any other living man.

Large organizations such as:

Westinghouse Electric & Manufacturing Co.	Brooklyn Chamber of Commerce
New York Telephone Co.	Philadelphia Chamber of Commerce
Bell Telephone Co. of Pennsylvania	Philadelphia Electric Co.
American Institute of Electrical Engineers	Philadelphia Gas Works Co.
New York	Ladies Agency Corporation

have had the training conducted in their own offices for their members and executives.

This book is a direct result of Dale Carnegie's experience, the only working manual of its kind ever written to help people solve their daily problems in human relationships.

SEND NO MONEY

Try Dealing THIS WAY with People
—just for FIVE Days!

The book is sweeping the country. It is on every best-seller list. It is one of the largest selling books of non-fiction of the twentieth century!

When you get your copy simply read it; there are no "exercises" to be practiced. Then try for five days Dale Carnegie's simple method of dealing with people. Judge for yourself, in your daily social or business life how easily whatever you do, say, or write can win the friendship and the hearty cooperation of others—instead of arousing resentment, friction, and either a negative response or no action at all.

It is not necessary to send any money now. You may pay for *How to Win Friends and Influence People* when it is delivered with the definite understanding that its price of only $1.96 will be refunded to you if you wish it. If this book does what we claim, it will mean more to you than ANY book you have ever read. If it doesn't, we do not want you to keep it. Mail the coupon at the left at once.

SIMON and SCHUSTER, Publishers
386 Fourth Ave.   New York City

ONLY $1.96
If you decide to keep it!

SIMON and SCHUSTER, Publishers
Dept. 103, 386 Fourth Ave., New York City

Please send me *How to Win Friends and Influence People*. I will pay postman only $1.96 plus few cents postage charges. It is understood that I may read it for 5 days and return it for refund if I then feel that it does not so every way live up to the claims made for it.

Name ....

Address ....

City .... State ....

☐ Check here if you prefer to enclose $1.96 WITH this coupon. In that case WE will pay the postage charges. The refund privilege applies of course.

NOTE If residents of New York City add to its City Sales Tax.

How Five Million Books Were Sold

This ad for Dale Carnegie's book, *How to Win Friends and Influence People*, was written by Victor Schwab, former president of the Schwab, Beatty and Porter advertising agency. The ad made a remarkable record. After preliminary tests proved its selling power, it was published in a long list of newspapers and magazines. The ad produced nearly 100,000 direct mail orders and started sales in bookstores that have amounted to over 5 million copies.

Do You Make These Mistakes in English?

Sherwin Cody's remarkable invention has enabled more than 100,000 people to correct their mistakes in English. Only 15 minutes a day required to improve your speech and writing.

MANY persons use such expressions as "Leave them lay there" and "Mary was invited as well as myself." Still others say "between you and I" instead of "between you and me." It is astonishing how often "who" is used for "whom" and how frequently we hear such glaring mispronunciations as "for MID able," "ave NOO," and "KEW pon." Few know whether to spell certain words with one or two "c's" or "m's" or "r's" or with "ie" or "ci," and when to use commas in order to make their meaning absolutely clear. Most persons use only common words—colorless, flat, ordinary. Their speech and their letters are lifeless, monotonous, humdrum.

Why Most People Make Mistakes

What is the reason so many of us are deficient in the use of English and find our careers stunted in consequence? Why is it some cannot spell correctly and others cannot punctuate? Why do so many find themselves at a loss for words to express their meaning adequately? The reason for the deficiency is clear. Sherwin Cody discovered it in scientific tests which he gave thousands of times. *Most persons do not write or speak good English simply because they never formed the habit of doing so.*

What Cody Did at Gary

The formation of any habit comes only from constant practice. Shakespeare, you may be sure, never studied rules. No one who writes and speaks correctly thinks of *rules* when he is doing so.

Here is our mother-tongue, a language that has built up our civilization, and without which we should all still be muttering savages! Yet our schools, by wrong methods, have made it a study to be avoided —the hardest of tasks instead of the most fascinating of games! For years it has been a crying disgrace.

In that point lies the real difference between Sherwin Cody and the schools! Here is an illustration: Some years ago Mr. Cody was invited by the author of the famous Gary System of Education to teach

SHERWIN CODY

English to all upper-grade pupils in Gary, Indiana. By means of unique practice exercises *Mr. Cody secured more improvement in these pupils in five weeks than previously had been obtained by similar pupils in two years under old methods.* There was no guesswork about these results. They were proved by scientific comparisons. Amazing as this improvement was, more interesting still was the fact that the children were "wild" about the study. It was like playing a game!

The basic principle of Mr. Cody's new method is habit-forming. Anyone can learn to write and speak correctly by constantly using the correct forms. But how is one to know in each case what is correct? Mr. Cody solves this problem in a simple, unique, sensible way.

100% Self-Correcting Device

Suppose he himself were standing forever at your elbow. Every time you mispronounced or misspelled a word, every time you violated correct grammatical usage, every time you used the wrong word to express what you meant, suppose you could hear him whisper: "That is wrong, it should be thus and so." In a short time you would habitually use the correct form and the right words in speaking and writing.

If you continued to make the same mistakes over and over again, each time patiently he would tell you what was right. He would, as it were, be an everlasting mentor beside you—a mentor who would not laugh at you, but who would, on the contrary, support and help you. The 100% Self-Correcting Device does exactly this thing. It is Mr. Cody's silent voice behind you, ready to speak out whenever you commit an error. It finds your mistakes and concentrates on them. You do not need to study anything you already know. There are no rules to memorize.

Only 15 Minutes a Day

Nor is there very much to learn. In Mr. Cody's years of experimenting he brought to light some highly astonishing facts about English.

For instance, statistics show that a list of sixty-nine words (with their repetitions) make up more than half of all our speech and letter-writing. Obviously, if one could learn to spell, use, and pronounce these words correctly, one would go far toward eliminating incorrect spelling and pronunciation.

Similarly, Mr. Cody proved that there were no more than one dozen fundamental principles of punctuation. If we mastered these principles, there would be no bugbear of punctuation to handicap us in our writing.

Finally he discovered that twenty-five typical errors in grammar constitute nine-tenths of our everyday mistakes. When one has learned to avoid these twenty-five pitfalls, how readily one can obtain the facility of speech which denotes the person of breeding and education!

When the study of English is made so simple, it becomes clear that progress can be made in a very short time. *No more than fifteen minutes a day is required.* Fifteen minutes, not of study, but of fascinating practice! Mr. Cody's students do their work in any spare moment they can snatch. They do it riding to work or at home. They take fifteen minutes from the time usually spent in profitless reading or amusement. The results really are phenomenal.

Sherwin Cody has placed an excellent command of the English language within the grasp of everyone. Those who take advantage of his method gain something so priceless that it cannot be measured in terms of money. They gain a mark of breeding that cannot be erased as long as they live. They gain a facility in speech that marks them as educated people in whatever society they find themselves. They gain the self-confidence and self-respect which this ability inspires. As for material reward, certainly the importance of good English in the race for success cannot be overestimated. Surely, no one can advance far without it.

FREE — Book on English

It is impossible in this brief review, to give more than a suggestion of the range of subjects covered by Mr. Cody's new method and of what his practice exercises consist. But those who are interested can find a detailed description in a fascinating little book called "How You Can Master Good English in 15 Minutes a Day." This is published by the Sherwin Cody School of English in Rochester. It can be had by anyone, free upon request. There is no obligation involved in writing for it. The book is more than a prospectus. Unquestionably, it tells you of the most interesting stories about education in English ever written.

If you are interested in learning more in detail of what Sherwin Cody can do for you, send for the book "How You Can Master Good English in 15 Minutes a Day."

Merely mail the coupon, a letter or postal card for it now. No agent will call. SHERWIN CODY SCHOOL OF ENGLISH, 8811 B. & O. Building, Rochester 4, N. Y.

The Longest-lived of All Mail Order Ads

This ad by Max Sackheim ran in various publications for 40 years. The reason it was repeated so often is because in all that time, nobody was able to write an ad that produced as many sales. Note the formula: (1) The headline offers a free lesson in English, and (2) the copy starts off by giving the reader a free lesson and then switches into sales copy. This ad is discussed in greater detail in Sackheim's book, *My First Sixty Years in Advertising* (Prentice-Hall, Inc., 1970).

"We could live on the money I'm spending for railroad fares! What do you say we try it?"

≈ The Greatest Reason in the World ≈

WHY did you buy life insurance?" I asked him.

"Well," he said, "it was because once I met a young person coming up the stairs of an apartment house with her arms full of packages, one of them dangling from a slender string. I didn't think she'd mind, so I offered to help her. At the door of her apartment, I saw that she was quite pretty. She still is.

"Because late one night, while she and I were waiting at a dimly lighted railway station for the Owl to take me home, I said, 'We could live on the money I'm spending for railroad fares! What do you say we try it?' We did, and it worked.

"Because one day I was offered a job by another company, and when I told my boss, he promised me ten dollars more a week if I'd stay. When I told her of

the boss's generosity, she said, 'What do you mean, generous? If he knew you were worth that much to him, he should have paid it to you before he had to.' So I quit and took the new job.

"Because one night she woke me up and said, 'I think I'd better go.' We went, and the last I saw of her that night, she was being trundled down a long corridor in a wheelchair, in spite of her protests that she could walk. When I saw her the next morning, she was lying very still and white and with the sweetish smell of ether on her breath. A nurse came in and asked, 'Wouldn't you like to see him?' But I wasn't interested in babies just then—not even our own.

"Because one autumn evening, while we were driving leisurely along a country road, we came upon a

small white cottage, its windows ablaze with the light of the setting sun. She said, 'What a place this would be for us!' Yes, what a place it has been for us!

"It's because of these memories, and many others that I wouldn't tell you and that wouldn't interest you even if I did, that I bought life insurance.

"And if the premiums could be paid in blood, instead of money, pernicious anemia would be a pleasure."

. . .

Moral: Insure in The Travelers. All forms of insurance. The Travelers Insurance Company, The Travelers Indemnity Company, The Travelers Fire Insurance Company, Hartford, Connecticut.

A Famous Ad for Life Insurance

"We could live on the money I'm spending for railroad fares. What do you say we try it?" This caption printed under the above picture gives a clue to the heart-throbbing story told in this ad. It is the story of a courtship, a marriage and a birth—and why one man bought life insurance. The secret of its success is its sincerity. This ad for The Travelers Insurance Company ranked number one in readership in magazines. It was praised by insurance men, advertising men, and insurance buyers. Requests for copies came in for years.

Voted the Ad Writers' Favorite

This ad by Carl Spier for Hamilton watches was published during the Christmas shopping season for many years. A group of 100 well-known ad writers were asked to name which famous ad they would most like to have written themselves. This ad received the largest number of votes. The Hamilton Company received hundreds of letters praising the ad. "I copied it for a note to my wife (with her Hamilton)," wrote one man. Letter after letter ends with "My next watch will be a Hamilton."

*"Can he really play?" a girl whispered.
"Heavens no!" Arthur exclaimed. "He
never played a note in his life."*

They Laughed When I Sat Down
At the Piano
But When I Started to Play!~

ARTHUR had just played "The Rosary." The room rang with applause. I decided that this would be a dramatic moment for me to make my debut. To the amazement of all my friends, I strode confidently over to the piano and sat down.

"Jack is up to his old tricks," somebody chuckled. The crowd laughed. They were all certain that I couldn't play a single note.

"Can he really play?" I heard a girl whisper to Arthur.

"Heavens, no!" Arthur exclaimed. "He never played a note in all his life. . . But just you watch him. This is going to be good."

I decided to make the most of the situation. With mock dignity I drew out a silk handkerchief and lightly dusted off the piano keys. Then I rose and gave the revolving piano stool a quarter of a turn, just as I had seen an imitator of Paderewski do in a vaudeville sketch.

"What do you think of his execution?" called a voice from the rear.

"We're in favor of it!" came back the answer, and the crowd rocked with laughter.

Then I Started to Play

Instantly a tense silence fell on the guests. The laughter died on their lips as if by magic. I played through the first few bars of Beethoven's immortal Moonlight Sonata. I heard gasps of amazement. My friends sat breathless—spellbound!

I played on and as I played on I forgot the people around me. I forgot the hour, the place, the breathless listeners. The little world I lived in seemed to fade—seemed to grow dim—unreal. Only the music was real. Only the music and visions it brought me. Visions as beautiful and as changing as the wind blown clouds and drifting moonlight that long ago inspired the master composer. It seemed as if the master

musician himself were speaking to me—speaking through the medium of music—not in words but in chords. Not in sentences but in exquisite melodies!

A Complete Triumph!

As the last notes of the Moonlight Sonata died away, the room resounded with a sudden roar of applause. I found myself surrounded by excited faces. How my friends carried on! Men shook my hand—wildly congratulated me. Everybody was exclaiming with delight—plying me with rapid questions. . . . "Jack! Why didn't you tell us you could play like that?". . . "Where did you learn?"—"How long have you studied?"—"Who was your teacher?"

"I have never even *seen* my teacher," I replied. "And just a short while ago I couldn't play a note."

"Quit your kidding," laughed Arthur, himself an accomplished pianist. "You've been studying for years. I can tell."

"I have been studying only a short while," I insisted. "I decided to keep it a secret so that I could surprise all you folks."

Then I told them the whole story.

"Have you ever heard of the U. S. School of Music?" I asked.

A few of my friends nodded. "That's a correspondence school, isn't it?" they exclaimed.

"Exactly," I replied. "They have a new simplified method that can teach you to play any instrument by mail in just a few months."

How I Learned to Play Without a Teacher

And then I explained how for years I had longed to play the piano.

"A few months ago," I continued, "I saw an interesting ad for the U. S. School of Music—a new method of learning to play which only cost a few cents a day! The ad told how a woman had mastered the piano in her spare time at home—and without any teacher! Best of all, the wonderful new method used, required no laborious scales—no heartless exercises—no tiresome practising. It sounded so convincing that I filled out the coupon requesting the Free Demonstration Lesson.

"The free book arrived promptly and I started in that very night to study the Demonstration Lesson. I was amazed to see how easy it was to play this new way. Then I sent for the course.

"When the course arrived I found it was just as the ad said—as easy as A.B.C.! And, as

the lessons continued they got easier and easier. Before I knew it I was playing all the pieces I liked best. Nothing stopped me. I could play ballads or classical numbers or jazz, all with equal ease! And I never did have any special talent for music!"

Play Any Instrument

You too, can now teach yourself to be an accomplished musician—right at home—in half the usual time. You can't go wrong with this simple new method which has already shown 350,000 people how to play their favorite instruments. Forget that old-fashioned idea that you need special "talent." Just read the list of instruments in the panel, decide which one you want to play and the U. S. School will do the rest. And bear in mind no matter which instrument you choose, the cost in each case will be the same—just a few cents a day. No matter whether you are a mere beginner or already a good performer, you will be interested in learning about this new and wonderful method.

Send for Our Free Booklet and Demonstration Lesson

Thousands of successful students never dreamed they possessed musical ability until it was revealed to them by a remarkable "Musical Ability Test" which we send entirely without cost with our interesting free booklet.

If you are in earnest about wanting to play your favorite instrument—if you really want to gain happiness and increase your popularity—send at once for the free booklet and Demonstration Lesson. No cost—no obligation. Right now we are making a Special offer for a limited number of new students. Sign and send the convenient coupon now—before it's too late to gain the benefits of this offer. Instruments supplied when needed, cash or credit. U. S. School of Music, 1631 Brunswick Bldg., New York City.

Pick Your Instrument

Piano	'Cello
Organ	Harmony and Composition
Violin	Sight Singing
Drums and Traps	Ukulele
	Guitar
Banjo	Hawaiian Steel Guitar
Tenor Banjo	
Mandolin	Harp
Clarinet	Cornet
Flute	Piccolo
Saxophone	Trombone
Voice and Speech Culture	
Automatic Finger Control	
Piano Accordion	

U. S. School of Music,
1631 Brunswick Bldg., New York City.

Please send me your free book, "Music Lessons in Your Own Home," with introduction by Dr. Frank Crane, Demonstration Lesson and particulars of your Special Offer. I am interested in the following course:

Have you above instrument? ....

Name ....
(Please write plainly)

Address ....

City .... State ....

An Ad That Started a New School of Advertising

This ad sells a correspondence course in piano playing. It was included in Julian Watkins' book *The 100 Greatest Advertisements*. For many years the theme "They laughed, etc." has been adopted by advertisers. For example: "They laughed when I sent away for free color film, but now my friends are all sending away, too!" Editor's note: This ad, written by John Caples, was cited when he was elected to the Copywriters Hall of Fame.

They Grinned When the Waiter Spoke to Me in French

—but their laughter changed to amazement at my reply

WE HAD dropped into Pierrot's for dinner—Pierrot's, that quaint French restaurant where the waiters speak nothing but French. Jack Lejeune, who boasted a smattering of French, volunteered to act as interpreter.

"Now tell me what you want to eat," announced Jack grandly, after we were seated, "and I'll 'parley' with the waiter."

With halting French phrases and much motioning of hands, Jack translated our orders to the waiter. Finally Jack turned to me.

"What's yours, Fred?" he asked.

"Virginia ham and scrambled eggs," I replied. Jack's face fell. He knew that my order would be difficult to translate into French. However, he made a brave effort.

"Jambon et des——et des——" but Jack couldn't think how to say "scrambled eggs." He made motions as if he were scrambling eggs in a frying pan, but the waiter couldn't get what he was driving at.

"I'm afraid you'll have to order something else, Fred," he said finally. "I can't think of the word for 'scrambled eggs.'"

Everybody smiled—everybody except me. With great ceremony I beckoned to the waiter. "I'll explain my order to the waiter," I said. A chuckle ran around the table.

"Fred can't speak French, can he?" I heard a girl whisper to Jack.

"No—he never spoke a word of French in his life," came the answer. "But watch him. This will be funny. He'll probably give an imitation of a hen laying an egg."

A Tense Moment

The waiter addressed me. "Qu'est-ce-que vous voulez, Monsieur?" he asked.

There was a pause. All eyes were on me. I hesitated—prolonged the suspense as long as possible. Then in perfect French I said to the waiter: "Donnez-moi, s'il vous plaît, du jambon aux oeufs brouillés—jambon de Virginie."

The effect on my friends was tremendous. The laughter stopped. There were gasps of amazement. In order to heighten the effect, I continued for several minutes to converse in French with the waiter. I asked him all sorts of questions—what part of France he was from—

how long he had been in America, and many other queries. When I finally let the waiter go, everybody started firing excited questions at me.

"Fred! Where did you learn to speak French like that?" "Why didn't you tell us you could talk French?" "Who was your teacher?"

"Well, folks," I replied, "it may sound strange, but the truth is I never had a teacher. And just a few months ago I couldn't speak a word of French."

"Quit your kidding!" laughed Jack. "You didn't develop that knowledge of French in a few months. I thought it took years to learn to talk like that."

"I have been studying French only a short while," I insisted. And then I told them the whole story.

How I Learned French Without a Teacher

"Did you ever hear of the House of Hugo?" I asked.

Jack nodded. "That's that famous Language Institute over in London, isn't it?"

"Yes," I replied. "They've been teaching languages for over a century. Thousands of Europeans have learned foreign languages in a surprisingly short time by their 'at-sight' method."

"But what's that got to do with your learning French?" asked Jack. "You haven't been over there taking lessons from the House of Hugo, have you?"

"No, I couldn't go to the House of Hugo, so the House of Hugo came to me," I replied quizzically.

My Friends Look Startled

"Here's what I mean," I said. "The authorities of the House of Hugo got together recently and decided to condense their knowledge of language instruction—their experience in teaching French—the secrets of their wonderful method into a course of printed lessons—a course which anyone could study at home.

"This course turned out to be the most ingenious method of learning French ever devised. It was simply marvelous. It enabled people to learn French in their own homes, in an incredibly short time.

"I can scarcely believe it myself, but just a few months ago I didn't know a word of French. Now I can speak and understand French when it is spoken to me. And I didn't study much—just a few minutes a day. There were no laborious exercises to do—no tiresome rules—no dull class-room drills. It was actually fun learning. Everything was so clear, so simple, so easy. Honestly, the Hugo 'At-Sight' French Course is the most remarkable thing of its kind I have ever seen!"

Try It 5 Days FREE

This story is typical. You, too, can now learn French at home—quickly, easily, pleasantly—just as thousands of others are doing by the celebrated Hugo 'At-Sight' Method. Twenty-four fascinating lessons, carefully planned. The most ingenious method of learning French ever discovered. Whole generations of language-teaching experience in all the leading European cities are behind this French course.

The wonderful thing about this simplified Hugo method is that it makes you *your own teacher*. At home—in minutes that might, otherwise be wasted—you learn phrase by phrase, sentence by sentence, to speak the language correctly and well. To be able to speak French is decidedly a cultural attainment, and is recognized as such. Use those spare minutes to master French this fascinating Hugo way!

No money is necessary now. We shall be glad to send you the complete course FREE FOR 5 DAYS so that you may see it and judge it for yourself. Within the free examination period you have the privilege of returning the course without cost or obligation, or keeping it as your own and sending only $2 as a first payment, and thereafter $2 a month until the full price of $12 has been paid.

You are the judge. Simply return the course within 5 days if you are not fascinated and delighted with it. If you act promptly, a valuable French-English Dictionary, containing 45,000 words, will be included without additional cost.

We urge you to clip and mail this coupon today. Doubleday, Page & Co., Dept. F-522, Garden City, New York.

An Ad That Became a Conversation Piece

This ad employs the same theme as the "Piano" ad on the page opposite. It was successful in selling a correspondence course in French. The ad was kidded by cartoonists and joke writers. For example, one version read: "They laughed when I spoke to the waiter in French—but he came right back with some Scotch." Another: "They were surprised," remarked the gentleman who never tipped, "When the waiter spoke to me at all." Said the ad manager: "We don't mind being kidded. The most kidded ads are often the most successful."

The Rolls-Royce Silver Cloud—$13,550

"At 60 miles an hour the loudest noise in this new Rolls-Royce comes from the electric clock"

*What makes Rolls-Royce the best car in the world? "There is really no magic about it—
it is merely patient attention to detail," says an eminent Rolls-Royce engineer.*

Special showing of the Rolls-Royce and Bentley at Salter Automotive Imports, Inc., 9009 Carnegie Ave., tomorrow through April 26.

Effective Salesmanship in Print

This advertisement, written by David Ogilvy, created a sensation. It was the most talked-about ad of its time. Ad men tore it out of publications and pinned it to their walls as a model of salesmanship. Said Ogilvy: "Factual advertising like this outsells flatulent puffery. The more you tell, the more you sell. Notice the very long headline—and 719 words of copy, all facts." Said the senior Rolls-Royce executive when he read the headline: "We really must do something to improve our clock."

If you are a careful driver you can save money on Car Insurance

LIBERTY MUTUAL'S money-saving plan for careful motor car owners is summed up in these nine words: "Careful drivers are entitled to lower automobile insurance cost."

Here's how it works: By barring dangerous drivers and selecting only careful drivers, we have fewer accidents. This means fewer losses to pay. Furthermore, you avoid paying large commissions to insurance salesmen on new policies or renewals. The savings which result from this plan come back to you. More than 41 million dollars in dividends have been so returned to policyholders by Liberty Mutual since it started 23 years ago.

Our promises are backed by resources of more than 29 million dollars. Your car insurance is handled without bother or red tape. Claims are dealt with promptly.

You are invited to send for the free money-saving booklet below. We will notify you promptly *whether you are eligible for a policy.* No obligation on you or on us. Merely clip the coupon and receive the facts.

7 Good Reasons why you should insure with Liberty Mutual

1 You are identified with reputable, careful drivers. Liberty Mutual's clients are selected, not merely solicited. They are the most careful automobile drivers in the country. You profit by that association in dollars and cents.

2 You do not have to help pay for costly accidents caused by dangerous, reckless drivers.

3 Savings effected by careful selection of careful

No car can be safer than the man at the wheel. And no driver can feel 100% safe without adequate insurance on his car. If you are a consistently careful driver, we believe you are entitled to car insurance at lower cost. With us, you do not have to pay the same price for automobile insurance as dangerous, reckless drivers. Here is the way our plan works: Selected drivers, hence fewer accidents and fewer losses—savings returned to you.

drivers, and savings resulting because your premiums do not go to pay large commissions to salesmen on new policies or renewals are returned to you. In 23 years at least 20% annually has been so paid back to policyholders.

4 Your company is the largest, strongest mutual casualty insurance company in the U. S. It has grown steadily in size and strength, in good times and in bad.

5 Your company operates from coast to coast. Liberty Mutual service is as close as your telephone.

6 Your car insurance is handled without bother or red tape. Claims are settled fairly and promptly.

7 It is *your* company. *Mutual* companies are owned and operated by their policyholders.

IF YOU LIVE IN NEW YORK

Leading men in this city are in our company. We can refer you to many careful drivers in your neighborhood who have Liberty Mutual car insurance. Most of our business has come from one man telling another. We would like to have 1,000 more carefully-selected policyholders here. If you are a careful driver, you can become one of the 1,000, and you may save money on car insurance, as your neighbors do.

Why not take the first step right now? Without obligation to you or to us, please send for the free money-saving booklet offered below. We will send the facts promptly on receipt of the coupon. Then you and we can decide.

LIBERTY MUTUAL
INSURANCE COMPANY

NEW YORK: 10 East 40th Street, Phone CAledonia 5-3100   Brooklyn: 187 Joralemon Street, Phone CUmberland 6-9050
Newark: 20 Clinton Street, Phone MArket 2-9920

(Offices open evenings until 9:00 o'clock) Nation-wide service

LIBERTY MUTUAL—writes Workman's Compensation, Automobile, and all other forms of Liability Insurance; also Burglary Insurance and Fidelity Bonds. All forms of Fire Insurance written through the United Mutual Fire Insurance Co.

Copyright 1935, L. M. I. Co.

CLIP AND MAIL THE COUPON BELOW

LIBERTY MUTUAL INSURANCE COMPANY
10 East 40th Street, New York, N. Y.

Without obligation, please mail me your Free Booklet which shows exactly how much careful drivers can save on car insurance.
T. 3-35

Name_____

Address_____

Town where car is kept_____My present policy expires_____

Make of car____No. of Cyls____Body Type____Model No.____Year____

A Pioneer in Insurance Advertising

This ad started a new school of insurance advertising by offering lower cost insurance to a special group, in this case, careful drivers. The copy says: "Liberty Mutual's clients are selected, not merely solicited." Note the panel (above the coupon) with the heading "If You Live in New York." This localizing of newspaper ads helps to increase coupon response.

An Ad that Started a Cigarette Revolution

This ad was written by Rosser Reeves, former chairman of Ted Bates, Inc. Said Reeves: "The ad worked like no other I have ever seen. When the campaign started, Viceroy Cigarettes were a little-known brand. Monthly sales were small. With these 130 words of copy, monthly sales jumped to 50 million ... to 100 million ... to 200 million ... and on up. The client enlarged the factory to meet consumer demands. These 130 words created a revolution in the cigarette industry for company after company has now moved in with other filter-tip brands."

Index